Degree of Change

NCTE Editorial Board: Jamal Cooks, Deborah Dean, Ken Lindblom, Amy Magnafichi Lucas, Bruce McComiskey, Duane Roen, Vivian Vasquez, Anne Elrod Whitney, Kurt Austin, Chair, ex officio, Emily Kirkpatrick, ex officio

Degree of Change
The MA in English Studies

Edited by

MARGARET M. STRAIN
University of Dayton

REBECCA C. POTTER
University of Dayton

National Council of Teachers of English
1111 W. Kenyon Road, Urbana, Illinois 61801-1096

Staff Editor: Bonny Graham
Interior Design: Jenny Jensen Greenleaf
Cover Design: Pat Mayer
Cover Image: Ingram Publishing/iStock/Thinkstock

NCTE Stock Number: 10799; eStock Number: 10805
ISBN 978-0-8141-1079-9; eISBN 978-0-8141-1080-5

©2016 by the National Council of Teachers of English.

All rights reserved. No part of this publication may be reproduced or transmitted in any form or by any means, electronic or mechanical, including photocopy, or any information storage and retrieval system, without permission from the copyright holder. Printed in the United States of America.

It is the policy of NCTE in its journals and other publications to provide a forum for the open discussion of ideas concerning the content and the teaching of English and the language arts. Publicity accorded to any particular point of view does not imply endorsement by the Executive Committee, the Board of Directors, or the membership at large, except in announcements of policy, where such endorsement is clearly specified.

NCTE provides equal employment opportunity (EEO) to all staff members and applicants for employment without regard to race, color, religion, sex, national origin, age, physical, mental or perceived handicap/disability, sexual orientation including gender identity or expression, ancestry, genetic information, marital status, military status, unfavorable discharge from military service, pregnancy, citizenship status, personal appearance, matriculation or political affiliation, or any other protected status under applicable federal, state, and local laws.

Every effort has been made to provide current URLs and email addresses, but because of the rapidly changing nature of the Web, some sites and addresses may no longer be accessible.

Library of Congress Cataloging-in-Publication Data

Names: Strain, Margaret M., editor. | Potter, Rebecca C., editor. |
  National Council of Teachers of English.
Title: Degree of change : the MA in English studies / edited by
  Margaret M. Strain and Rebecca C. Potter.
Description: Urbana, Illinois : National Council of Teachers of English,
  [2016] | Includes bibliographical references and index.
Identifiers: LCCN 2016027930 (print) | LCCN 2016044801 (ebook) |
  ISBN 9780814110799 (pbk.) | ISBN 9780814110805 (eISBN) | ISBN
  9780814110805
Subjects: LCSH: English philology—Study and teaching—United States. |
  Graduate students—United States. | English teacher—Training of. |
  Universities and colleges—Curricula—United States.
Classification: LCC PE68.U5 D44 2016 (print) | LCC PE68.U5 (ebook) |
  DDC 420.71/1—dc23
LC record available at https://lccn.loc.gov/2016027930

For my family, always
—*Margaret M. Strain*

For John M. Potter and Marilyn Carey Potter,
thank you
—*Rebecca C. Potter*

CONTENTS

ACKNOWLEDGMENTS ix

INTRODUCTION: DEGREE OF CHANGE xi
    Margaret M. Strain

I Disciplinary Shifts

1 *The Locally Responsive, Socially Productive MA in Composition*...3
    Kory Lawson Ching, Tara Lockhart, and Mark Roberge

2 *English Online/On the Line: The Challenges of Sustaining Disciplinary Relevance in the Twenty-First Century*........22
    Kristine L. Blair

3 *Academic Capitalism, Student Needs, and the English MA*..41
    Mark Mossman

4 *But Can You Teach Composition? The Relevance of Literary Studies for the MA Degree*.......................59
    Rebecca C. Potter

II Programmatic Transformations

5 *From Political Constraints to Program Innovation: Professionalizing the Master's Degree in English*...........79
    Kaye Adkins

6 *Boundary Crossings and Collaboration in a Graduate Certificate in Teaching Writing* 99
    Steve Fox and Kim Brian Lovejoy

7 *TextSupport: Incorporating Online Pedagogy into MA English Programs*...................................120
    Abigail G. Scheg

— vii —

CONTENTS

8 Crafting a Program That Works (for Us): The Evolving
Mission of the Master's in English at Rutgers University–
Camden 138
William T. FitzGerald and Carol J. Singley

9 "There and Back Again": Programmatic Deliberations
and the Creation of an MA Track in Rhetoric and
Composition 157
Hildy Miller and Duncan Carter

III Changing Student Populations

10 Student Ambitions and Alumni Career Paths: Expectations
of the MA English Degree 179
Ann M. Penrose

11 Disciplining the Community: The MA in English and
Contextual Fluidity 197
James P. Beasley

12 An MA TESOL Program Housed in the English
Department: Preparing Teacher-Scholars to Meet
the Demands of a Globalizing World 215
Gloria Park and Jocelyn R. Amevuvor

13 When the MA Is Enough: Considering the Value of
Graduate Education................................... 234
Sharon James McGee, Rebecca Burns, Kisha Wells, Nancy Thurman
Clemens, and Jeff Hudson

Afterword 253
Adam Komisaruk

INDEX 265

EDITORS 275

CONTRIBUTORS 277

ACKNOWLEDGMENTS

We wish to thank Bonny Graham, senior editor of the NCTE Books Program, as well as our anonymous reviewers for their careful readings, thoughtful recommendations, and sustained support of this project. This book is all the stronger for their collaboration.

Introduction:
Degree of Change

Margaret M. Strain
University of Dayton

The history of higher education in the United States is one of admixture. The first American colleges initially followed a British educational model, with a prescribed classical curriculum characterized by lecture, recitation, and disputation. Undergraduate students finished their course of study by earning a baccalaureate degree. Those who completed advanced work (sometimes with a thesis) graduated with a master of arts, the highest postsecondary degree awarded. In the nineteenth century, the German university, with its expanded curricula, scientific approaches to research, and disciplinary organization, appealed to a new nation experiencing urbanization, industrial growth, and western expansion. American education reformers began calling for the creation of "universities" to remedy the limitations of liberal arts colleges. A vital part of this educational revision was the addition of the PhD as the culminating degree. In many cases, institutions imposed a graduate university structure onto existing undergraduate and masters-granting schools (e.g., Harvard and Yale). The opening of Johns Hopkins University in 1876 marked the first American institution conceived according to the German university model (Parker; Berlin). With this shift, the PhD supplanted the MA as the benchmark preferred terminal degree (Storr 47–56).

The rise of the new university in the United States had important consequences for higher education. It created a hierarchical relationship between the PhD and the MA. The tiered system also gave rise to a distinction in the purpose of graduate education—a

— xi —

INTRODUCTION

tension that troubles us still—and that is the difference between, as Bernard Berelson puts it, "graduate *education* and graduate *training*" (i.e., the pursuit of knowledge for its own sake and preparation for a profession) (8). Masters programs provided graduates with coursework in areas such as education, engineering, commerce, technology, medicine, fine arts, and journalism and led to employment in various professional fields. In the field of English studies, the MA offered training for teachers and educational administrators. A PhD in English signaled more rigorous scholarship in the study of literature, with the end result of reproducing the next generation of academic scholar-leaders. The MA in English studies thus came to be seen in two ways: as either a stepping-stone to, or, failing that, a "consolation prize" (Bartlett 26; Dalbey 17) for those who did not qualify for, the proper end of graduate education: the doctorate.[1]

In the twentieth century, the master's degree, though diminished by its now medial position in higher education, never lost its value as a training ground for newly enfranchised learners (e.g., women, African Americans) and those seeking additional credentials (Stimpson 146; Steward). Indeed, especially after World War II, the number of master's programs in the United States far outstripped doctoral ones. In fact, despite the growing preference for a PhD-wielding professoriate, the master's remained the highest degree held by the majority of American college and university faculty members until the latter part of the twentieth century. Judith Glazer reports, for example, that in 1959–1960, "only 40 percent of faculty held PhDs" (10). Today, the number of faculty with PhDs has increased: 60 percent of full-time faculty and instructional staff and 18 percent of part-time faculty and staff hold the degree. Still, those with a master's as their highest degree remain strong at 26 percent of full-time and 52 percent part-time faculty ("Full-Time and Part-Time Faculty"). Closer to home, the Modern Language Association's (MLA) Ad Hoc Committee on the Master's Degree reports that "close to half (49.1%) of all those teaching English in colleges and universities hold a master's as their highest degree" (3). These statistics suggest that the MA continues to hold its stature as a professionalizing degree within the academy—and beyond it. Increasingly, the MA in English is a required or preferred degree for a number of "alt-ac" positions in

— xii —

Degree of Change

nonprofit and government organizations, publishing, education, and library sciences (*Chroniclevitae.com*).

Additionally, the MA has taken on new purposes without ever abandoning its foundations. Associate and baccalaureate degrees provide students with a general education grounded in the humanities and social and natural sciences, but for those who require specialized preparation, the undergraduate degree is insufficient. Advanced study exposes teachers to curricular innovation and, just as important, intellectual engagement. And while many doctoral programs expect their candidates to have a master's prior to matriculation, the percentage of students who earn the MA with the PhD goal in mind is small. Indeed, the MA continues to outpace the PhD in appreciable numbers. The National Center for Education Statistics projected that by the 2020–21 academic year, the number of MA degrees to be awarded would reach 865,000 ("Actual . . . Master's Degrees") compared to 106,100 doctoral degrees ("Actual . . . Doctor's Degrees"). These figures reflect degrees awarded in multiple fields. Still, the sheer number of graduates across many disciplines invites greater attention to the value of the MA.[2]

The MA is, after all, the entry into graduate study. It is the place where students engage in the specialized work of their disciplines, hone critical thinking and writing skills, participate in the theoretical and philosophical conversations within their fields, produce original research, and enter a professional community. It is also the degree that motivates students to continue or discontinue further study. If we consider the degree as a site where career trajectories are shaped, if not defined, the binary between the MA as a "training ground" and the PhD as "serious academic study" breaks down. That is, if we see the MA only as preparation for other work, we overlook the importance of what happens in these programs and with this unique population of students. Clearly, there is a purpose to the MA—and all the more reason to examine the degree more closely.

In contrast, the mission and identity of the PhD in English studies remain relatively stable. Disciplinary exchanges about the doctorate regularly appear as discussion topics at annual MLA and Conference on College Composition and Communication (CCCC) meetings and in other venues. From time to time,

— xiii —

INTRODUCTION

scholars have turned their attention to the MA—as an offshoot of conversations about the doctorate (Gaylord; Giordano) or as a special topic for a journal (Bartlett; Wright).[3] But these efforts do not capture the significant changes and expansion the MA in English has undergone in the last twenty years, not the least of which include the creation of track systems within existing programs, the development of online courses and programs, and an increase in international student enrollments.

Two studies have drawn attention to these changes. In 2011 the ADE Ad Hoc Committee on the Master's Degree published the results of two questionnaires it circulated to PhD-granting and MA-granting institutions. The authors of "Rethinking the Master's Degree in English for a New Century" encourage departments to engage in programmatic and disciplinary conversations on topics such as content-based versus skills-based curricular models, the viability of certificates, and best practices for hiring MA graduates for non-tenure-track positions (2). According to their data, literature remains a specialization in nearly 95 percent of reporting institutions, while concentrations in composition, rhetoric, and writing (38 percent), creative writing (20 percent), and English as a Second Language (ESL) (16 percent) are growth areas (Table 3). The committee regards the diversification among MA programs as evidence of the field's "responsive[ness]" (8) to disciplinary and external factors. At the same time, the committee poses an understandable question: is the "diffusion" affecting the "identity of the MA in English" (8)? We would respond by noting that concerns about fragmentation and identity are less a cause for disciplinary concern and more an astute observation about the unique character of the MA. The MA, more than the PhD, is positioned in a dynamic contact zone—a place where disciplinary knowledge, student need, and local exigencies interact and where disciplinary identity is constantly negotiated.

John S. Dunn Jr. and Derek N. Mueller's 2013 "Report on the 2012 Survey of Programs" created for the Master's Degree Consortium of Writing Studies Specialists suggests contemporary trends and provides statistical snapshots of the present state of the degree. Targeting programs in writing studies and related fields, Dunn and Mueller raise questions about a range of issues: the age and size of programs, student recruitment and enrollment,

Degree of Change

the specialization of faculty, and postgraduate career opportunities, to name a few. Their findings echo the trend found by the ADE Ad Hoc Committee on the Master's Degree concerning the number of MA graduates who seek academic employment as community college instructors, followed closely by those who obtain writing-related careers in the public sector; those who pursue doctoral work in writing rank third (16). While it may serve those of us in the English professoriate to see the MA as a segue to doctoral work, the numbers tell us that many of those graduating with an MA in English do not see the PhD as their primary goal. This is not for lack of ability, as the "consolation prize" narrative might imply. Rather, graduates have come to see how the study of writing, literature, and language translates into meaningful everyday work within and beyond the academy. Dunn and Mueller's findings also concur with the MLA's ADE report concerning the expansion of existing programs and the inauguration of new ones. When asked to name the official start date of their program, 27 percent of those who responded to the question reported 1980–1989 (15). Clearly, diversification is not so new; it has been unfolding for nearly three decades. Rather, as a discipline, we have only begun to recognize and deal with the consequences of these changes, especially within the contact zone where disciplinary knowledge, student needs, and local exigencies converge.

Degree of Change: The MA in English Studies argues for a fuller consideration of the contemporary state of the MA in English and for new dialogue about its pivotal role in higher education. In doing so, the collection takes up some of the challenges programs face: creating curricula that reflect distinct institutional missions, rethinking how to compete in digital learning environments, and preparing graduates to thrive in global communities. The book also explores the inextricable link between local exigencies and broader, more complex concerns. In an effort to serve students and community needs (a long-standing hallmark of the degree), graduate educators must balance institutional identities alongside faculty resources and state accreditation boards. Many of the programs in existence today owe their strength to faculty commitment and creativity in the face of difficult material realities. The impetus to earn higher degrees and credentials shows no signs of slowing down (Fairfield), yet this trend raises ethical concerns about labor. Are we overproducing MA grads? This question echoes one doctoral programs asked not so long ago about the number of students they admitted each year. Today, the potential for exploiting MA graduates remains a critical concern as more holders of MAs are hired for adjunct employment. In a glutted market, individuals with MAs face positions with low pay, no benefits, and no job security. Shouldn't conversations about such issues *begin* at the level of the MA, especially in departments where the MA in English serves as a stand-alone degree?[4]

Many of the authors represented in this collection—seasoned and newcomer—are those working on the front lines of curricular and institutional change, particularly in the secondary schools and community colleges. Thus, we see this collection of value to department chairs, graduate program administrators, faculty, and students interested in the conversations about and direction of the MA in US higher education. The cluster of chapters in each section features a prevailing theme. As the title of the first section suggests, "Disciplinary Shifts" examines MA programs as a generative force—at once administrative, interdisciplinary, and political—for change in English studies. The authors in the second section, "Programmatic Transformations," examine the responsive, dynamic, and not unproblematic interactions between MA programs and the constituencies with whom they work within and beyond the university. The scholars ask us to consider the values and assumptions that underpin these connections. Finally, "Changing Student Populations" offers a glimpse into the lived experiences of graduate students themselves in the programs and in the field. The writers highlight some of the varied occupations the MA degree has opened for them and reveal the sometimes surprising ways these individuals draw on their MA experiences. In his afterword, Adam Komisaruk takes the chapters as a point of departure to suggest where the future of the degree might be headed. While the essays here do not reflect the entirety of the energy, labor, and diversity that MA programs in English possess, we are excited to explore some of the possibilities within these pages.

Degree of Change

Part I: Disciplinary Shifts

MA programs by design and by circumstance are dynamic, ecological systems. They operate within complex academic networks even as they extend into public and civic spaces. The chapters in the section "Disciplinary Shifts" highlight the uniquely contextual and always rhetorical relationships that MA programs maintain with public, institutional, and programmatic constituencies. The authors of "The Locally Responsive, Socially Productive MA in Composition" take seriously the charge to serve both their graduate population and regional constituencies, which are often community colleges. They also complicate the proposition offered by Peter Vandenberg and Jennifer Clary-Lemon that "MAs can function on relatively autonomous ground, enabling community-based pedagogies that exploit intra- and interdisciplinary flexibility to link students to local exigencies and opportunities" (277–78). Kory Lawson Ching, Tara Lockhart, and Mark Roberge do so by identifying the "ethical and thorny dilemmas" that arise when newly hired MA instructors find that their graduate preparation is at odds with the skills they need as instructors in community colleges. Moreover, the curricular expectations of many community college English departments do not reflect contemporary perspectives on writing studies. How do faculty in MA programs grapple with these challenges? Ching, Lockhart, and Roberge account for the multilayered ways they attempt to negotiate the competing demands of each stakeholder while remaining socially productive.

In "English Online/On-the-Line: The Challenges of Sustaining Disciplinary Relevance in the Twenty-First Century," Kristine L. Blair confronts head-on several concerns facing English graduate education: declining tenure lines, faculty reticence in adapting to changing student needs, and institutional pushes to reach more diverse student populations. What impact do these disciplinary issues have on often-overlooked master's programs? In answer, Blair recounts her department's development of a fully online MA in English geared to public school teachers and writing professionals. While online courses are common forms of distance education, Blair explains how this initiative, because its success rested

— xvii —

on the investment of the entire English faculty (not merely those involved in writing and new media studies), engendered fruitful discussions about the future of the MA, the importance of digital pedagogies for English studies, and the tactical considerations of administering an online graduate program.

As some critics have lamented, the master's degree has been known for its credentialing function rather than its conferral of "mastery" in the field (Berelson 189). Mark Mossman sees untapped opportunity in this reality. In "Academic Capitalism, Student Needs, and the English MA," Mossman cites the number of fields that now require advanced degrees of new hires as they seek graduates with specialized skills and expertise. Shelia Slaughter and Larry L. Leslie and Slaughter and Gary Rhoades term the role of the university in this enterprise *academic capitalism,* and it is here that Mossman is most concerned with the entrepreneurial implications of this phenomenon for the MA in English. He proposes a new vision for the degree—one that embraces its role in the "New Economy"—a position he argues it has tacitly held for decades.

As I have noted, one of the major institutional developments within MA programs has been the emergence of curricular concentrations or the inauguration of programs devoted to writing studies. Students and prospective employers see a ready market for graduates prepared to move into writing-related and teaching careers. Coursework in writing studies, notwithstanding its other merits, is perceived as a pragmatic, even advantageous training for one's career. Can the same be said of generalist MA degrees or those programs with concentrations in literature? Has English studies failed to make a case for the relevance of literary studies for future teachers? Rebecca C. Potter takes up these questions in her essay, "But Can You Teach Composition? The Relevance of Literary Studies for the MA Degree." Using data from a survey of English department chairs from community colleges, Potter examines the assumptions these employers hold about the MA degree in literature, finding it lacking as a preparation for teaching in their departments. She also tackles a more troubling issue—the relative silence within the field of English studies generally to make an argument for its humanistic value to stakeholders outside

– xviii –

Degree of Change

the academy. This conversation, she rightly claims, is one worth having.

Part II: Programmatic Transformations

The essays in "Programmatic Transformations" introduce us to the demographic and geographic diversity across individual programs. In each instance, the authors highlight the unique circumstances that motivate their programs, whether it is a response to a state mandate, the need for curricular and programmatic reform, or an alternative to traditional program delivery. In doing so, they remind us of the "silent success" the degree has achieved in its openness to new fields of study, alternative instructional technologies, interdisciplinarity, nontraditional students, and professionalization, to name a few (Conrad, Haworth, and Millar 314). Four years after its change in designation from Missouri Western State College to Missouri Western State University (MWSU), MWSU inaugurated its master of applied arts in written communication in 2009. Charting that journey in "From Political Constraints to Program Innovation: Professionalizing the Master's Degrees in English," Kaye Adkins employs the theory of ecocomposition to highlight how state, professional, institutional, and departmental discourses converged in the design and implementation of this new degree. Discursive ecology is an especially useful lens for understanding how the linguistic transactions were shaped by MWSU's material environment. Adkins asks us to consider how some of the traditional strengths of MA programs such as teaching, literacy, and literature might be reimagined for alternative academic and nonacademic settings.

Steven Fox and Kim Brian Lovejoy present another look at programmatic diversity in their essay, "Boundary Crossings and Collaboration in a Graduate Certificate in Teaching Writing." In the state of Indiana, educational reformers are calling for changes to state laws that undermine or eliminate the requirement for a master's degree for middle and secondary teachers. In its place, they favor district or school initiatives that shift the purpose of teachers' continuing education from the teachers' own enrichment

— xix —

INTRODUCTION

to ways instructors can foster *student* achievement. The difference between the two is substantial. In a move that unites the partnerships they have forged with the Hoosier Writing Project, the Indiana Teachers of Writers, and their university resources, Fox and Lovejoy detail the development of a Certificate in Teaching Writing in their department. While not replacing their MA, the growing twenty-hour program brings together middle, high school, and college teachers to create opportunities for collaboration, critical dialogue, and action research.

Like many MA graduates, Abigail G. Scheg completed courses in traditional literary studies, writing pedagogy, and a bit of creative nonfiction. She also came to her first job with teaching experience. What she found missing from her graduate education was attention to teaching in online environments, an ability many academic employers presume new hires possess. In "TextSupport: Incorporating Online Pedagogy into MA English Programs," Scheg argues for "the necessity of theoretical and practical preparation for using technology" (122) at the MA level.[5] In the early days of computer-assisted instruction, many of us learned on the job how to teach writing in classrooms ill-fitted for the task. Face-to-face (F2F) teaching was changing even then. Today, technologies are ubiquitous educational tools, but F2F pedagogies are not sufficient preparation. Facing pressures from "above," programs frequently adapt to offer training in the areas in demand, such as ESL, writing instruction, and online education, but without adequate faculty expertise in these areas. Programs across the country are facing these pressures, made real and explicit in this collection.

Most people find change discomfiting. It destabilizes us, and therefore we resist it even in the face of the opportunity for something better. William T. FitzGerald and Carol J. Singley locate their MA in English program in exactly this position. The MA in the English department at Rutgers University–Camden maintains a confident identity as a stand-alone program serving the south Jersey area. It is also a regional campus, part of the State University of New Jersey, with New Brunswick as the flagship institution. Recent events have converged that propel the faculty to undertake curricular and institutional revision, and for a traditional program based on literary studies, this presents a sea

— xx —

change. The situation the authors describe echoes the challenges of many stand-alone MA programs. FitzGerald and Singley provide readers with a candid look at some of the avenues before them and invite us to ponder what such change means for the mission of Rutgers–Camden.

Hildy Miller and Duncan Carter, in "'There and Back Again': Programmatic Deliberations and the Creation of an MA Track in Rhetoric and Composition," chronicle a journey of sorts. Having completed an undergraduate curriculum revision with an enhanced focus on rhetoric, Miller and Carter began to consider the interrelationship between their undergraduate major and a new MA program in rhetoric and composition. Should the program be a stand-alone MA or a track within the existing MA in English? The authors' institutional quandary is one shared by departments across the country as evidenced by the proliferation of MA majors and stand-alone programs in recent years. Miller and Carter chart five critical questions and responses that led them to see the efficacy of creating a track. Ultimately, the decision the faculty made had less do with matters of form. Rather, they began to see "this choice as a rhetorical problem, as a process in which we must reflect deeply on the many layers of faculty's disciplinary identities" (172). Their critical questions are a useful heuristic for others contemplating changes to their MA program.

Part III: Changing Student Populations

Most, if not all, of the evaluations and recommendations we read in our professional publications about the master's degree reflect the perspectives of deans, chairs, faculty members of national organizations, and other institutional administrators. These voices are shaped and motivated by the continued viability of graduate education. They share a united concern, of course, for the pathways their students take after graduation and caution us to mind the gap "between students' aspirations and employment outcomes on the one hand and MA programs' stated goals and curricular requirements on the other" (ADE Ad Hoc Committee 1). They are mindful too that while many students complete an MA in English and later pursue a career in teaching, that is not to say the program

INTRODUCTION

itself has equipped them to do so. The authors in Part III answer the proverbial question about post-MA careers and offer critical responses to disciplinary and institutional stakeholders. These are the voices of recent MA graduates and the faculty who mentor them. In an ideal world, these individuals would sit down at a large round table to share their viewpoints. But failing that, we have much to gain by regarding how the degree has informed their life decisions and professional relationships. At the same time, the studies presented in this section offer insight into the ways MA graduates have navigated the disjunction between "employment outcomes" and their programs' "curricular requirements."

Ann M. Penrose takes the helm as director of graduate studies at her institution and begins asking critical questions: What is our admissions philosophy? Does it align with our program goals? What are these goals? Her chapter, "Student Ambitions and Alumni Career Paths: Expectations of the MA English Degree," presents the preliminary findings of two surveys she circulated to current students and graduates of their MA in English—a program that offers specializations in five areas and shares a disciplinary home with an MS in technical communication and an MFA in creative writing. This firsthand feedback, Penrose notes, "enable[s] us to go beyond our personal impressions and anecdotal reports . . . [and] represent students' goals and expectations" (181) in forging a program that produces not only "good writers but also critical thinkers and thoughtful humanists" (194). Graduate faculty mentoring by individuals who are informed about workforce options is essential to guiding prospective graduates toward a variety of career paths (see Moore and Miller).

The master's degree has also demonstrated its capacity for community outreach and engagement. Vandenberg and Clary-Lemon, seeking to underscore the importance of the MA in writing, have noted the degree's "responsiveness to local conditions" (268) and "distinctive flexibility" (275). In their view, the MA in writing is equally poised to build intra- and interdisciplinary relationships, thereby strengthening its disciplinary and institutional position. James P. Beasley explores how the qualities that Vandenberg and Clary-Lemon identify as integral to a new understanding of the MA in writing apply to the MA in English. Not only that, but Beasley shows how the dynamic interplay between

— xxii —

Degree of Change

the degree and its constituencies (e.g., other disciplines, community partners, university administrators) is multidimensional. In sum, he underscores the dialogic, contextual fluidity of the MA in English and the impact it has on graduate students.

One of the most pressing literacy issues in a time of global communications is meeting the needs of second language learners. We hear this message at all educational levels. A few MA programs do offer ESL as a specialization (ADE Ad Hoc Committee 33). Still, only 39 (20 percent) of the 200 MA-level Teachers of English to Speakers of Other Languages (TESOL) programs in the United States reside in Departments of English, as noted by Gloria Park and Jocelyn R. Amevuvor in "An MA TESOL Program Housed in the English Department: Preparing Teacher Scholars to Meet the Demands of a Globalizing World."[6] The others are found in Departments of Linguistics, Foreign Languages, Education, Curriculum and Instruction, even International Studies. In what ways does an MA TESOL program based in an English department distinctly shape the preparation of its graduates? How does the program support those who are not native English speakers learning how to work with diverse domestic populations but instead international, multilingual graduate students hoping to teach English and present their thesis research in their home countries? Park and Amevuvor offer insights into these questions in an analysis of their program.

As we know, there are many ways to evaluate the worth of an MA program. It can be assessed quantifiably through financial support for teaching assistantships and tuition reimbursement, graduate student job placement, even Carnegie Foundation rankings. In "When the MA Is Enough: Considering the Value of Graduate Education," Sharon James McGee, Rebecca Burns, Kisha Wells, Nancy Thurman Clemens, and Jeff Hudson explore the intrinsic benefits of a teaching of writing specialization that is part of a stand-alone program. McGee admits that when she initially imagined this chapter, she had intended to interview graduates for their input. As co-writers with McGee, these authors take on an agency and self-reflexivity missing in the reports of academics long removed from their own graduate student days. Each speaker—from a soldier teaching Afghan girls in Kabul, to a National Writing Project instructor, to an assistant professor

INTRODUCTION

at a community college, to a preschool teacher now working with developmental writers—reminds us of the values an MA in English confers that we cannot quantify, such as the beauty of language in all its forms, respect for difference, the importance of literacy, and the uniqueness of human expression. While surveys and statistical data tell us that the largest number of MA graduates go into teaching, these authors demonstrate just how often graduates enter teaching environments nothing like the settings in which they were trained as teaching assistants at elite colleges or universities.

Together, the contributors to *Degree of Change* demonstrate the vibrancy and diversity of the faculty, administrators, and graduates who make the master of arts in English a degree that is at once a significant part of our educational heritage and an exciting part of our educational future. Now, as in the past, MA programs enculturate new student populations, train teachers, and provide vocational training for administrators and professionals. The essays reveal that the number of graduates entering professions other than teaching remain small. Increasing numbers are finding positions in community colleges and the field of English education; there is also a growing international demographic of graduate students who will return to teach English in their home countries. These chapters provide a vivid portrait of the diverse labor MA graduates undertake that previous reports on the status of the degree do not. At the very least, they call us to reconsider the old narrative of the MA as simply a stepping-stone to a PhD.

At the same time, challenges that the MA has traditionally met are reframed in new iterations. The creation of MA programs in writing studies and TESOL is not the only way the MA has diversified. It is not uncommon to see degree programs that offer endorsements or certificates in specialty areas to better equip graduates for marketplace demands. Yet our contributors reveal the many challenges that the shifting marketplace has created for MA programs in English. Are faculties keeping up? Are they preparing their master's students to teach in the online classroom, the diverse classroom with a majority of nonnative speakers, the economically stratified classroom? The answer is probably not.

Finally, the authors show us the ways in which the MA degree has embraced a kind of hybridity. While stand-alone programs in

— xxiv —

literature exist, the mission and curricula of many others reflect global literacies, cross-disciplinary connections, and pedagogies sensitive to digital course delivery. These issues pose more urgency given the economic climate, the rise of international US universities, and increased demand for online education. Clearly, there is much work to do. The essays in this collection provide a road map for that future.

Acknowledgments

I wish to thank Patrick Thomas for his thoughtful comments, useful recommendations, and abundant goodwill in reading several iterations of this introduction.

Notes

1. On the second-place status of the MA in English, see also Allen and Duyfhuizen.

2. In 2007 the ADE Ad Hoc Committee on Staffing reported that "close to half (49.1%) of all those teaching English in colleges and universities hold a master's as their highest degree" (qtd. in ADE Ad Hoc Committee on the Master's Degree 3). This percentage (which was taken from a 2004 national study of postsecondary faculty [2004 National Study]) prompted the ADE Executive Committee to take a "hard look" at the MA (3). Ten years after these data were first released, we can presume that MA graduates represent an even greater percentage of postsecondary teachers.

3. See the 2005 special issue of *Rhetoric Review* edited by Stuart C. Brown, Monica F. Torres, Theresa Enos, and Erik Juergensmeyer devoted to MA programs in rhetoric and composition studies.

4. MA programs not attached to PhD programs are often referred to as "terminal" or, alternatively, "stand-alone." Throughout this collection, authors use both.

5. According to the ADE Ad Hoc Committee on the Master's Degree, coursework in technology or digital humanities is not a requirement in more than 75 percent of the reporting MA programs (see their Table 5).

6. For a breakdown of the concentrations *within* MA-granting programs, see the ADE Ad Hoc Committee on the Master's Degree report (33). The responses in Table 3 may reflect MAs attached to doctoral programs.

Works Cited

"Actual and Projected Numbers for Doctor's Degrees Conferred by Postsecondary Degree-Granting Institutions, by Sex of Recipient: 1995–96 through 2020–21." Table 35. *Projections of Education Statistics to 2020.* (NCES 2011-026). By William J. Hussar and Tabitha M. Bailey. Washington, DC: NCES, 2011. 75. Web. 14 Aug. 2013.

"Actual and Projected Numbers for Master's Degrees Conferred by Postsecondary Degree-Granting Institutions, by Sex of Recipient: 1995–96 through 2020–21." Table 34. *Projections of Education Statistics to 2020.* (NCES 2011-026). By William J. Hussar and Tabitha M. Bailey. Washington, DC: NCES, 2011. 74. Web. 14 Aug. 2013.

ADE Ad Hoc Committee on the Master's Degree. "Rethinking the Master's Degree in English for a New Century." *Modern Language Association.* MLA, June 2011. Web. 14 Aug. 2013.

Allen, Don Cameron. "The Intermediate Degree in English." *Bulletin of the Midwest Modern Language Association* 1.1 (1968): 1–2. Print.

Bartlett, Anne Clark. "Is It Terminal? Re-Evaluating the Master's Degree." *Journal of the Midwest Modern Language Association* 37.2 (2004): 26–29. Print.

Berelson, Bernard. *Graduate Education in the United States.* New York: McGraw, 1960. Print.

Berlin, James A. *Writing Instruction in Nineteenth-Century American Colleges.* Carbondale: Southern Illinois UP, 1984. Print.

Brown, Stuart C., Monica F. Torres, Theresa Enos, and Erik Juergensmeyer, eds. Spec. issue of *Rhetoric Review* 24.1 (2005): 5–127. Print.

Chroniclevitae.com. The Chronicle of Higher Education. Web. 24 Apr. 2016.

Conrad, Clifton F., Jennifer Grant Haworth, and Susan Bolyard Millar. *A Silent Success: Master's Education in the United States.* Baltimore: Johns Hopkins UP, 1993. Print.

Dalbey, Marcia A. "What Good Is the MA Degree?" *ADE Bulletin* 112 (1995): 17–20. Print.

Dunn, John S., Jr., and Derek N. Mueller. "Report on the 2012 Survey of Programs." *Master's Degree Consortium of Writing Studies Specialists*. Master's Degree Consortium of Writing Studies Specialists, 19 Feb. 2013. Web. 14 Feb. 2014.

Duyfhuizen, Bernard. "Betwixt and Between: The Master's Program and a Field of Dreams." *ADE Bulletin* 112 (1995): 21–24. Print.

Fairfield, Hannah. "Master's Degrees Abound as Universities and Students See a Windfall." *New York Times*. New York Times, 12 Sept. 2007. Web. 23 Sept. 2014.

"Full-Time and Part-Time Faculty and Instructional Staff in Degree-Granting Institutions, by Field and Faculty Characteristics: Fall 1992, Fall 1998, and Fall 2003." Table 269. *Digest of Education Statistics 2011*. (NCES 2012-001). By Thomas D. Snyder and Sally A. Dillow. Washington: NCES, 2012. 393-94. Web. 14 Aug. 2013.

Gaylord, Mary M. "On the Outside Looking In: Some Thoughts about the MA Degree." *PMLA* 115.5 (2000): 1267–69. Print.

Giordano, Michael J. "Revaluing the Master's Degree." *PMLA* 115.5 (2000): 1271–73. Print.

Glazer, Judith S. *The Master's Degree: Tradition, Diversity, Innovation*. Washington: Association for the Study of Higher Education, 1986. Print.

Moore, Cindy, and Hildy Miller. *A Guide to Professional Development for Graduate Students in English*. Urbana: NCTE, 2006. Print.

Parker, William Riley. "Where Do English Departments Come From?" *College English* 28.5 (1967): 339–51. Print.

Slaughter, Shelia, and Larry L. Leslie. *Academic Capitalism: Politics, Policies, and the Entrepreneurial University*. Baltimore: Johns Hopkins UP, 1999. Print.

Slaughter, Sheila, and Gary Rhoades. *Academic Capitalism and the New Economy: Markets, State, and Higher Education*. Baltimore: Johns Hopkins UP, 2004. Print.

Steward, Doug. "The Master's Degree in the Modern Languages since 1966." *Profession* (2004): 154–77. Print.

Stimpson, Catharine R. "Graduate Education: The Nerve Center of Higher Education." *What Is College For? The Purpose of Higher Education.* Ed. Ellen Condliffe Lagemann and Harry Lewis. New York: Teachers College, 2012. 132–55. Print.

Storr, Richard J. *The Beginnings of Graduate Education in America.* New York: Arno, 1969. Print.

2004 National Study of Postsecondary Faculty (NSOPF:04) Report on Faculty and Instructional Staff in Fall 2003. National Center for Education Statistics. (NCES 2005-172). Washington, DC: May 2005. Web. 23 Feb. 2011.

Vandenberg, Peter, and Jennifer Clary-Lemon. "Advancing by Degree: Placing the MA in Writing Studies." *College Composition and Communication* 62.2 (2010): 257–82. Print.

Wright, Erika. "Graduate Degree on the Margins: Educational and Professional Concerns of the MA Student." *Journal of the Midwest Modern Language Association* 37.2 (2004): 30–36. Print.

I

DISCIPLINARY SHIFTS

CHAPTER ONE

The Locally Responsive, Socially Productive MA in Composition

KORY LAWSON CHING, TARA LOCKHART, AND MARK ROBERGE
San Francisco State University

In their article "Advancing by Degree: Placing the MA in Writing Studies," Peter Vandenberg and Jennifer Clary-Lemon note that MA degrees in composition are viewed primarily as an "entryway to the doctorate" (259). They argue convincingly for a new conception of the MA, not as a mere academic stepping-stone to further graduate study but instead as "a much more responsive and diverse degree" (265). While a composition PhD program is designed primarily to support the production and reproduction of composition as a scholarly discipline and therefore "depends predominantly on research specialization to feed the academic marketplace" (265), an MA program in composition can be more agile in its responsiveness to local conditions and the diverse needs of its students and other stakeholders. An MA program might concentrate, for example, on preparing its graduates for teaching careers at local educational institutions, or for specific kinds of professional writing in various contexts, rather than (or in addition to) future success in a PhD program. For Vandenberg and Clary-Lemon, the MA should therefore be viewed as "a locus of situated, locally responsive, socially productive, problem-oriented knowledge production" (259).

While we agree that an MA program in composition presents many opportunities to be "locally responsive," it has been our experience, as faculty teaching in such a program, that it can also be a site of tensions between competing visions of what it means to be "socially productive," especially with regard to the practices of teaching composition. Even as we strive in our MA program

– 3 –

to be responsive to the needs of our graduate students, many of whom go on to serve as teachers in Bay Area community colleges, we as a faculty find ourselves running into thorny ethical and professional dilemmas. In this chapter, we respond to Vandenberg and Clary-Lemon's characterization of MA programs by exploring how one program has attempted to be receptive to the needs of our region's stakeholders and institutions while maintaining our professional and intellectual allegiances to the scholarly field of composition studies. We argue that, as composition scholars and researchers, our understandings of what constitutes socially productive pedagogy can differ from the kinds of situated teaching practices that graduates of our MA program are asked to engage in as community college teachers. Our MA program, therefore, is often a site of tension, one that requires very specific "problem-oriented knowledge production" as well as significant programmatic self-examination and curricular experimentation.

As we have already suggested, the MA composition program at San Francisco State University (SFSU), where we teach, serves primarily to prepare graduates to teach composition and reading courses at the two-year college level. Our graduate courses focus on theory, research, and pedagogy, with special attention to teaching in local community colleges and student populations in our geographic area. In addition to the MA in composition, we offer two graduate certificates. Our first certificate, "Teaching College Composition," consists of four courses and primarily serves students who are concurrently enrolled in related MA programs (English literature, creative writing, Teaching English as a Second Language) but who want additional specialization in writing pedagogy. Our second four-course certificate, "Teaching Post-Secondary Reading," serves both concurrently enrolled students in related MA programs and local community college teachers who want to obtain further specialization in reading instruction. Thus, while our program is occasionally a stepping-stone to PhD programs, most of our work is focused on preparing graduate students to take teaching positions locally.

Given these demographics, local responsiveness might seem to be a straightforward endeavor for our program. As a faculty, we know our graduate students' backgrounds, experiences, and career goals. We know many of the community colleges where

— 4 —

The Locally Responsive, Socially Productive MA in Composition

our graduates will end up teaching. We know much about the community college student populations whom our graduates will be teaching. And, as active scholars in the field of composition, we know what current research and theory say about how these graduate students should be trained to teach.

Indeed, local responsiveness *can* sometimes be straightforward, as illustrated by recent changes we made to our program's capstone project. Previously, the culminating experience for our composition MA was a traditional five-chapter thesis, typically based on a yearlong qualitative research project, followed by a formal thesis defense. Feedback from our graduates who were teaching at local community colleges made it clear to us that this type of traditional academic project was not preparing them to teach and was not helping them serve their students. Nor did these teachers feel that the project had helped them become the "reflective practitioners" our program encouraged (Schön). In short, we had been treating our own MA program as if it were primarily a stepping-stone to PhD-level research.

The locally responsive and socially productive solution was simple and straightforward: we replaced the thesis capstone with a portfolio project that fed directly into students' professional development as teachers. The portfolio now includes (1) teaching materials, including a detailed plan and rationale for a college-level composition course, as well as a statement of teaching philosophy; (2) an article-length writing sample aimed at potential publication in a pedagogy-oriented journal; and (3) a reflective essay in which students discuss how the portfolio represents their work as both teachers and scholars. In addition, the high-stakes thesis defense has been replaced with guided support throughout the portfolio process. These solutions have benefited all stakeholders: graduate students see it as much more useful to their own preparation for teaching, community colleges see the fruits of graduates' work when graduates include parts of their portfolio in their job applications, and we faculty find the process much more success-oriented and rewarding. These strategic changes have allowed us to bring the culminating experience more in line with current values and models of effective teacher development—achieving a socially productive end consistent with our disciplinary values—while at the same time being locally responsive to our graduates' particular needs.

More often than not, however, local responsiveness is not so straightforward. If an MA program is going to be responsive within its local context, it needs to develop as full an understanding of that context as it can. The needs of various stakeholders must be taken into account, even if some of those needs conflict with one another: What should our MA program be accomplishing? What local needs should we be responding to? To gain a more nuanced understanding of the ways our MA program might serve as "a locus of situated, locally responsive, socially productive, problem-oriented knowledge production," we embarked on a qualitative study of our graduates. As a faculty, we were particularly interested in focusing on the bridge between our MA program and our local community colleges. We began in 2009 by contacting alumni, surveying them about their current employment, their perceived level of preparation for that employment, and any other feedback they wished to offer us. After analyzing survey responses, however, we found we needed richer data in order to understand the complexities and tensions that arose in the survey information; we therefore began conducting in-depth interviews each year with recent alumni who are within their first five years of community college teaching assignments. These hour-long, semistructured interviews follow a protocol of questions focusing on the compatibility between the preparation they received in our program(s) and the "real-world" issues they face in local community colleges. A study such as this provides empirical data that can serve as a jumping-off point for critical reflection, curricular change, dialogue with local stakeholders, and even further theorizing within our discipline.

In the remainder of this chapter, we address three areas of tension that have emerged from this study in order to highlight the kinds of challenges that can arise when an MA program attempts to be a "a locus of situated, locally responsive, socially productive, problem-oriented knowledge production." In the first area, which involves preparing our graduates to work with diverse student populations, we believed we were doing a state-of-the-art job in teacher preparation, yet we discovered significant mismatches between the scholarly work we were doing in our graduate seminars and the experience that graduates faced when they entered community college classrooms. In the second area—preparing our graduates to work with grammar and language development issues—we discovered that research and theory in our field were often in conflict with teachers' site-specific classroom experiences and the institutional expectations of some local community colleges. In the third area, of preparing and certifying community college reading teachers, we discovered a knot of tensions that required delicate negotiation: state mandates about reading instruction, the curricular structure of reading courses at community colleges, our own scholarly training in literacy education, and graduate students' expectations that they will be able to step right into a job teaching reading. All of this was further complicated by the fact that "reading" is itself a thorny and contested notion among traditional cognitivists, literacy educators, and critical theorists. Our purpose in this chapter is to explore some of the challenges involved in shaping a composition MA program that respects the situated needs of our graduates and community while still upholding our shared understanding of our field's pedagogies.

Working with Diverse Student Populations

As program faculty, we are steeped in critical theory, multiculturalism, and notions of social justice. Our curriculum strongly emphasizes linguistic and cultural diversity throughout our seminars, and some seminars focus on working with specific student populations such as basic writers and second language students. It is therefore surprising that the first eleven graduates of our MA program we interviewed—while laudatory of the program in general—repeatedly noted that they felt unprepared to deal with the vast range of diversity in community college English classes. Interviewees mentioned the following:

- ◆ Although SFSU is highly diverse, area community colleges are even more so, and diverse in different ways.

- ◆ Teachers struggled in their first few years to accommodate the variety of student abilities, noting the wide range of skill levels and the broad variety of student difficulties, characteristics, and motivations.

- ◆ Most alumni felt underprepared to deal with students with specific needs, such as older and returning students, students with learning disabilities, students with physical disabilities, students with mental problems, and returning veterans.

We find these teachers' call for more training in serving diverse students both reassuring and perplexing. We find it reassuring in that our recent graduates appear to be ideologically on the same page with the social justice orientation of our program and of the field of composition as a whole. These teachers are cognizant of—and care about—the multifaceted diversity that students bring to local community colleges. Rather than see it as deficit or an indicator that certain students should not be in college, they see diversity as a call to develop their teaching repertoires so they can better serve students.

Yet we find this call for more training perplexing given the curriculum of our program, which features a composition theory course taught from a critical perspective, a sociolinguistic course that emphasizes working with linguistically and culturally diverse students, and a seminar in working with developmental readers and writers at the community college level. Still, graduates of this program want even more preparation for working with basic literacy students. Because our program is firmly rooted in the field of composition, our paradigm features an imagined student trajectory through developmental writing classes, first-year composition, the associate of arts (AA) degree and— hopefully—transfer to a four-year institution. *Academic literacy*, while ill-defined and contentious, is a central trope of our field. For our field, "equity and access" means equity and access to a traditional academic path, terminating in a BA or higher. However, this imagined trajectory does not fit the realities of many local community college students, and it often imagines a more homogeneous class in terms of ability. A more explicit and realistic discussion of the writing and reading abilities of many two-year college students and how those abilities might require adaptation of the strategies

The Locally Responsive, Socially Productive MA in Composition

and philosophies taught at SFSU might help MA students better anticipate challenges.

We also found that teachers might benefit from a greater understanding of different *kinds* of diversity. Beyond issues of cultural and ethnic diversity, MA students wanted more preparation for serving perhaps the widest swath of diverse students imaginable—students who often require intensive, individualized instruction or accommodation. This preparation seems to necessitate a combination of knowledge: conceptual understanding of disabilities and assistive teaching strategies, emotional understanding of issues such as trauma or PTSD, and practical knowledge to handle the associated issues brought on by the combination of student density and diversity. Given our particular locale, our program could do more to simulate how MA students might plan for incredibly diverse classes, including using classroom management strategically.

It is also possible that increased awareness of a range of student motivations would further enhance understanding of the two previous areas of concern. While one segment of the community college population uses the two-year degree as a path to transfer to a four-year institution, other students pursue vocational or enrichment aims and some drop in and drop out of the community classroom at will. Acknowledging and discussing this range of motivations seems important given the teaching contexts of our graduates; recognizing the diverse aims and motivations students have can likewise contextualize the different abilities and challenges students bring to the classroom. This issue could be addressed not only by explicit discussion of the range of student motivations and academic trajectories, but also by assignments that ask MA students, as future teachers, to consider how those different motivations might shape students' engagements with activities and assignments.

Working with Grammar and Language Development Issues

The second area of interviewees' concern—grammar and language issues—presents a marked contrast to the issue of diversity. In the case of diversity, teachers appear to be on the same page as the program; they value working with diverse students and simply want more preparation to do so. Both program and alumni appear to agree that for an MA teacher preparation program to be "locally responsive" and "socially productive," it must prepare teachers to work effectively with diverse populations in the local context. By contrast, in the area of grammar and language, there appears to be a strong tension between the program—which is anchored in the field of composition studies—and new teachers, who are now anchored in the world of community college English.

Over the past forty years, the field of composition has moved away from formalist concerns and an emphasis on grammatical correctness toward more social views of writing that emphasize the relationships between reader, writer, text, and world (see, for example, Richard Fulkerson). A common trope pervading the field is that if a teacher focuses on *what* students want to say and *whom* they want to say it to, "the grammar will take care of itself." Many in the field see the explicit teaching of grammar as an archaic relic, a gatekeeping mechanism that is a barrier to equity and access (for example, Mina Shaughnessy's notion of "guarding the towers"), or even a form of linguistic oppression (Conference on College Composition and Communication).

So we were surprised to find that the majority of those we interviewed expressed a strong wish that they had done more grammar work during their MA program. Interviewees who had taken a now-discontinued grammar-focused course in our program found it to be one of their most valuable experiences, and those who had not taken such a course said they regretted it.

These interviewees represent a broad cross section of recent alumni, not a group of "grammar mavens" who somehow managed to hold on to formalist and prescriptivist views of language while going through the program. Like most of our MA students, the majority of our interviewees eagerly problematized traditional grammar-focused instruction while in their graduate classes. However, they seemed to undergo something of an ideological turnabout once they began teaching at the community college level. We wondered what prompted this dramatic change in perspective.

The Locally Responsive, Socially Productive MA in Composition

One possible explanation might be found in the pressures that teachers face in some community college English departments. Our MA program prepares students for a twenty-first-century world of language ideology, but teachers sometimes find themselves teaching in English programs that are firmly rooted in dated yet persistent notions of language and literacy. This is evident in the formalist curriculum of some community colleges, which continue to offer a sequenced progression of skills-oriented courses, starting with sentence-level grammar, then a course on paragraph writing, and then a course on essay writing.

This tension is particularly evident in our recent programmatic decision to eliminate what was once a prerequisite course, Grammar and Rhetoric of the Sentence. This course was introduced in the 1970s as a progressive step away from traditional metalinguistic grammar teaching, which taught *about* grammar structures rather than teaching students how to *use* grammar structures. It also represented a step away from the traditional heavy emphasis on error correction. The course was based on Christensen's generative sentence rhetoric, focusing on ways that students could improve their syntactic maturity in writing and enhance their stylistic repertoires.

In time, what was progressive became retrograde; as Robert Connors notes, the field of composition moved away from sentence-level grammar, and many of our faculty began to see the course as an impediment to the intellectual development of our graduate students because it often gave students the impression that *teaching writing* is synonymous with *teaching grammar*. So we decided to eliminate the requirement—to the great pleasure of most graduate students, who found the course to be tedious, difficult, and out of touch with the world of writing.

But this decision was not met with universal approval. There was some grumbling among program alumni and current students who had taken the course. For many of them, it represented a kind of rite of passage, a chance for them to finally nail down (for themselves) the more esoteric ins and outs of English grammar. The decision has also been met with consternation from some community college hiring committees and departments staffed with former program graduates who feel that our program has suffered due to the movement away from grammar instruction.

— 11 —

This difference in views has created a tension between our desire to be both locally responsive and socially productive. To be socially productive, we need to move teachers away from a myopic focus on grammar teaching. Yet at the same time, teachers themselves say they want and need more preparation in understanding and teaching grammar. This tension is further exacerbated by administrative and curricular pressure from some local community colleges to emphasize grammar. In fact, some community college English courses have learning outcomes that specifically include grammar features. It is also possible (though not evident from our interviews) that community college teachers feel pressure from their students to teach grammar, since some students may equate writing instruction with grammar instruction.

Another related tension lies at the fissure between first language (L1) and second language (L2) writing instruction. While our composition MA program strongly emphasizes diversity, the program (and the scholarship informing our curriculum) tends to focus on the racial, ethnic, cultural, linguistic, and socioeconomic diversity of native speakers of English. Paul Matsuda refers to this phenomenon as the disciplinary division of labor: in its research, theory, and pedagogy, the field of composition is oriented toward native-English-speaking students, while the field of TESOL is oriented exclusively toward nonnative speakers. Unfortunately, this disciplinary division does not mirror the demographics of local community colleges, where the student population (even in "mainstream" English classes) consists predominantly of multilinguals and English learners.

It is therefore not surprising that interviewees' concerns about grammar teaching often focused on multilingual students. These teachers find themselves working with a student population that was not the focus of their teacher training. The MA program thus faces a challenge unlike that of diversity: in the case of training teachers to work with diversity, the program can simply broaden its curriculum; but in the case of training teachers to work with multilingualism, the program can only go so far before straying into the realm of TESOL, a field that is already represented at SFSU by a separate MA TESOL program.

The Locally Responsive, Socially Productive MA in Composition

This small examination of teachers' views on grammar presents many fruitful questions and avenues for our program to explore:

1. How can an MA composition program balance the scholarly and ideological demands of the field with the real-world demands that graduates face when they go on to teach at community college?

2. How can we train graduate students to be socially productive agents of change while at the same time preparing them to work within the traditional curricular and institutional structures of community college English departments?

3. Finally, how can we create genuine scholarly conversations between MA composition programs and local community colleges that go beyond a didactic, top-down, "we-know-what-is-best" message, and instead see local community colleges and teachers as funds of knowledge that can inform our scholarship and our field as a whole?

Preparing Students to Teach Reading

In addition to the tensions our first two examples have explored, a third arose in our MA program. An outside pressure— in this case, state legislation—created both a need and an opportunity to be locally responsible and socially productive. In 1988, California State Assembly Bill 1725 was signed into law as part of large-scale changes to the community college system. This bill specified that community college reading instructors must possess either an MA degree in education with a specialization in reading or an MA degree in another teachable subject (such as English or ESL) with an additional twelve units of coursework in adult reading instruction. In response to AB 1725, many teachers scrambled to meet the new requirement to become officially certified. To meet this new need, SFSU's sole faculty member who specialized in reading designed a twelve-unit Certificate in Post-Secondary Reading (PSR), which was approved by the faculty senate that same year. For more than fifteen years, SFSU was the only university to offer such training. The program thus showed its local responsiveness by moving quickly and effectively to fulfill this newly legislated need.

Although the PSR certificate was originally created in response to an external legislative mandate, the program eventually strove to be socially productive in terms of advancing the field as well. Motivated by a theoretical commitment to integrating reading and writing instruction to better serve SFSU's undergraduate program, the PSR certificate entered a second phase, spearheaded by the collaboration between our reading specialist and our developmental writing specialist (see Goen & Gillottee-Tropp; Goen-Salter). Courses and curriculum were revised to capitalize on research in the field, and the innovative program became well known in California for its approach to integrated reading and writing (IRW) instruction at both the undergraduate and graduate levels. More students were drawn to SFSU to gain the MA in composition or the PSR certificate, knowing it would increase their preparation and marketability on the community college job front. Some of these MA students, in turn, went on to create IRW programs of their own at the community colleges where they landed jobs, influencing undergraduate curricular change, writing centers, and program administration while simultaneously advancing the field's understanding of literacy theory and pedagogy.

The passage of this legislation has thus, over the last twenty-five years, prompted a complex symbiotic relationship between our graduate curriculum and California's community colleges. In many ways, creating and maintaining such a certificate epitomizes the "locally responsive and socially productive" nature of our program: we showed leadership at the local level by creating a program of study valued by community colleges and the state at large (as represented by the legislature), and we strengthened that program theoretically in ways that moved scholarship in the field, and local teachers, forward.

There are both benefits and challenges to continuing to offer a certificate that, at its heart, is a legislative requirement. A clear benefit is that our MA students who graduate with the certificate are in high demand by community colleges across the state, as most writing instructors are also expected to be able (and be certified) to teach reading, including the stand-alone reading courses that often remain in place at community colleges. Community

The Locally Responsive, Socially Productive MA in Composition

colleges and other California state universities have greater awareness of our program; students, too, are aware of the program and constitute a continuous stream of new applicants. Last, we have stronger connections to community colleges and their faculties via our graduates who have circulated out.

Yet, like any certification grounded in vocational aims, our PSR certificate walks a fine line: we need to fulfill students' desire (and the state's requirement) for "usable" strategies and practices that can be applied to the community college classroom, yet we are also professionally committed to theorizing and contextualizing those strategies so that teachers become reflective practitioners instead of "best practice" replicators. Although this is a tension also felt in the larger MA program as a whole, due to different populations and divergent goals it arises particularly among students who enroll in the PSR courses. Helping to certify students from other MA programs (such as English literature, creative writing, TESOL), as well as returning community college teachers seeking further credentials, positions us as locally responsive in that we help our graduates improve their marketability as community college teachers. However, this sort of pragmatism has contributed to such high enrollments in our certificate courses that we have to stretch our faculty thin in order to staff them. Since there is course overlap between our MA program and the certificate programs, there are also sometimes stark differences in motivation among the students in those courses. Certificate students from other MA programs are occasionally surprised to find that composition is more than a collection of teaching tips and techniques, and they sometimes resent having to engage with theories and scholarship in a field that holds little intrinsic interest for them. It is a challenge, then, to design courses with the academic rigor we deem appropriate for our composition MA students while at the same time satisfying the expectation of practicality that many of our certificate students seem to hold.[1]

In addition to needing to strike a professionally responsible balance between legislated, vocational "training" and academic scholarship in our PSR certificate courses, we continue to face several ethical challenges instructive to other MA programs. Central among these are, first, the issues of program stewardship and, second, a lack of articulation between community college

— 15 —

and four-year institutions that plays out in teacher training. These issues are interrelated and have raised many questions for our faculty over the years.

First, the question of program stewardship. Innovative and locally responsive program initiatives are often spearheaded by a single faculty member who sets up the program or curriculum, guides the direction of that program, and stays on top of scholarship relevant to that program. This was the case at SFSU, with our one faculty member who initially built (and taught much of) our PSR certificate. When this faculty member retired, we were faced with an important staffing problem that went beyond logistics and into the realm of ethics: when faculty turnover occurs, should others in the program who may have different interests and different areas of expertise take over stewardship of that program? In our case, we want to continue to offer the PSR certificate since it responds to a clear community need, allows our program to fill a niche that few other programs have been able to fill, and has been socially productive in terms of moving local curricula forward. On the other hand, we no longer have faculty with specialization in postsecondary reading, and as our faculty's expertise changes, we want to have the flexibility to offer new courses that better match expertise. As Richard E. Young and Irwin R. Steinberg note, "Institutional resources" such as "faculty members whose interests and training are relevant to the . . . program" are crucial to program sustainability (397). Each time our faculty makes subtle changes to the PSR certificate, we must negotiate our self-imposed allegiance to this legislation alongside our desire to remain flexible, nimble, and offer courses that better fit our current faculty's training and interests.

The question of program stewardship intersects with a second tension MA programs might encounter as they respond to outside pressures: lack of articulation between those outside pressures (in our case, legislation pertaining to community colleges) and their own programs and expertise. When the certificate program was instituted, SFSU still maintained separate remedial reading and writing courses, and so the faculty who taught in the MA and certificate courses had experience with stand-alone reading courses similar to those found at some community colleges. However, as we updated and improved our undergraduate cur-

The Locally Responsive, Socially Productive MA in Composition

riculum to integrate reading and writing, we no longer offered stand-alone reading courses. This move was a positive one for our undergrads, but it had the consequence of removing from our own institution the kinds of courses we are preparing students to teach at two-year colleges.

By phasing out remedial courses on our own campus, we have lost an institutional resource or fund of knowledge that once supported this aspect of the certificate program. Beyond removing opportunities for our PSR certificate students to observe and teach in stand-alone reading courses on our own campus, this change has had a more substantial effect on faculty, who now no longer have opportunities to teach the kinds of courses they are preparing our certificate students to teach. Many faculty members have expressed ethical qualms about and reluctance in training students to teach the stand-alone reading courses they themselves do not teach (or, indeed, may never have taught).

Tensions like these raise questions about the relationship between institutional resources and a program's ability to be both locally responsive and socially productive. The tenure-line faculty who teach the graduate curriculum have been educated in PhD programs, and they work in an institutional context that is notably different from the ones in which their students will likely teach. The kind of apprenticeship in teaching common in PhD programs does not provide a good model in this context. We may in fact be able to maintain a program that continues to fill the certification needs for our region, but changes in the higher education landscape may ultimately affect the quality—and therefore the productiveness—of that work.

Both of these ethical challenges, combined with the professional challenges we face in balancing the practical and the theoretical, have prompted our faculty to continually study our program, our decisions, and the experiences of our graduates, revising as necessary along the way. In many ways, the ethical and professional challenges we have detailed in this chapter have necessitated that we gather even more information about our graduates' experiences and build stronger connections and bridges with our surrounding stakeholders, particularly community colleges. Nonetheless, changes to our faculty makeup, and even to our undergraduate programs, since they offer opportunities for students and faculty alike, suggest that we may have to reconsider the way we can be responsive to local needs. Significantly, such changes have led us to recognize and negotiate the important differences between an academic program like the composition MA, wherein faculty are expected to have a scholarly interest in the subjects they teach, and a certificate program, which tends to have a much more applied or practical focus.

Conclusions: Negotiating Responsiveness

As the tensions we've described indicate, MA programs, more than PhD programs, house competing populations and their pursuant interests, demands, and desires. Students join our MA classes for a host of reasons, and it is our job to find ways to build on these diverse interests while still making each course and program requirement productive for everyone. Sometimes we can be locally responsive to these needs by drawing on scholarship in the discipline: our work educating students about social justice and access, cultural diversity and critical pedagogy, and reading theory and pedagogy has fulfilled these goals for many of our students. In other areas, such as traditional grammar instruction, we must negotiate conflicts between local contexts that deem such work necessary and a field of scholarship that remains skeptical of its efficacy. In still other areas, our curriculum may choose to respond to legislation at a statewide level, intimately affecting how and what we teach and affecting our larger context as our graduates ripple out to new institutions.

As we work to strengthen our program, we have found it helpful to build as many bridges as possible with those stakeholders we value most, which allows us to learn more about how we might respond, adapt, or innovate. For example, in response to reports from alumni, we created partnerships with local community colleges to offer onsite internships in which our students can shadow experienced teachers and even have opportunities to teach, while at the same time taking a course on our campus dealing with key issues in community college instruction. This internship opportunity serves our students—as they learn firsthand about the locations and students where they might teach—and it serves the community colleges, since they want to see us producing more graduates who are "knowledgeable and enthusiastic" about teaching in that context (Boroch et al. 20). Moreover, this partnership has opened additional channels of communication between our faculty and the two-year colleges we attempt to serve, both by preparing teachers and by providing a system in which local knowledge can feed back into and inform our program.

Like our MA program, all graduate programs are works in progress and must continually ask whether they are being responsive to the local needs of their students and communities while simultaneously balancing disciplinary and professional commitments. As we have suggested, though, it is not always possible to be all things to all people, and difficult choices sometimes have to be made among competing professional and ethical principles. This includes the ways in which "socially productive" choices, such as promoting current educational theory, might sometimes be at odds with "local" demands or desires. In providing a snapshot of one MA program, the challenges it has faced, and the reflective principles guiding its ongoing development, we have illustrated part of Vandenberg and Clary-Lemon's argument: that terminal MA programs should focus less on preparing students for the PhD and more on identifying and addressing local or regional needs. Program self-assessment and self-reflection, combined with feedback mechanisms such as internships, local conferences, or increased partnering with alumni, are some specific ways programs can pinpoint these needs and show the way forward. For us at San Francisco State, the primary local need is preparing community college teachers and doing our part to support the democratic mission of access and equity in public higher education. For other schools, it might be developing strong professional writers to meet the needs of area businesses. Whatever the trajectories of our graduates, we need to ensure that the work we do prepares them to make meaningful contributions to their communities and to society at large. Through situated, localized responses aimed at strengthening relationships within their local context, MA programs can not only serve their students and their communities, but they can also continue to enhance our understanding of the various and crucial roles that MA programs play in advancing both our knowledge and our society.

Note

1. It is, of course, worth noting that students from different programs and with different expectations contribute to the vitality and energy of these courses, sometimes expressly by bringing other perspectives, expertise, needs, and motivations.

Works Cited

Boroch, Deborah, et al. *Basic Skills as a Foundation for Student Success in California Community Colleges*. Sacramento: Research and Planning Group for California Community Colleges, 2007. Print.

California State Assembly. *Assembly Bill No. 1725*. 1988–1989 reg. sess. Sacramento: OSP, 19 Sept. 1988. Web. 1 July 2015.

Christensen, Francis. "A Generative Rhetoric of the Sentence." *College Composition and Communication* 14.3 (1963): 155–61. Print.

Conference on College Composition and Communication. "Students' Right to Their Own Language." *College Composition and Communication* 25.3 (1974): 1–32. Print.

Connors, Robert J. "The Erasure of the Sentence." *College Composition and Communication* 52.1 (2000): 96–128. Print.

Fulkerson, Richard. "Composition at the Turn of the Twenty-first Century." *College Composition and Communication* 56.4 (2005): 654–87. Print.

Goen-Salter, Sugie. "Critiquing the Need to Eliminate Remediation: Lessons from San Francisco State." *Journal of Basic Writing* 27.2 (2008): 81–105. Print.

Goen, Sugie, and Helen Gillotte-Tropp. "Integrating Reading and Writing: A Response to the Basic Writing 'Crisis.'" *Journal of Basic Writing* 22.2 (2003): 90–113. Print.

Matsuda, Paul Kei. "Composition Studies and ESL Writing: A Disciplinary Division of Labor." *College Composition and Communication* 50.4 (1999): 699–721. Print.

Schön, Donald A. *The Reflective Practitioner: How Professionals Think in Action*. New York: Basic Books, 1983. Print.

The Locally Responsive, Socially Productive MA in Composition

Shaughnessy, Mina P. "Diving In: An Introduction to Basic Writing." *College Composition and Communication* 27.3 (1976): 234–39. Print.

Vandenberg, Peter, and Jennifer Clary-Lemon. "Advancing by Degree: Placing the MA in Writing Studies." *College Composition and Communication* 62.2 (2010): 257–82. Print.

Young, Richard E., and Erwin R. Steinberg. "Planning Graduate Programs in Rhetoric in Departments of English." *Rhetoric Review* 18.2 (2000): 390–402. Print.

CHAPTER TWO

English Online/On the Line: The Challenges of Sustaining Disciplinary Relevance in the Twenty-First Century

KRISTINE L. BLAIR
Youngstown State University

A 2009 ranking of graduate-level English programs developed by *U.S. News & World Report* defined the utility of an advanced degree in English in the following way: "Earning a master's degree or Ph.D. in English can improve your writing skills, sharpen your analytical abilities, and broaden your literary knowledge." In chronicling the list of approximately 135 top-ranked programs in the country, the areas of study included eighteenth- through twentieth-century British literature, African American literature, American literature before and after 1865, gender and literature, literary criticism and theory, and medieval and Renaissance literature. Given these emphases, it isn't surprising that the presumed goal of a master's degree is preparation for PhD programs in literary studies that in turn prepare students for careers as future literature faculty. Current economic conditions have influenced the move away from full-time positions to more part-time positions, which has resulted in staffing undergraduate English courses in many programs with contingent labor, including non-tenure-track faculty who possess the master's degree.

According to the Modern Language Association's Executive Committee of the Association of Departments of English (ADE), "While the profession shares a well-developed sense of doctoral programs as preparation for postsecondary teaching, there is far

English Online/On the Line

less awareness of the role master's programs have played in sup-
plying candidates for postsecondary faculty positions, especially
the already large and still growing cadre of full- and part-time
teachers holding non-tenure-track appointments" (ADE Ad
Hoc Committee on the Master's Degree 1). These deteriorating
material conditions have impacted the overall value of a master's degree that, rather than preparing students for a full-time
academic career, may instead be preparing them for second-class
academic status and, far worse, the unemployment line. For
instance, in chronicling the development of a master's program
in professional writing, Susan M. Hunter, Elizabeth J. Giddens,
and Margaret B. Walters note that the newer "trend in looking
beyond a traditional notion of English studies has gained strength,
in part, because it responds to a perennial question: How can
English studies prepare students for lives and careers outside of
academe?" (153–54). As these authors assert, there needs to be
better support for and tracking of master's level students who
do not seek academic careers or educational advancement or
who take positions that do not allow them to apply the skills the
degree is meant to foster. Similarly, the ADE report "points to
a gap between students' aspirations and employment outcomes
on the one hand and MA programs' stated goals and curricular
requirements on the other" (1).

Part of the problem is one of audience awareness: all too many
faculty members continue to believe that the students enrolling
in graduate-level English courses are all on the same academic
career path—one that is more rhetoric than reality. A decline in
the number of undergraduate English majors (Steward) impacts
the numbers of students enrolling in traditional English programs
as defined by the *U.S. News & World Report* survey. Yet, as the
ADE report suggests, enrollment in master's programs, even in
the humanities, is growing, in part because the cultural capital
of a bachelor's degree in the current economic climate is limited,
and many students require advanced certification and training,
particularly in areas such as education. But the ADE further notes
that "such growth does not necessarily mean that English departments automatically profit, whether financially, educationally, or
intellectually, from the establishment or expansion of master's

programs" (4). Indeed, while numbers of programs and students may grow, resources may not, because of the ongoing lack of opportunities for English departments to document their success in attracting students able and willing to self-fund. A related problem is delivery; to be as accessible as possible, both the curriculum and the mode in which faculty develop and deliver graduate-level content to more diverse student populations mandate that programs shift from the brick-and-mortar classroom to the fully online classroom.

To provide a context for these issues and concerns, I chronicle the development of the online Master's Plan II (nonthesis) in English at Bowling Green State University (BGSU), one of the few fully online programs in the discipline. Approved for distance delivery in 2008, this master's program primarily targets public school educators in need of advanced certification but has attracted a range of professional audiences as well. As part of this case study, I overview the economic exigencies that prompted development of the degree, including declining enrollments in traditional face-to-face graduate seminars in English literature and the resulting push at both the institutional and state levels to diversify our audience by expanding modes of delivery at both the undergraduate and graduate levels.

In addition to these exigencies, this chapter addresses the need to redefine English studies for twenty-first-century students, stressing the master's degree as something other than a first step to the PhD or a niche program that enables graduate faculty to teach courses in their specialty areas as opposed to courses that enhance students' marketability outside the academy. Even as scholars have acknowledged the role of technology in enhancing our overall relevance as a field (Selfe 72; Smith), the topic of online learning can be a contentious one in departments of English, in part because of the perceived gap in quality of interaction between face-to-face and virtual delivery. Among faculty colleagues, there can exist a certain nostalgia not only for traditional delivery modes but also for traditional literary content that meshes more with teacher-centered as opposed to student-centered goals.

Regardless of these ideological rifts within our unit, I document the ways in which the development of this degree plan has led to productive conversations among faculty about the future

English Online/On the Line

of master's level education in English and about how to develop and deliver curricula that prepare graduate students for a range of academic and professional careers, especially because of concerns about the overall utility of the MA in English (Steward). This chapter describes specific learning outcomes for the program that balance the emphasis on literary studies (the continual focus of many English MA programs) with other disciplinary emphases such as rhetoric and writing and technical communication. Despite the potential of these outcomes, the sustainability of this initiative depends on faculty development models that help graduate educators become more aware of the ways in which the signature pedagogies and outcomes of English studies can and should be remediated through online delivery to the benefit of real students we serve rather than the ideal ones we imagine we do.

The Master's Plan II Program

As online course development gained momentum across BGSU's campus, in part through the implementation of the Blackboard course management system as well as through the development of a distance learning center titled IDEAL (Interactive Distance Education for All Learners), our own department experienced initial success in the delivery of online graduate courses to non-residential populations in northwest Ohio. In summer 2002, we began by offering five fully online graduate seminars across programs (linguistics, literature, rhetoric and writing, and scientific and technical communication), hoping to attract a middle and secondary school teacher audience in need of generalist training in English studies. Because this group has been required to seek certification beyond the bachelor's degree, they are often the group from whom our graduate office receives the most queries about course offerings. As a computers and writing specialist and director of graduate studies at the time, I was heavily involved in the process of migrating graduate seminars online, talking with faculty about the enrollment exigencies for online teaching, and creating a unit-specific team development model (Alvarez, Blair, Monske, and Wolf) that paired graduate students trained in an online course I developed and taught, "Online Learning for

English Educators," with individual faculty teaching online for the first time, working together to migrate curricular content and learning the course management system.

After the initial pilot offerings in 2002, we began to regularly offer online graduate seminars each summer, which were not only consistently enrolled but also frequently created a situation in which demand exceeded available space. Because of this demand, once I was appointed English department chair in 2005, my primary goal was to create a fully online master's program to bolster what were at the time limited enrollments in some graduate-level courses, notably in technical communication, and that ultimately led to the discontinuation of the face-to-face MA in that program in favor of a four-course certificate program in international scientific and technical communication. Thus, I worked with our Graduate Committee to revise our English MA Plan II, a generic 33-credit hour, nonthesis option with only three specific course requirements, into a more defined degree option with several tracks beyond the original three-course requirement, including one in English language arts that allows students to complete the degree in a fully online sequence of courses across programs. Although the majority of these courses are in English, the emphasis on language arts in the public schools also permits us to include interdisciplinary elective options in departments such as Teaching and Learning (College of Education), American Culture Studies, Women's Studies, Theatre and Film, and others within the College of Arts and Sciences. And unlike our MA Plan I in Literary and Textual Studies, a long-standing face-to-face program clearly designed for those students pursuing academic careers, our MA Plan II English Language Arts is one that attracts a range of nonresidential populations, specifically those whose finances, work, and/or family responsibilities do not always allow for full-time study during the standard academic year. Equally important, these students often are not pursuing the doctorate; therefore, a degree that offers more breadth of training in English studies seemed an appropriate option for fully online delivery.

Even with the difference in student populations among our programs (a rhetoric and writing PhD, an MFA in creative writing, the master's in literature, an online certificate in technical communication, and a certificate in Teaching English as a Second

English Online/On the Line

Language), our courses frequently enroll both residential and nonresidential students, in part because of similar requirements across programs. Rather than view this as a liability, we saw it as a strength, particularly because it ensured that courses would sufficiently fill and counteract our initial enrollment problems. Moreover, online course delivery could also benefit academic year residential students in need of more flexible schedules, notably in the summer when they may study and work outside of Bowling Green because of limited funding opportunities. Despite these different populations, we initially did not expect the enrollments for our online graduate courses to exceed the cap of fifteen students. Instead, we believed that consistent and fully online delivery leading toward the Plan II MA would attract new student learners to advanced study in English. And ultimately, in our emphasis on public school educators, we believed we would provide a valuable service to the population of northwest Ohio.

"If You Build It": Challenges in Implementation

Student Demand

Once the degree was approved in 2007, promotion for the program was inconsistent in that the distance learning office did not have the marketing staff to advertise the program, and as a result, courses initially filled, as predicted, because of hybrid populations. A course such as "Literary Theory and Criticism" often had three distinct populations: doctoral students in rhetoric (through fall 2010), residential master's students in literary studies, and the slowly growing number of fully online students accepted to the program. Part of the challenge in attracting students was that our market of public school educators had often been out of undergraduate school for some time, and we began to discover that some of the standard benchmarks for graduate applicants—academic writing samples, current letters of reference from those who were able to observe applicants as students, and the ever intimidating Graduate Record Exam—often deterred individual applications. To account for such issues, we soon updated our requirements to allow students to substitute Praxis II English Language Arts licensure exams or the equivalent licensure

— 27 —

measurement and accepted a balance of professional, supervisor, and academic reference letters. We also migrated in a course titled "Graduate Writing" (ENG 6040), meant to be a refresher or introduction to the expectations of advanced academic and professional writing. Similar concerns accompanied the portfolio capstone experience and the stated faculty presumption that written projects would adhere to MLA (Modern Language Association) style, whereas work in linguistics, rhetoric, education, and technical communication frequently relies on APA (American Psychological Association) style.

To encourage even more flexibility and to accommodate nontraditional students, in contrast to our annual fall admissions cycle for all other programs, we developed rolling admissions deadlines: July 1 for fall, October 1 for spring, and March 1 for summer. This would prove to be a tactical mistake in program management, for as word of the program spread, enrollments began to increase, and by the fall of 2010, we had more than fifty students at various stages of the degree. Because these students were entering the program at different times and applying later than other students and not as part of a controlled cohort, courses were not always available in sequence and, very often, due to the hybrid population, space in remaining online courses could not be guaranteed. To counteract this problem, we have since returned our application cycle to the same fall deadlines as other programs, though this choice countered the expectation by deans and enrollment management administrators that we expand our capacity if at all possible, an issue that has led to faculty concerns about quantity over quality.

Faculty Resistance

In an effort to provide incentives and rewards to BGSU faculty migrating courses online, the university initially provided development funds of $2,000 and the technological support of the distance learning center, recently renamed the Center for Online and Blended Learning (COBL). While such development funds are no longer provided, faculty teaching online courses continue to receive a $1,000 stipend for each online course, and online courses are part of the standard teaching load rather than an expected overload. The financial incentives led a number of faculty to teach online courses at both the graduate and undergraduate levels, responding to student demand for a shift in summer session offerings to fully online delivery and the faculty's realization that face-to-face summer courses would not sufficiently enroll to run. Nevertheless, given the academic labor issues and concerns about the ability of online courses to foster the standard curricular objectives of English graduate study, newer literature faculty not privy to initial conversations about the online degree expressed resistance. Although we addressed this concern by removing pretenure faculty in literature from online graduate rotations, this move represented a double standard because pretenure faculty in rhetoric and writing regularly taught graduate and undergraduate courses online without complaint or difficulty. Literature faculty claimed their courses were too theoretically complex for critical reading and discussing online. Literature courses were deemed more difficult to teach than doctoral-level seminars in rhetoric, which were in turn labeled more pedagogical and less theoretical. Of equal concern was the fact that a number of literature faculty did not want to focus on courses such as The Teaching of Literature, preferring instead to teach special topics courses in their literary specialties. Rather than bringing our programs together, the degree was reinscribing dated biases and binaries between literary studies and rhetorical studies (Scholes).

As discussions progressed, another concern emerged that revealed some inherent presumptions about students the faculty preferred and expected to serve, in this case residential students dedicated to university-level careers as literature professors and not practicing language arts teachers or other working professionals. Yet, as Jacques Berlinerblau has argued, the problem facing humanities faculty in general is their failure to engage multiple internal and external audiences, particularly at the graduate level:

> The public redemption of the humanities that I have in mind begins in graduate school. The change will occur when we persuade apprentice humanists to engage their audience and then equip them with the tools to do so. Who composes that audience? In order of importance: students, scholars not in one's field, and cultivated laypersons.

In many ways, English is no different from other disciplines in which faculty prefer to teach courses directly in their area of expertise and to assign and read texts that have concrete connections to their scholarly agenda. Certainly, the connection to a cohort of graduate students is an important part of their roles as researchers, mentors, and advisors. Nevertheless, the belief that the online MA students were inherently inferior to the face-to-face MA students revealed an elitism and ultimately a short-sightedness about the importance of English studies beyond the academy that, as Berlinerblau suggests, limit the ability to engage with and address the needs of real twenty-first-century learners whose professional circumstances warrant new delivery modes, not more of the same.

Admittedly, there are technological limits on engagement as well, and faculty across programs expressed legitimate concern about the ability to meet curricular objectives through a course management system like Blackboard. Although most faculty used Blackboard as a supplement to face-to-face instruction, many had never used its various presentation, communication, and assessment features for fully online instruction. Therefore, they had little to no experience enhancing the traditional Blackboard course shell by integrating more multimodal, interactive Web 2.0 tools that would be more engaging than the text-driven communication and assessment that this particular course management system tends to privilege. Although online writing specialists such as Scott Warnock support course development through user-friendly systems, he also advocates that faculty spend time developing needs assessments that align learning activities with the types of tools that foster them most effectively and establish "the right mix" (20). Most faculty in English had not pursued professional development opportunities in teaching with technology outside the department through COBL or our Center for Teaching and Learning, and they tended to focus more on the increase in workload than on the potential benefits of online education. Therefore, their understanding of the potential for digital tools to foster the signature pedagogies of English studies, often via whole-class and small-group discussion and student facilitators, was overshadowed by the presumption of loss rather than gain.

English Online/On the Line

Fostering Change

Writing about the need for an emerging set of principles in developing both innovative and rigorous distance education models, Lawrence Ragan asserts that "the techniques and artistry of the craft may change depending on the constraints of time and place, but the desired student goal, a marked and measurable change in behavior, [are] clearly the same" (10). In other words, as Ragan's article title suggests, "Good Teaching Is Good Teaching," and the same strategies that foster student success in face-to-face environments can and should be implemented in online environments. My goal as department chair (my term ended in 2014) was to help our faculty see that it is possible to develop and deliver online graduate curricula in ways that mesh with stated learning outcomes. In discussing the pros and cons of online master's study in literature, W. R. Owens suggests that the "asynchronous nature of the medium can enable students to produce more measured and thoughtful contributions" (41). As more and more faculty teach online, including literature faculty, who received direct pressure from the dean of the college to share the responsibility of online graduate teaching in the program, the process has become demystified, and though many do continue to voice concerns about workload, others express surprise at the quality of discussion and the student initiative that occurs in online forums. A faculty member (Begum) in our literature program forwarded a student response that supports this view:

> Just wanted to give you feedback on your question regarding the non-graded discussion board. I loved that it was not part of the graded material. It really did free me up to respond genuinely to the papers I did read. You made it clear in your syllabus that you expected us to participate regularly that was enough, I think, for a graduate course. I didn't feel like I was interacting with the others in our class because I "had" to, as a result, I feel that my posts were more authentic. I want to say, too, that this class has restored my feelings about online instruction. Your posts on the announcement board kept you "present" in our class.

— 31 —

If "good teaching is good teaching," then it follows that bad teaching in face-to-face environments can translate into bad teaching in online environments. There have been concerns about instructional performance across programs in terms of timeliness of response or overall online presence of those faculty who might not prioritize their online students equally with their face-to-face populations. Although some faculty have voiced critiques of students who may initially enroll in an online course with the perception that it will be less rigorous and then drop the course when they see the actual workload involved, faculty themselves may not always see their online courses as meaningful. Given *Chronicle of Higher Education* headlines such as "Why Online Education Won't Replace College—Yet" (written by a philosophy professor), there remains a bias that perceives face-to-face teaching and therefore face-to-face students as more important. A related issue is one of ownership: because the online students are literally not visible, faculty often do not perceive them as "our students" but as external clientele, leading to a continual caste system in which some students are deemed more ideal than others. This has led to problems in securing faculty to serve as portfolio capstone readers for the online cohort; as a result, in fall 2012 we developed a rotation of faculty from across participating programs to serve, a process in place for many other types of course schedules in the department.

To counteract these biases, our department has engaged in a number of quality control measures, along with both department- and university-level professional development forums, including a fully online training course for faculty new to teaching online, developed and delivered by COBL instructors. But because so many courses in English have already been migrated to online delivery, it became equally important to develop a faculty peer observation system that better accounted for the ways in which faculty interact with students online and the types of tools that facilitate these processes. Our guidelines were heavily influenced by the Quality Matters program, which provides a rubric of standards ("Program Rubric") that include such aspects as learning objectives (competencies), instructional materials, learner interaction and engagement, accessibility, and course technology. And because tenure and promotion review require peer observa-

English Online/On the Line

tion, this process also ensured that faculty were recognized and rewarded for their online teaching successes.

Another important form of professional development has been the meetings of faculty across programs; faculty have met to share not only the whats of online English pedagogies but also the hows and the whys, as Warnock suggests. For instance, one meeting was facilitated by a literature faculty member who discussed the teaching of a literary theory course online, stressing the importance of clarifying difficult concepts upfront via mini-lectures in PowerPoint. Because of the complexity of readings and the difficulty in grasping the language of theory, the instructor addressed workload concerns, which then led to a productive discussion of managing both presentation and assessment processes. Several important outcomes arose from this session, including the need to allow students to play more of a facilitator role in discussion forums and the need for faculty not to feel as though they have to respond to every online comment to be "present" (both a pedagogy and a workload issue).

Faculty also discussed the ability to rely on other tools besides Blackboard to move away from what Owens has acknowledged as the text-based form of online communication, allowing students to have opportunities to present orally and engage in debate (42). Certainly there are tools that allow for that, including Skype, podcasting software, and other freeware and Web 2.0 applications. A follow-up workshop led by a faculty member in creative writing emphasized the role of audio podcasting to deliver content and the availability of units on campus to assist with the design and development of audio modules and commentary. In fairness to our faculty, this is often the area in which campus-wide faculty development and instructional technology units are limited, in part because of the desire to offer training in the tools that are institutionally supported, typically the course management system, as opposed to open source and other social media tools that would foster higher levels of interactivity.

Regardless of our success in delivering the degree and graduating students over the last several years, the challenges we continue to face are multiple. Based on our annual assessment report (Edminster), program completers have expressed concerns about the ability to enroll in required courses in a timely way given that

— 33 —

these courses are typically only offered once a year. In addition, students have expressed a desire for courses more relevant to their teaching duties, moving from purely theory-based treatments to pedagogical assignments that include more lesson planning. All programs have, as a result, engaged in more curricular discussion about ways to make courses as pragmatic as possible while still meeting programmatic learning outcomes.

Moreover, the university has made a shift from Blackboard to Canvas as the supported learning management system, and while training is available, faculty must take the initiative to sign up for and attend such forums to better develop not only functional technological literacies but also critical and rhetorical technological literacies (Selber 25) that will allow them to understand the role that a range of digital tools play (or not) in fostering presentation of content, communication between students and between students and faculty, as well as student self-assessment and more faculty-driven modes of evaluation. To that end, a recent workshop encouraged faculty to develop professional development plans for determining where they are in terms of their techno-pedagogical competencies, where they need be, and how, through training, peer observation, and curricular modification, they are going to get there. Not getting there is simply not an option, due to both ongoing student demand and the university's mission to attract fee-paying students. While not every course in the online program is geared toward college-level instruction, our "Teaching of Writing" and "Teaching of Literature" courses have the potential to prepare students not only for the curriculum and pedagogy of writing and literary studies but also for the ways those factors are migrated and potentially transformed online. The likelihood of these future faculty teaching online in either community college or four-year university settings is strong, given increasing numbers of job descriptions that call for experience in distance education.

Conclusion

Just as faculty make presumptions about the ideal student population, the problem facing English and other humanities faculty

English Online/On the Line

is the presumption about their ability to innovate and engage; Hearn and Gorbunov quote a 1999 study by Massey-Burzio that typifies this constituency as "ignorant, skeptical, or wary of the new technology and its opportunities; they mostly opt for the old and customary methods" (22). While writing studies specialists are often early adopters of technology, literary studies specialists haven't been as focused on digital pedagogies. More recently, however, the growth of the digital humanities and increasing attention paid to scholarly production in virtual spaces suggest we should look to organizations such as MLA and the Conference on College Composition and Communication (CCCC) to establish a stronger relationship between technology and both research and teaching. MLA Past President Sidonie Smith makes this call to action in her 2010 MLA newsletter column:

> Our students will be disadvantaged if they do not graduate from doctoral programs as skilled teachers, adept at engaging classes of various sizes and different mixes of students and versed in scholarship on student literacies and learning environments. . . . Furthermore, they will need facility in digital composing, melding words, images, moving images, and sound. Many of them will produce digital scholarship that doubles as teaching tools, requiring sophisticated pedagogical approaches to concept design and platform use.

Smith makes a strong connection between research and teaching, something that English faculty committed to emerging work in the digital humanities should not ignore in the current emphasis on the role of technology and Web 2.0 in the consumption and production of scholarship. And given mandates for increasing external funding to support graduate education at BGSU and other research-intensive institutions, the humanities cannot afford to be left behind or left out of these conversations. Indeed, Hearn and Gorbunov question, "How have humanities departments responded to the advent of new technologies? Can we identify cases of successful and 'profitable' responses by humanities departments and new technologies?" (21).

Despite the challenges in implementing our own degree, there is no doubt that it represents a profitable response. We are still one of the few online MA programs in BGSU's College of Arts and

Sciences, and our efforts to recruit fee-paying students has had a positive impact on our face-to-face programs in that the department received approximately $60,000 for additional graduate student stipends for our residential programs. Our documented "growing pains" notwithstanding, we have become a model for others at our university seeking to migrate programs online out of economic necessity, student demand, overall decreases in graduate stipends, and the need to generate a population of fee-paying professional students to augment the funded students who, from the university's perspective, represent costs. To accommodate such necessity and demand, we have since developed another fully online MA track, this one in professional writing and rhetoric; we are now actively recruiting our first cohort.

One factor that diminishes the perception of success is the inability of some English faculty to let go of the presumption that online learning environments are inherently inferior, and that nothing can be done curricularly or pedagogically to make these spaces just as intellectually rigorous as face-to-face environments. Certainly, a continual challenge is the larger academic debate on this subject, with higher administration perceived as in the business of online courses for the financial rewards and faculty resistant to online learning on the grounds of academic rigor. In "Don't Confuse Technology with College Teaching," Pamela Hieronymi laments the move of MIT, Harvard, Berkeley, and Stanford toward online education, presuming that digital delivery privileges mere transmission of information or ideas as opposed to more genuine learning, and that it ultimately reduces technology's benefit to grammar checking and quiz development. For Hieronymi,

> It is as though elite educators . . . decided to pretend that if we just let those seeking an education talk among themselves (in grammatically felicitous sentences), they will somehow come to express difficult ideas in persuasive arguments and arrive at coherent, important insights about society, politics, and culture.

Ironically, the process Hieronymi describes is perhaps one of the great benefits of online education: it fosters participation by all students, not merely the few who are vocal in a face-to-face

English Online/On the Line

setting, and it balances the responsibility for knowledge-making between faculty and students as co-facilitators. This is the essence of graduate education in English and inevitably makes online delivery more, not less, conducive to such a student-centered seminar-style approach.

Another presumption to jettison is the belief that the singular role of English faculty is to train students to be mirror images of themselves as educators. Instead, our responsibilities as English educators should include modeling successful online pedagogies for future populations of public school and college-level educators who will increasingly be expected to assume these responsibilities, as the following email plea to the online discussion list TechRhet indicates:

> I'm teaching online English Comp for the first time. Does anyone have any quick and dirty instructions/help/files that will help me jump start my education on this form of delivery? I have a few weeks yet, but still am starting to freak out about this. (Freckleking)

One way to assist instructors like Freckleking is to foster a department-specific learning community (Alvarez et al.) comprising both experienced and novice online teachers committed to exploring the possibilities and constraints of online learning and collectively determining the training and resources required to be successful. Our online courses must serve as models of presentation and communication in not only academic settings but professional ones as well; effective and ethical online writing and communication practices are important aspects of today's workplace culture. While the responsibility for overall technology integration has often been relegated to computers and writing specialists within rhetoric and composition or to English education specialists (Tulley and Blair 445), this charge can and should extend to the whole of English studies in an effort to engage with nontraditional students, who are becoming less the exception and more the norm, even at residential universities such as BGSU.

At both the undergraduate and graduate levels, educational access is a significant issue for institutions, and all faculty must realize that changing economic realities lead many students to

— 37 —

community colleges and many working professionals to online degrees that meet their needs as place-bound, job-dependent adults requiring alternative models to the brick-and-mortar classroom. It is vital that English studies, given both its status as a hallmark of the liberal arts and the limited job prospects for those working in the profession, align itself with this mandate. Although online education at the graduate level may be the exception rather than the norm in English studies, and may initially be uncomfortable for faculty and graduate students alike, our experience at BGSU is that students are better prepared as a result of functioning as students in true distance settings and having firsthand experience in online classroom management in their role as co-facilitators. Inevitably, we must remediate and transition our profession into a new model of higher education that both emphasizes professionalization and sustains the relevance of a language arts degree beyond the academy. This commitment impacts not only our future but also the future of the students we serve within twenty-first-century learning environments.

Works Cited

ADE Ad Hoc Committee on the Master's Degree. "Rethinking the Master's Degree in English for a New Century." *Modern Language Association*. MLA, June 2011. Web. 5 Aug. 2012.

Alvarez, Deborah M., Kristine Blair, Elizabeth Monske, and Amie Wolf. "Team Models in Online Course Development: A Unit-Specific Approach." *Educational Technology and Society* 8.3 (2005): 176–186. Print.

Begum, Khani. "FW: Received Papers." 3 Aug. 2012. Email.

Berlinerblau, Jacques. "Survival Strategy for Humanists: Engage, Engage." *Chronicle of Higher Education*, 5 Aug. 2012. Web. 8 June 2016.

Edminster, Jude. MA II Online Track Assessment Report. 15 July 2012. Unpublished report. Print.

Freckleking. "Teaching English Comp Online." Message posted to TechRhet Discussion List. 6 Aug. 2012. Web. 22 Aug. 2012.

Hearn, James C., and Alexander V. Gorbunov. "Funding the Core: Understanding the Financial Contexts of Academic Departments in the Humanities." *Tracking Changes in the Humanities: Essays on Finance and Education.* Ed. Malcolm Richardson. Cambridge: American Academy of Arts and Sciences, 2005. 1–46. Print.

Hieronymi, Pamela. "Don't Confuse Technology with College Teaching." *Chronicle of Higher Education,* 13 Aug. 2012. Web. 8 June 2016.

Hunter, Susan M., Elizabeth J. Giddens, and Margaret B. Walters. "Adding Value for Students and Faculty with a Master's Degree in Professional Writing." *College Composition and Communication* 61.1 (2009): W153–74. Web. 10 June 2016.

Owens, W. R. "Master's Level Study in Literature at the Open University: Pedagogic Challenges and Solutions." *Teaching Literature at a Distance: Open, Online, and Blended Learning.* Ed. Takis Kayalis and Anastasia Natsina. London: Continuum, 2010. 33–43. Print.

Quality Matters. "Program Rubric." *QualityMatters.org.* Quality Matters Program, 2010. Web. 10 June 2016.

Ragan, Lawrence C. "Good Teaching Is Good Teaching: An Emerging Set of Guiding Principles and Practices for the Design and Development of Distance Education." *Cause/Effect* 22.1 (1999): 10–22. Web. 10 June 2016.

Scholes, Robert. *Textual Power: Literary Theory and the Teaching of English.* New Haven: Yale UP, 1985. Print.

Selber, Stuart A. *Multiliteracies for a Digital Age.* Carbondale: Southern Illinois UP, 2004. Print.

Selfe, Cynthia L. "Toward New Media Texts: Taking up the Challenges of Visual Literacy." *Writing New Media: Theory and Applications for Expanding the Teaching of Composition.* Ed. Anne Frances Wysocki, Johndan Johnson-Eilola, Cynthia L. Selfe, and Geoffrey Sirc. Logan: Utah State UP, 2004. 67–110. Print.

Smith, Sidonie. "Beyond the Dissertation Monograph." *MLA Newsletter* 42.1 (2010): 2–3. Web. 13 June 2016.

Steward, Doug. "The Master's Degree in Modern Languages since 1966." *ADE Bulletin* 136 (2004): 50–68. Print.

Tulley, Christine, and Kristine Blair. "Remediating the Book Review: Toward Collaboration and Multimodality across the English Curriculum." *Pedagogy* 9.3 (2009): 441–69. Print.

U.S. News and World Report. "Best English Programs, Top Humanities Schools, US News Best Grad Schools." *usnews.com*. U.S. News and World Report, 2009. Web. 13 June 2016.

Warnock, Scott. *Teaching Writing Online: How and Why*. Urbana: NCTE, 2009. Print.

CHAPTER THREE

Academic Capitalism, Student Needs, and the English MA

MARK MOSSMAN
Western Illinois University

If we consider the skill-driven employment sectors of the global economy, then the English MA is now the most significant degree conferred in English studies—more than either the bachelor's or the doctorate.

I make this assertion within the context of what Shelia Slaughter, Gary Rhoades, and Larry L. Leslie have defined as the new paradigm in contemporary higher education, that is, "academic capitalism." Slaughter and Rhoades specifically note that the development of an academic capitalism has effected radical changes in pedagogical practice and/or course delivery, faculty and staff behaviors, intellectual property ownership and distribution, basic university funding strategies, and larger long-term planning initiatives. More than these changes, though, the major effect that academic capitalism has produced in the last twenty years is curricular: increased development and conferral of terminal master's-level degrees and postbaccalaureate certificates in such areas as the health sciences, management and administration, business and communications technologies, and education. These degrees are often delivered within a distance-learning format and linked directly to the development of credentials and/ or licensure for future employment, salary increases, and other industry-specific concerns.

The conferral of graduate degrees and certificates in English has failed to keep pace with those professional fields just noted. Yet, despite the downward turn in numbers of degrees conferred, paradoxically, English studies is still recognized in practice as

– 41 –

being a vital field, perhaps the most vital field in the contemporary university, especially in the humanities. Again and again, "English," and the curricular requirement of English courses, is made central in discussions in higher education concerning student acquisition and articulation of those basic skills by workers in almost all sectors of the economy—skills such as literacy, critical thinking, analytical reading, and critical writing. Far from exile on the margins, "English" is in reality central in this new order of academic capitalism in higher education. With this in mind, I argue that the future of the MA in English rests on two related points: (1) the degree should shift in its function and engage more actively in the political, cultural, and historical exigencies that shape its present existence in a market economy, and (2) despite increasingly intense pressures, the MA degree should continue to engage political/cultural/historical issues as *objects* of study.

Academic Capitalism and the Business of Skill

In the final chapter of his book *Nice Work If You Can Get It: Life and Labor in Precarious Times* (2009), Andrew Ross tells of being a member for one year of Shanghai's American Chamber of Commerce and of his experience of the Chamber's several "social mixers" in Shanghai during this period. Among the crucial points of Ross's story is his amazement at the number of representatives from US universities pursuing financial capital in China. Ross writes,

> I came to realize that, as a representative of an American University, I was not at all out of place in this environment. My institutional employer and its brand were perfectly at home in this watering hole for profit-chasing, cost-cutting investors pursuing a lucrative offshore opportunity.
>
> It's one thing to joke in the faculty lounge about our universities going off in pursuit of emerging global markets, and yet another to be handed business cards in one such emerging market by corporate reps who want to do business. My personal experience in China helped me to understand how easy it is, in practice, for our academic culture to meld with the normalizing assumptions and customs of modern business culture. (192)

Academic Capitalism, Student Needs, and the English MA

The final chapter of *Nice Work* suggests that higher education is designed now to meet a very wide set of expectations, one primary expectation being the securing of capital and institutional or brand-name expansion through corporate networking on a global scale. Without question, such corporate behaviors are now normalized and necessary for the contemporary higher education institution's success. These behaviors likewise cohere with the expectations of both students and larger North American and eurozone economies.

In *Mission and Money: Understanding the University*, Burton A. Weisbrod, Jeffrey P. Ballou, and Evelyn D. Asch confirm the complicated dynamic of these relationships that Ross's experience in China illustrates. Higher education now functions in a worldwide culture of contradictory expectations, declining skill, budgeting crises, and fierce competition. The authors explain:

> For parents, higher education is vital to their children's lifetime careers, on the one hand, but is a major financial drain on family resources, on the other. For public policy-makers, higher education is many things—a fundamental element of their constituents' demands for economic opportunity, a crucial element of the struggle for equality of access to learning and prosperity, a magnet for attracting business and industry, and a source of national, state, and local pride. But it is also a social service—and increasingly so. (xiii)

Key to my argument here is a recognition of our current place in the academy as workers in English studies. The contemporary postsecondary institution is viewed by many stakeholders as a global business, a promise of prosperity, a vehicle for social equality, and a practical social service. These notions concerning the purpose of higher education run askew from what Catharine R. Stimpson and many others in English have argued, which is that "educational institutions exist in order to apply and extend to their communities the values of teaching, learning, and the creative yet rigorous search for the truth" (35). Though these values are certainly present in the minds of our students, their parents, and their families, they are not primary, and only one part of the larger purpose of investing in the higher education system.

— 43 —

In this context, Shelia Slaughter and Gary Rhoades define academic capitalism as a shift away from the "public good knowledge/learning regime," the paradigm under which we in English studies still clearly operate and through which we, arguably, drive many of our MA students toward low-paid teaching positions with little advancement opportunities. Now, according to Slaughter and Rhoades, higher education is being defined and practiced through an entirely different set of notions, expectations, and values in alignment with profitable enterprise and the shared development of capital (8). In their words, this paradigm shift means that now "professionals, who still portray themselves as independent, are aligning themselves with the market and corporate elites, backgrounding the state and the public domain" (8). The result is that "new," often private or corporate, often international "networks" are being built and fully exploited that "connect them [higher education faculty] with the market economy, spanning boundaries between public, nonprofit, and market organizations" (38).

Let me put it another way. The best-suited response by the higher education institution to the dynamics of a global economy is believed to be a reorientation of the mission of higher education itself. No matter what the school may be (private or liberal or public, prestigious or inclusive, two-year or four-year, technical or comprehensive or research or ivy), the orientation is now to be production-driven, heavily regulated, and widely networked in practice. A school's successes are tied less to the diversification of student and faculty populations, or political and social perspectives, than directly to the narrow budgetary issues of the expenditure and acquisition of funds and the regulated placement of graduates into those networks that will further contribute to increased funds for the institution itself. Most prevalent now is the understanding that a completed course, a defined major, and a conferred degree are all credentials that will lead to employment in one of the sectors of the New Economy (see Jacobs).

We in English understand ourselves through an entirely different set of conditions. But in the day-to-day practice of a twenty-first-century educational institution—and this now includes the day-to-day practices of our professional lives in departments of English—knowledge and learning are defined less as the building

— 44 —

Academic Capitalism, Student Needs, and the English MA

blocks of intellectualism and discovery and more as the acquisition of specific credentials that confirm the possession of a particular, usable skill set that in turn equips the individual for participation in the New Economy. We have known for years that most students go to school on the belief that doing so will allow them to get a job and to acquire a measure of self-determination in finding that job; higher education institutions have now created an environment in which the primary mission is to reinforce and confirm this notion.

Most colleges and universities in the United States have now completed a decades-long process of transformation, having remade themselves in various ways in order to serve the monetary promise of an American education. This makeover has included everything from the push to offer more online or distance courses and to establish interdisciplinarity to strategic attempts to forge partnerships with external public and private entities or stakeholders and the development of undergraduate and graduate curricula that serve those constituencies directly. Postsecondary institutions, especially community colleges and the many regional state colleges and universities, understand their purpose as service to their immediate regions. The main requirement of that service is to place graduates, the gift of a job for those students who graduate.

This major paradigm shift in learning and knowledge dissemination in the United States is constituted by a conscious reorientation of the higher education institution itself. Andrew Ross's story cited earlier suggests that higher education is now a global industry made up of numerous entities competing in the New Economy. It is not the outside pressure of a potential customer that has generated this shift, nor is it entirely the demands of entities outside of higher education. It is the institution itself that has turned students into, in effect, traded commodities. This shift has been required by reductions in state funding and, simultaneously, an increase in external funding opportunities for many public institutions. In a critique of higher education's apparent embrace of NPM (New Public Management) philosophy and practice, Chris Lorenz writes that in the past thirty years, "the societal relevance of the universities demanded by critical students was turned on its head to become economic relevance to business and industry in the knowledge society" (600).

— 45 —

I assert that, in many ways, "English" is situated at the center of these exchanges in higher education and the discussions surrounding them. For example, the teaching of writing at the public higher education institution falls within these new developments and regulations. When one considers our discipline in this light and that the vast majority of courses offered in "English" are first-year writing or composition courses taught by graduate students or graduates with the MA degree, the English MA is the degree most directly engaged in these changes.

Much contemporary master's-level education is being built within this new higher education context and on these credentialing, entrepreneurial activities—that is, responding directly to the marketplace with credentials for the postbaccalaureate student rather than development in and knowledge of the research dynamics of the academic discipline itself. Though this is admittedly controversial to say, what it means for the English MA is that many of our students—and our potential students—are much more concerned with professionalization than with the latest work on Arthurian legend or postcolonial theories of globalization. Whether we like it or not, we are in the age of academic capitalism. In general, graduate students enrolling in the English MA are less concerned about learning, perspective, and research in the humanities and more concerned with the possible career choices available to them with the skill sets that an MA or, eventually, a PhD will provide. MA students are pursuing the credential needed to get the job—whether that job is at the community college (using pedagogical skills to teach up to twelve courses a year) or working for a regional business (using professional writing, reading, and speaking skills to build up a career) or, after the PhD, at the four-year college or university (where they will become what we have become—professionals engaged in a competitive, production-oriented environment).

There is clear evidence to support this claim. In 2005, Judith Glazer-Raymo provided a thorough analysis of the contemporary master's degree, asserting that "the master's degree exemplifies the diversity and complexity of graduate education in the twenty-first century" (vii). The report then documents the rising importance—empirically and philosophically—of the master's

Academic Capitalism, Student Needs, and the English MA

degree in the United States and catalogs how the degree embodies a restructuring of the disciplines themselves. This rise in the significance of graduate education—specifically the great shift toward the master's degree—concerns both professionalization *and* the increased commodification of education itself. Glazer-Raymo's account, combined with the work of Slaughter, Rhoades, Leslie, and many others, suggests that it is unlikely that the trend toward an academic capitalist knowledge/learning regime will stop. As Glazer-Raymo also reports on the master's degree:

> Four mechanisms will continue to propel the professionalization of master's education and its pivotal role in the marketplace: technological advances, global partnerships, mandates for accountability, and the permeability of disciplinary and institutional boundaries. Whereas the arts and sciences had been central to the university mission throughout the twentieth century, professional programs now predominate throughout the degree hierarchy. The geographic proximity of universities and workplaces, part-time and weekend courses, employer subsidies, and virtual campuses further enhance the marketability of the master's degree. (viii)

Glazer-Raymo concludes that "the Master's Degree is evolving as an *entrepreneurial* credential with the potential to alter the direction of graduate education in the liberal arts and sciences as well as in the professions. . . . [The master's degree is] more responsive to the marketplace than to traditional academic environments" (5; italics mine).

The drive to credential individuals with specific skill sets is rooted in academic capitalism—that being the business of skill. It is a powerful position, for in its contemporary form, higher education in the United States is at the center of a New Economy built primarily on the skill sets involved in the manipulation of information and knowledge. In theory, and increasingly in practice, the business that specializes in "higher ed" or "skill" has a tremendous amount of structural control over the entire process and thus is in a position to profit significantly in the current economic climate.[1] The higher education institution is one entity in the New Economy that can direct and manipulate "product"

– 47 –

(the graduating student) and, as a result, the business of the New Economy as a whole. Students need degrees (or credentials) to get jobs; the employer (whether public or private) needs personnel with degrees (or appropriate skill sets) to do its work; the higher education institution sits at the start and at the end of this process.

Integral to the skill set the university delivers (and which is vital to the New Economy) are critical writing and critical reading. The teaching of these skills is not usually housed in education or business but in the humanities, and in English specifically. There are three essential areas of production that guarantee the English MA's continued relevance to academic capitalism. These are first-year writing programs, WAC/WID programs, and general education programs. The crucial point here is that a great majority of the courses in these programs, and the associated skill sets, are taught most often by individuals with English MAs.

When we ignore the work that our MA students typically do and instead build our master's degrees primarily around the more traditional modes of discovery and content that fuel the delivery of most baccalaureate programs in English, we ultimately deflate the MA holder's professional position as a teacher of writing and deflate our own work as a discipline. This is because the stated purpose of a traditional focus is often contradictory and poorly articulated and therefore read by those outside of the immediate field as functionally irrelevant—concerned with cloudy ideals and the often vague possibility of "moving on" to a PhD program rather than emphasizing the hard necessity of mastering skills in order to do the job. Though it is significant, the diversification and deep, constant consideration of content does not have the overwhelming importance often presumed. Whether it be the insertion of postcolonial texts into a curriculum rather than the works of Empire, or graphic novels rather than the narratives of the Brontës, none of those vital book conversations in our disciplines matters as much on the transcript or résumé as the inclusion of functional skill sets in the curriculum so that the curriculum as a whole is understood as a deeply relevant training instrument that has a defined, marketable purpose for those students who move through it on their way to a career.

Academic Capitalism, Student Needs, and the English MA

Trends in Graduate Education and the Work of English

The previous section ended by suggesting that through the vehicle of the MA program English studies can better articulate its relevance in the New Economy, in the function of an academic capitalism, and in the skills-oriented work now being done across contemporary postsecondary education. These assertions may be read as controversial. Yet the currently documented state of English—namely, its diminishment as a field of graduate study—is not. The statistics on the English MA are remarkable. While master's-level education becomes more prevalent in the larger academy, enrollment in English MA programs is declining. Amazingly, there has been little research published on this trend. Doug Steward reports in a 2004 article:

> The overall number of master's degrees granted in the field of English has remained almost constant over the last three and a half decades, wavering around 6,000 degrees per year. . . . To represent the decline in degree conferrals in these fields solely in terms of numbers of degrees, however, disguises the fact that these fields' percentage shares of all master's degrees granted have slipped markedly. English's share slipped to 1.18% in 2001, less than a third of its 4.46% share in 1966. . . . In other words, as a share of all master's degrees granted, *master's degrees in English have declined by 72% in the past three and a half decades, those in foreign languages by 80%.* (154–55; italics mine)

In the midst of a boom in the conferral of master's degrees in the United States, the MA in English has lost a great percentage of those new students. Instead, students are gravitating toward sectors in postbaccalaureate education most directly tied to the New Economy and an academic capitalism. According to the National Center for Education Statistics (NCES), the most prominent graduate degrees conferred in 2006–2007 were the following:

> At the master's degree level, the largest numbers of degrees were in the fields of education (177,000) and business (150,000). The fields with the largest number of degrees at the doctor's

— 49 —

degree level were health professions and related clinical sciences (8,400), education (8,300), engineering (8,100), biological and biomedical sciences (6,400), psychology (5,200), and physical sciences (4,800). (238–39)

Note again that English, as well as most of the traditional arts and sciences, is simply nowhere to be found in these data. Most of the degrees conferred, more than 300,000 master's degrees, feed into the well-networked academic capitalist industry or commercial structures, such as education, business, and the health professions.

Unlike those colleges, schools, and departments already networked into the New Economy, in institutions of higher education, English studies envisions itself as operating outside of the dynamics of an academic capitalism. Philosophically, the humanities are in an oppositional posture that pushes against the structure of academic capitalism and that often pits faculty oriented toward one set of values and purposes against administrators oriented toward an entirely different set of values and purposes, creating a binary that is on both ends destructive and, as Stanley Aronowitz describes it, "self-deceptive" (45). Both the internal, field-specific debates and this resistance to "the outside" have led to a lack of coherence in the curriculum of most master's degree programs in English. These programs often fail to address the actual needs of master's-level students and the requirements of the New Economy within which these students and these programs function. As the discipline seems unable to recognize what students need, it is not surprising that this same discipline creates programs that are unclear, at best, in how they are preparing students for the world outside of the academy.

The response from English to these larger issues has almost always focused on undergraduate education or the PhD. When there has been work done on the function of the English MA, it has been out of necessity and often extremely local in nature. Sometimes this work has resulted in major curriculum revision, sometimes in productive, broader discussions in such forums as Association of Departments of English (ADE) summer seminars for chairs and graduate directors, and sometimes in an article published in *College English, PMLA, Profession,* or *The ADE Bulletin.*

Academic Capitalism, Student Needs, and the English MA

Often such responses from English have ended, as Frank Donoghue notes, in "histrionics" (1). These histrionics have arisen because there is no national-level, coherent commitment to bridge what we do in English studies to new economic structures. Consider the real numbers provided by the NCES report and by Steward's article, both of which clearly demonstrate the English MA's current marginal place in US graduate education, along with Robert Scholes's moment of quiet rage in his 1996 classic on revising English studies curricula:

> What this society *wants* of those who graduate from its schools and colleges with degrees in the humanities—as opposed to what many of those who claim to speak for it *says* it wants—are, at worst, docility and grammatical competence, at best, reliability and a high level of textual skills. What this society does *not* want from our educational institutions is a group of people imbued with critical skills and values that are frankly antagonistic to those that prevail in our marketplaces, courts, and legislative bodies. (19)

Though accurate in its assessment of US society, more than anything Scholes's writing articulates anger with the circumstances of US higher education and English's place in it. Despite the many pages that follow the preceding quote, the revision of English did not work. It is within this frame that Donoghue writes:

> Too many observers now describe the current state of higher education, particularly of the humanities, as a crisis. I wish instead to characterize it as an ongoing set of problems, a distinction that might first appear only to be semantic. The terms of the so-called crisis, from the academic humanistic perspective, are always the same: corporate interests and values are poised to overwhelm the ideals of the liberal arts and to transform the university into a thoroughly businesslike workplace. (1)

Our responses have failed to articulate the set of problems themselves and have been built on faulty assumption, hysteria, and a willful self-marginalization rather than on an actual engagement with the reality of what has been happening for decades in the higher education industry.

Such engagement begins with the revision of the English MA—the degree structure that produces the largest percentage of personnel teaching in English and humanities-oriented departments. Just as we are a discipline housed in a larger economic realm dominated by an academic capitalist regime, we are now within this realm a discipline not of PhDs but of MAs. English studies is not being conducted primarily by professors with PhDs; it is being conducted—articulated every day—in general education courses and first-year writing courses by adjunct, part-time, or full-time non-tenure-track instructors with MAs.[2] As Donoghue notes, "Even professors familiar with these categories would likely be surprised to learn that tenured and tenure-track professors currently constitute only 35 percent of college teaching personnel and that this number is steadily falling" (56).

It is at this juncture of academic labor, diminished enrollment, and academic capitalism that the work of the English MA must begin. Revision is all the more necessary given our place in higher education—those first-year writing courses and general education courses constitute real capital for the humanities disciplines and guarantee a role for English studies in the current academic capitalist learning regime. In these terms, the MA in English must be recognized now as central to English studies. If up to 65 percent of college teaching personnel can now be constituted by MAs rather than PhDs, then right now the MA is already functioning as such.

In its current form, however, the MA is structured either as a preparatory or predoctoral degree or as the consolation degree for students unable to finish the doctorate. As a result, this major degree of graduate education, this degree that is seeing a boom in the academy, is understood by English faculty, by incoming students, and by potential students as a degree without an immediate purpose and without any immediate market value. While the rest of higher education shifts and gains in reorienting itself to those increases in graduate-level enrollments, increases by students who desire a marketable credential, English falls behind—despite the need for our discipline in the contemporary university structure.

This can all change. I have suggested that the master's degree must be transformed into a structure that is less about political, cultural, and historical perspective and more about concrete

Academic Capitalism, Student Needs, and the English MA

bridges that lead directly into new economic structures. The degree must be focused, in its curriculum and in its wider function, not as either a predoctoral center or a kind of finishing school, but as a degree focused on the development of skill sets that clearly translate into marketable credentials. The MA degree must unite two very different curricular orientations. We must develop a skills-oriented curriculum that is built for professional competence and that is able to articulate those competencies in an effective way. Through this work, the MA in English can be turned into one of the primary degree structures in the New Economy while simultaneously, through its continued, tradition-based emphasis on interdisciplinarity, made into a degree that can in itself produce sweeping levels of transformation on multiple levels. It can achieve this status both in the graduate student enrolled in the MA program and in the wider circle that the now credentialed professional, the "super-product" (able to teach and train effectively in higher education and also, if desired, work in other New Economy sectors) will then influence and, indeed, control. To be clear, given the context of our current cultural practices, values, and assumptions, the MA degree is unique in that it does indeed have the potential to empower all of the students enrolled in it.

Obligations and Solutions: Pedagogy and Professionalization

Simply by being the highest degree possessed by most postsecondary teachers of the humanities, the MA is significant and influential in its practice. It is now in a period of intense transformation. Already the degree is being understood and used by many graduates in English as a credential for the academic, public, or private sector marketplace rather than as a period of intermediate training for further study in the discipline itself. Our MA students are directly engaged in the New Economy, and they often understand much more than we do the MA degree's role and potential function in those contemporary networks within which higher education now functions.

— 53 —

The work of our profession now is to engage this transformation, to examine it, and then to change it so that graduate study in English becomes more professionalized and recognized as the commodity that in so many ways it already is. The graduate program, especially at the masters-only institution, should come to constitute a professionalizing center. No matter how repellent this may seem to many of us, I want to stress that in mismanaged ways this degree already functions in these terms and within this context.

The English MA should be rebuilt in curricular content so that it is organized primarily around a pedagogy of skill sets that can legitimately radiate out into other areas. In its function as a terminal credentialing structure, I am arguing for a degree that possesses a professionalism that differs from such credentialing degrees as the MBA or the MAT. Ours will be a professionalism that privileges issues of social justice and the development of skills that speak to the larger social values our discipline already engages and has engaged for a long time—skills and values that engage, for example, sustainability and ecological issues and thus can now prepare graduates for work in emerging green industries; or skills and values that engage gender, race, sexuality, disability, and other kinds of somatically oriented issues and thus can now prepare students for possible careers in various kinds of social service and health industries; or skills and values that engage those overarching pedagogical and larger classroom issues that can now prepare students for possible careers in secondary or postsecondary education; or skills and values that require deep analysis of cultural constructs—like race—and that can now prepare students for possible careers in law and other discourse- or public policy–oriented endeavors; or skills and values that encompass the work on texts, new media, and new technology issues that can now prepare students for possible careers in emerging New Economy sectors. Through curriculum revision, in addition to that percentage of English MA students who will go on to a PhD program, we can develop a large percentage of professionals who are equipped with the skills and value sets to transform environments and conditions, and who also, significantly, have

Academic Capitalism, Student Needs, and the English MA

the publicly recognized credentials that will allow them immediate entrance into those kinds of environments where those skill sets and values are highly sought assets.

This position deepens, I think, the arguments of John Guillory and many others[3] that the English MA should be rebuilt with a defined purpose and inherent coherency. Gerald Graff's work on the university and its everyday practices in the classroom defines what I mean:

> For American students to do better . . . they need to know that summarizing and making arguments is the name of the game in academia. But it's precisely this game that academia obscures, generally by hiding it in plain view amidst a vast disconnected clutter of subjects, disciplines, and courses. The sheer cognitive overload represented by the American curriculum prevents most students from detecting and then learning the moves of the underlying argument game that gives coherency to it all. (3)

In a very focused way, the English MA is now a microcosm of what Graff sees in all of the academy—an incoherent clutter of subjects and subdisciplines that obscures from our MA students the meaning of this work and the thing that will enable them to succeed in any environment—that is, deep reading skills, the mastering of argumentative discourse, and the development of both persuasive writing and speaking skills. Possessing skill in what Graff defines as "the underlying argument game" is the key into the New Economy and all of its forms and practices; it is the skill our MA students can "master," and therefore it is the credential they can use to enter and excel within the New Economy.

What will such changes look like, and how can Graff's notion of possessing the power to argue be best delivered in the English MA program? For the sake of brevity, I list the following possibilities for revision:

- ◆ Documenting an emphasis on rhetoric in each graduate course in tangible ways (such as syllabi, assignments, etc.) that demonstrate to future employers how the graduated student is credentialed in specialized discourse;

- Developing in the program, or with the larger school or college, entrepreneurial courses that work specifically on professionalization and career-oriented issues; these courses could include units on job placement training or graduate-level service learning projects that link directly to prospective employers;

- Developing individual, interdisciplinary 12–16 credit hour post-baccalaureate certificate structures;

- Adjusting admission requirements to provide more accessibility to returning, nontraditional students while simultaneously improving standards—this can be done by revamping and broadening the definition of application requirements such as the writing sample or the goals statement;

- Increasing accessibility by developing online course offerings and other distance learning options;

- Changing the exit option structure of the program so that it requires students to do work that forms a practical bridge to employment or into a PhD program; and

- Developing a three-year MA program that is able to better serve the student through more intense and elaborate credentialing activities, such as a semester or even yearlong internship program with external stakeholders.

In all of these possible revisions there is one overriding requirement: the English MA is a degree that must engage academic capitalism and become a bridge to the New Economy. English studies should willfully participate in this transformation of higher education, for in doing so those academic discourses and research products that are not necessarily oriented toward the production of skill—those discourses of inquiry, of opposition, of deep analysis, of intense theoretical speculation, those discussions of Oscar Wilde's fabulous excess, for example, or of Coleridge's Imagination, or of Said's brilliantly coherent politics, or of Butler's logics of performance, or of the simple furthering of experience in the mad, wild ways of a visionary William Blake, or a defiant Audre Lorde, or a sardonic Hunter S. Thompson—all of those discourses that define the work of English studies will transform, through their own intrinsic commitment to unfettered intellectualism, the current skill-based, openly utilitarian paradigm, the current "capitalist knowledge/learning regime" itself.

If English studies is able to build such bridges, then its relevance will be assured, as will the further transformation of the higher education institutions and the New Economy that now defines them.

Notes

1. This basic rationale is one of the many explanations for the emergence of successful online, for-profit institutions—educational corporations that specialize in servicing students and delivering to them quickly and at a reduced cost those skills they need. The University of Phoenix, for example, operates on this philosophy.

2. Certainly there is a large percentage of full-time instructors who have PhDs. The point is that the PhD is not a required credential for these positions, let alone a preferred qualification.

3. In many ways, I am agreeing with and furthering the position of Mary Gaylord, who writes on the future purpose of the MA: "A restrung and refurbished MA will not change the world overnight, but visible commitment from highly visible institutions to rigorously defined basic skills and knowledge, to user-friendly pedagogy, to the improvement of public secondary education, can only strengthen the image of what the humanities are and what they are good for" (1269).

Works Cited

Aronowitz, Stanley. *The Knowledge Factory: Dismantling the Corporate University and Creating True Higher Learning*. Boston: Beacon, 2000. Print.

Donoghue, Frank. *The Last Professors: The Corporate University and the Fate of the Humanities*. New York: Fordham UP, 2008. Print.

Gaylord, Mary M. "On the Outside Looking In: Some Thoughts about the MA Degree." *PMLA* 115.5 (2000): 1267–69. Print.

Glazer-Raymo, Judith. *Professionalizing Graduate Education: The Master's Degree in the Marketplace*. San Francisco: Jossey-Bass, 2005. Print.

Graff, Gerald. *Clueless in Academe: How Schooling Obscures the Life of the Mind*. New Haven: Yale UP, 2003. Print.

Guillory, John. "Preprofessionalism: What Graduate Students Want." *ADE Bulletin* 113 (1996): 4–8. Print.

Jacobs, Jane. *Dark Age Ahead*. New York: Vintage, 2005. Print.

Lorenz, Chris. "If You're So Smart, Why Are You under Surveillance? Universities, Neoliberalism, and New Public Management." *Critical Inquiry* 38.3 (2012): 599–629. Print.

National Center for Education Statistics. "Supplemental Table to Indicator 41: Graduate and First-Professional Fields of Study." Table A-41-1. *The Condition of Education 2009*. (NCES 2009-081). By Michael Planty et al. Washington: NCES, 2009. 238–39. Web. 13 June 2016.

Ross, Andrew. *Nice Work if You Can Get It: Life and Labor in Precarious Times*. New York: New York UP, 2009. Print.

Scholes, Robert. *The Rise and Fall of English: Reconstructing English as a Discipline*. New Haven: Yale UP, 1998. Print.

Slaughter, Shelia, and Larry L. Leslie. *Academic Capitalism: Politics, Policies, and the Entrepreneurial University*. Baltimore: John Hopkins UP, 1999. Print.

Slaughter, Sheila, and Gary Rhoades. *Academic Capitalism and the New Economy: Markets, State, and Higher Education*. Baltimore: Johns Hopkins UP, 2004. Print.

Steward, Doug. "The Master's Degree in the Modern Languages since 1966." *Profession* (2004): 154–77. Print.

Stimpson, Catharine R. "Asserting Our 'Brand.'" *Change: The Magazine of Higher Learning* 38.4 (2006): 30–35. Print.

Weisbrod, Burton A., Jeffrey P. Ballou, and Evelyn D. Asch. *Mission and Money: Understanding the University*. Cambridge: Cambridge UP, 2008. Print.

CHAPTER FOUR

But Can You Teach Composition?
The Relevance of Literary Studies
for the MA Degree

REBECCA C. POTTER
University of Dayton

As a site for transformative curricular and programmatic innovation, the stand-alone MA program (those graduate programs that do not offer a PhD) is where the changing desires and expectations of administrators, students, and faculty converge. For as the contributors to *Degree of Change* illustrate, it is at the MA level in particular that curriculum and program design is propelled by student interest and career ambition, faculty expertise, and administrative drive for revenue. The transformations inspired by this convergence have made an impact in shaping the ways a master's in the field of English studies is seen as preparatory training for future employment. Or I should say "fields" of English, since one thing *Degree of Change* underscores is how varied and multifaceted MA programs in English studies have become. Navigating this terrain can be daunting for faculty and students alike, which has led programs to rewrite the map of that terrain by establishing subdivisions within it, such as tracks and certificate programs, in order to better communicate to their students (and administration) what it is they do and offer through the MA (Miller and Carter; FitzGerald and Singley).

The report of the ADE Ad-Hoc Committee on the Master's Degree in English notes the reconfiguration of the traditional MA program that has taken place over the last several decades, observing that "a generation or so ago, 'English' might well have been defined as 'literature,' but no longer" (7). At the time of the ADE report, 2011, more than one-third of MA programs allowed

– 59 –

students to specialize in rhetoric and composition; half offered creative writing, either as a specialization or separate department; and more specialized tracks were offered in English as a Second Language, linguistics, and professional and technical writing (7). This trend toward granting degrees that denote specialization has only accelerated since then. Hildy Miller and Duncan Carter capture the effect of these changes in the field by illustrating how the contemporary MA program in English is facing a question of identity. This was made especially apparent when they went through the process of developing a track in rhet/comp for their already existing MA program.[1] The process required faculty to consider in what way the addition of a track in rhet/comp would affect both how they identified what they taught—how does this course fit with a certain track?—and how they identified *with* what they taught—how do I align with a certain track? These considerations influenced not only the role and purpose of the new track in rhet/comp, but also the role and purpose of the now distinct literature track.

Creating new tracks is further complicated by the need to match faculty strengths with the professional skills their students will need to succeed in their positions after graduation (Scheg; Park and Amevuvor). Ideally, matching requires addressing the myriad economic and community-centered constituencies that impact stand-alone MA programs serving local students and communities (Adkins; Ching, Lockhart, and Roberge). And it can provide the opportunity to respond to the changing demands of an academic marketplace in ways that reflect not just local but also global factors that are proving to be significant for MA programs in attracting a more diverse student body (Mossman; Fox and Lovejoy). Yet as this collection reflects, an overwhelming number of these discussions focus on writing and literacy (including language) and the development of programs that teach in these areas at the MA level. Many of the contributors to this collection are engaged with theoretical trends in writing studies that impact curricular innovation, and they examine ways that graduates of these programs are being asked to teach writing, or demonstrate writing as a professional skill. More striking for me, however, is not just the dynamic sense of creative engagement attached to the ways writing studies is transforming the MA in English, but

But Can You Teach Composition? The Relevance of Literary Studies

the concomitant sense that literary studies is still searching for a way to enter the discussion. Whereas in writing studies one easily finds a vibrant discourse concerning changes in the profession, the minimal contribution of literary studies to this discourse gives rise to the question, how does the more traditional MA in English, with its emphasis on literature, serve its graduate students? What is the role and place of the literature track in English studies at a time of increased professionalization? William FitzGerald and Carol Singley address these very questions in their analysis of how a traditional MA in English may indeed seek a restructuring that reflects that convergence of student, faculty, and administrative interests. And their insights are valuable in capturing how the process has led to more questions. Yet as they themselves point out, answers to these questions remain elusive.

Across academic disciplines, the MA has been commonly perceived as a professional degree (Strain xii–xiv), even when the program is not part of a professional school. It is not surprising, then, that MA programs in rhet/comp in particular present vivid insights into how English studies can maintain a commitment to humanistic scholarship without dismissing a consideration of how students use a college degree to secure a job. Kaye Adkins's description of the master's of applied arts (MAA) in written communication is a case in point. Housed in the English department at Missouri Western University, the aim of the program is for students to "graduate with a practical degree that enhances their ability to advance their careers" (85). Program design is aimed at providing students with the knowledge, skills, and experience to find work in various fields, although the most common is teaching. Adkins illustrates how difficult it can be to establish a program that meets workplace demands (often in the shape of state-mandated education requirements), student career aspirations (through which community needs are often conveyed), faculty expertise, and the mission of the department and university. Adkins also shows no hesitancy in using the term *knowledge work,* which reveals how the stand-alone MA is moving quickly in resolving a long-discussed demarcation between the academic pursuit of developing knowledge and the professional pursuit of doing work. Yet literary studies has been less inclined to follow suit. While students pursuing an MA in English literature may have interests different from those pursuing a degree in written communication, over half will work as secondary or postsecondary teachers, whose primary task is to teach writing. This fact demands that MA programs offering a literature track consider how the degree serves the professional needs of its students who do not pursue the PhD. Students in the literature track desire both to further their career aspirations and to follow their passion for humanistic study, and would ideally see both those desires met by their MA programs.

The 2011 ADE Ad Hoc Committee report points to this need to reconceptualize the MA degree by taking into account more fully "what an MA program's graduates do after receiving the degree" (6), especially in light of the fact that the majority go on to teach at the secondary and postsecondary levels. And mostly what they teach is first-year composition at two- and four-year colleges. It is also work that a number of graduates not only land, but also *seek;* this was a surprise to the committee, as was the number of faculty (49.1 percent) teaching English at the postsecondary level who hold a master's as their highest degree (20).[2] Statistical data show a continued trend in the majority of students who earn an MA degree in English choosing not to pursue the PhD, and that teaching at two-year or four-year colleges remains the primary career for those graduates.

This trend will most likely accelerate as community college enrollments continue to expand. Over the last forty years, their enrollment has expanded at four times the rate of four-year public and private colleges and universities. While student numbers then dropped from 2008 until 2013 (Desrochers and Hurlburt 2–3; Delbanco 123), efforts to make two-year colleges tuition-free are likely to accelerate enrollment increases in the future. Whether staffing the necessary courses with full-time faculty will keep up with that acceleration is less certain.

Yet if we look beyond the ADE Committee's report by interviewing students directly after they have finished an MA program, an even more complex trend emerges. In her interviews of recent graduates, Ann Penrose reveals how student ambitions are incredibly varied, indicating that master's-level study is a process that helps students figure out what that next career step might be. Nevertheless, Penrose identifies some common expectations that students who enter graduate study in English hold, and not just the students pursuing a writing track. Penrose reports that a small number (15 percent) found careers in professional writing (24 percent aspired to find work in that area);[3] yet students across the board express how improving their writing skill was a major factor behind pursuing the MA in English (183). No matter their specialization, students assessed that their skills in writing had indeed improved, and this had helped them secure a job, or would in the future. Students cited improved writing skills as a key professional benefit of their graduate study, and considered a higher level of writing literacy as an asset they took away from their studies.

It is important to acknowledge that students in these programs identify a professional value in studying English, including English literature. But the professional value they define is specifically an increased skill in writing. This aspect of literary study—how it improves writing skill—can be lost, however, in the eloquent and persuasive defense of literature as a humanistic pursuit that develops critical thought (Teres) and enables intellectual discovery that can be transformative for a student's understanding of life's experiences (Delbanco). That reading, understanding, and writing about the works of excellent authors can benefit a student's own writing ability and skill is a given. MA programs need to take up this issue more aggressively by making a better case for how courses in literature help graduate students improve their writing skills in ways that further their professional goals. That case has not been made as of yet. The question is whether literature departments will seek to do so in the future. The focus and structure of graduate study at the MA level may change significantly if we do not, especially when we consider how pursuing the literature track could be a disadvantage when graduates of MA programs seek employment as lecturers at two- and four-year colleges.

Assessing the value of the traditional MA degree with a focus on literary study calls for a consideration of how it functions as preparative training in a field, and thus benefits the students who pursue it. Considering the place of literary studies in the stand-alone MA program points to the programmatic split in English studies between rhet/comp and literature. In the area of program innovation and development, rhet/comp and literature are consistently discussed as not just two different tracks in the same department (if they are in the same department), but as representative of two separate constituencies, with separate faculty expressing different interests, goals, and approaches to graduate-level education. The division has led to a bifurcation in how students and academic employers (at both two- and four-year colleges) perceive the differences between rhet/comp and literature and points to what shapes those perceptions. A reconsideration of the place and purpose of literary studies at the MA level also must recognize that many graduate students do not see the MA as a stepping-stone to the PhD—or if they do, how many change direction while in their programs and expect that the degree they earn will be of value when they seek professional employment.

To address the ways an MA in English, and in literature specifically, is viewed by a graduate's likely employer, I conducted a survey in 2016 of English department chairs at two-year and four-year colleges. Usable survey results included those department chairs engaged in hiring at some level. Out of a pool of 137 surveyed, there were 101 usable responses. Some clear observations about the value of the literature track emerged. Primary among them are (1) a perceived split between different fields in English studies: rhet/comp (including professional writing), TESOL, creative writing, and literature, which MA programs tend to underscore through a track system or division between departments; (2) a distinct preference for graduates with a background in rhet/comp for future employment at community colleges and regional colleges, whose primary need is faculty who can teach lower-level composition; (3) a marked difference between the work experiences of the graduates from MA programs, most of whom will go on to teach high school English or composition at the college level, and that of the faculty for those programs, whose overwhelming work experience is typically limited to teaching their specialty at the university level; and (4) the lack of connection between literary studies and the professional future of its graduates at the MA level, which has led to a sense that the MA in English literature has less professional value, except as a stepping-stone to the PhD. These findings support the resounding conviction expressed through the contributions of this volume: that stand-alone MA programs are central to the development of

But Can You Teach Composition? The Relevance of Literary Studies

English studies today, training the majority of the field's practitioners and defining its purpose, forcing literature programs that offer the MA to rethink how it serves its students.

The survey attempted to assess how, when hiring, department chairs value the different areas of English studies, and more specifically how students who took the literature track compared with those whose educational focus was in rhet/comp. I distributed the survey electronically to 87 department chairs at two- and four-year colleges, and 50 department chairs at four-year colleges that staff lecturers and do not have a PhD program in English. Results were compiled separately for each group and compared. I received usable responses from 67 chairs of two-year colleges and 34 chairs of four-year colleges. There was very little deviation in the answer differentiation between the groups; results were similar in both cases. Therefore, results listed here represent compiled totals unless specifically noted. The results were also consistent and rather surprising in their measurement of hiring preferences.

When considering a job candidate for a position for which the MA is the highest degree required, department chairs at both two-year and four-year colleges expressed an overwhelming preference for candidates whose specialization was in rhetoric/writing studies. Respondents were asked to rank their preference for hiring in terms of first, second, third, and fourth when considering the following categories: a candidate with an MA in rhetoric/writing studies; a candidate from a generalist program with a majority of coursework in literature; a candidate with a degree in education; or a candidate with an MFA degree. There were 90 respondents, 61 from two-year and 29 from four-year colleges. Out of those 90 respondents, 65 (68 percent) ranked candidates who focused on rhetoric/writing studies over candidates with a focus on literature, or creative writing, or education. Creative writing was a distant second as a preferred specialization, with only 14 respondents choosing it over rhet/comp. Yet only 11 respondents preferred a candidate from a generalist program with a majority of coursework in literature over either rhet/comp or creative writing candidates. And while nearly half of department chairs considered those with a literature background their second preference (41 of 90), most of the respondents who had not listed rhetoric/writing studies first listed the field second, making skill

— 65 —

in writing either the first or the second choice for 79 out of the who responded.

There was one significant preference difference between two-year and four-year colleges. Two-year institutions prefer a candidate from a generalist program with a majority of coursework in literature over a candidate with an MFA degree (15 percent as opposed to 12 percent for those with the MFA). On the other hand, department chairs at four-year colleges would significantly prefer to hire someone with an MFA over a candidate with a focus on literary study. Out of 29 respondents, 18 ranked rhet/comp as their first choice, 7 preferred creative writing, and only 2 chose literature (one chose education). This can be explained by the number of PhD-holding faculty in these departments who predominantly teach literature. Department chairs at four-year colleges are hiring MAs primarily to teach first-year English to a large number of undergraduate students; literature courses are generally taught by faculty holding a PhD and specializing in a literary field. This explains why they would seek lecturers who have expertise in writing studies, but also exposes how the generalist degree that emphasizes literary study is perceived in the academic marketplace. Those who focus on literature are considered to be less equipped to teach writing when compared to their colleagues from rhet/comp.

This preference is borne out even further when department chairs were asked to compare rhet/comp and literature directly in terms of hiring preference. In hiring an instructor for a teaching position, respondents were asked if they would "highly prefer" or "somewhat prefer" a candidate in rhet/comp or literature, or if they had "no preference" between the two. More than 70 percent (60 of 84 responses) stated a preference for those with a degree in rhet/comp (39.0 percent highly preferred and 32.1 percent somewhat preferred rhet/comp), while only 13 (15 percent) preferred the literature focus (4.8 percent highly; 10.8 percent somewhat). Even more surprising, only 11 respondents (13 percent) found no significant difference between candidates with literature backgrounds and those with rhet/comp backgrounds. Comments provided with these questions paint a fuller picture in expressing how preference was based on departmental needs, how candidates whose coursework focused on literary studies still

But Can You Teach Composition? The Relevance of Literary Studies

have knowledge and experience in teaching writing, and how the primary concern is to "hire the best instructor we can," which includes more than a candidate's field of specialization. Yet despite acknowledging the many factors that are weighed in the hiring process, department chairs still prefer a candidate with a rhet/comp background over one with a literature background when the job is to teach first-year composition. And teaching composition is the job the majority of MA graduates in English pursue.

When asked who is best able to teach in their department, survey respondents clearly reflected departmental needs for staffing composition courses. Comments about the questions further emphasized that the vast majority of staffing needs were in the area of composition, and that demand was generally increasing, particularly at two-year colleges. Department chairs from two-year colleges especially noted that when considering the kind of writing instruction new hires will engage in, such as business and technical writing, professional writing, writing across the curriculum, or composition, first-year composition is by far the most relevant for their staffing needs. About 95 percent ranked that skill as first among all other considerations for potential hires. The finding is interesting because it reveals that even in the field of rhet/comp, areas of specialization such as technical writing are not in high demand at the instructor level. In fact, writing across the curriculum was ranked second in curricular need (53 percent of responses in this category), followed by creative writing (17 percent of responses) and then technical writing (16 percent). Just like their counterparts from the literature track, MA graduates in rhet/comp will be hired to teach lower-division writing to college students and may have little opportunity to teach in their area of specialty.

Given the advantage MA holders with a rhet/comp background seem to have over their counterparts from more traditional MA programs, faculty will need to reconsider whether their curriculum meets their students' professional goals, particularly in the face of academic shifts that continue to emphasize the importance of writing skills as an integral part of undergraduate education. Such an assessment also needs to address the variance between the curriculum of the MA program, what faculty learned and apprenticed while graduate students in their own PhD programs, and what knowledge is useful to the MA graduate who takes a position (either full-time or adjunct) in a community college or as a full-time lecturer (untenured) in a four-year college. The majority of faculty teaching graduate courses in stand-alone MA programs were educated in PhD-granting universities where the standard practice is for tenured and tenure-track faculty to teach just 5 percent of first-year writing courses.[4] In my review of faculty at fifteen universities with stand-alone MA programs in English, the faculty experience more closely resembles that of their PhD advisors than the future employment of the students they teach. The trend may be even more endemic among literature faculty teaching graduate classes in MA programs, who typically received a bachelor's and a PhD from highly ranked universities and have taught exclusively at the university level. In a given department, very few tenured faculty have attended and/or taught in a community college, and some may consider teaching composition to be a necessary evil. Many may not be required to teach composition at all. Very few have taught high school English. This is not to say that experience in these areas is necessary for faculty who train graduate students, but it does raise the question of faculty readiness to provide expert guidance in the kind of work that most of their master's students will undertake.

The disparity between what is taught in the graduate seminar and what is needed in the classroom has greatly influenced how the degree is perceived by English department chairs in a position to hire instructors to teach lower-level writing courses. Respondents to the survey for assessing hiring preferences were asked questions concerning whether graduate programs effectively prepared students to teach in their departments, and whether what students were learning in those programs was beneficial in preparing them to assume the position. The survey asked respondents if they thought "the coursework offered at existing graduate programs prepared students to teach in [their] department." Responses reflected a five-point scale (extremely well, well, adequately, somewhat, not at all). Two-thirds of respondents believed that graduate study did an adequate to poor job of preparing their graduates for teaching positions in their departments (52 of 75 responses falling in the adequate [36 percent], somewhat [28 percent] or not at all [5 percent] category).[5] Only two of the 75

But Can You Teach Composition? The Relevance of Literary Studies

responding thought that graduate-level coursework prepared students extremely well, while a larger number, but far from a majority, thought it prepared students well (21 responses, 28 percent).

While the majority of responses fell in the middle range, department heads generally found the coursework in a typical MA program to be lacking in relevance and preparation for the jobs graduates will undertake. Comments indicated this was especially true for courses in literature. When asked if the *scholarship* the applicants had done in their graduate programs was relevant to future success in the position offered, of the 76 who responded, not one marked the box "very relevant." Only slightly more than a third considered it relevant (28 responses), while under half considered the scholarship in graduate school sometimes relevant but often not (33 responses). A noticeable number of department chairs felt it was mostly irrelevant or completely insignificant to the work the new hire would be asked to do (13 percent).

The department chairs surveyed were consistent in their recommendations for the types of courses that would be useful: more courses in developmental English; courses in pedagogy that address teaching in a racially and ethnically diverse setting; more courses in teaching literacy and grammar; courses in teaching students "how to teach" and how to write. "The research PhD and R1 position is a rarity now," wrote one commentator, "not the norm nor what is necessary in most colleges and universities. We need well-rounded faculty members, not research prima donnas." But who is teaching the MA graduate? In English literature, the graduate seminar provides the opportunity for faculty members to engage deeply with research and scholarship in a more specialized course that culminates in working with students on research projects and enriching their own research endeavors. Such a course does not discuss pedagogy outright, nor does the graduate seminar resemble the classroom experience most graduates of MA programs will likely have in their future teaching positions.

The master's degree in English literature is indeed a training ground for practitioners in the field, and as such, seeks to avoid what the ADE Committee considers to be a danger for MA programs: the curriculum losing sync with the world around it (10). But staying in sync proves difficult, especially when programs

— 69 —

attempt to maintain the viability of English literature beyond the traditional brick-and-mortar classroom, suggesting that the master–apprentice relationship one still finds at the PhD level is not working for the stand-alone MA program. There may be many reasons for this, but primary among them is the difference between the kind of work faculty and their graduate students do; the career trajectories of the faculty and their graduate students are often quite different. Abigail Scheg's experience underscores this point. In relating her own experience as a recent graduate called on to teach online courses, Scheg not only points to the gap between what faculty do and what their graduate students end up doing, but she also reveals faculty inability to respond to the student need for skill and experience in online pedagogy (Scheg 122–25). When we consider that the need for online teachers of English is coming from local communities, we can see how programs might fail to be socially responsive in ways that are productive for their students and their location.

However, unlike PhD programs in literature, in which the seminar room is a training ground for becoming a professor in the field (albeit an elusive goal), the student in a stand-alone MA program will most likely follow a different career path. The "stepping-stone" metaphor so often used to describe the MA in English studies implies transience—that students will move on to other places and other things—as well as a sense of immovable tradition, a rock in a river of change. Few MA students become rocks in the river; most are moving on to different places and environments. And yet faculty in these programs may base their pedagogy on the master–apprentice model they experienced as graduate students and find that model extremely rewarding for them, as well as for some of their students. But this model fails to meet the needs of graduates who remain deeply connected to teaching locally. Faculty can overlook the reality that many of their graduate students in the stand-alone MA program will go on to find professional careers as teachers in environments that are deeply connected with their communities. It is this sense of social and cultural engagement that attracted them to literary studies as undergraduates and that guides their professional work after earning the MA degree.

But Can You Teach Composition? The Relevance of Literary Studies

The perception among department chairs hiring graduates of MA programs makes a special demand on literature faculty to articulate persuasively how literary studies improves writing skill and better prepares the graduate student to teach writing skills to others. In doing so, the MA in literature will reopen tremendous opportunity for English studies that other humanistic disciplines can envy. "English" is a sought-after skill, and the study of literature has remained one of the most vibrant pursuits and greatest delights of our students. Yet it is also the means to perfecting skill in critical thinking *and writing*. Literature provides an effective tool for teaching literacy skills. It has been and continues to be a highly effective way of teaching composition (albeit not the only way). Given that more graduates of MA programs will find jobs in teaching composition than in professional writing and will outnumber those continuing on to the PhD, it is imperative that a persuasive case be made for how literary study at the MA level better prepares those graduates for teaching composition.

Literary studies as a field needs to address, in a systematic and substantive way, how it is preparing graduates for work that is directly related to what they learned in the MA program, and in so doing we can learn a great deal from our colleagues in writing studies. How does literary studies at the master's level respond to Peter Vandenberg and Jennifer Clary-Lemon's call to develop programs that "view the MA degree as a locus of situated, locally responsive, socially productive, problem-oriented knowledge production grounded in humanistic and liberal arts traditions" (259). Ching, Lockhart, and Roberge reveal two keys reasons why the "locally responsive, socially productive" MA program is integral to the mission of master's-level study. First, faculty who have been astutely aware of the dynamic relationship between their program and the educational communities they serve have strived to develop their degrees to address the needs of regional and community colleges. "Locally responsive" and "socially productive" eloquently capture the aim and spirit of their endeavor. Second, situating locality and workplace in a responsive, even integrative relationship with the academy underscores the potential for MA programs in English to embrace social and civic engagement. It allows a program's faculty to connect knowledge as "production" with humanistic traditions. The synthesis affirms the movement

– 71 –

in MA programs to overcome traditional divisions that separate town from gown, or critical thought from practical skill.

Scholars and teachers in English have always acknowledged the importance of their work to increase literacy and critical thinking, not just by teaching those skills or practicing them in a professional environment, but also as an act of social justice. Skill in communication is without question a marketable commodity; it is also fundamental to political enfranchisement. The number of graduates of master's programs in English studies who use their degrees to engage in meaningful work that empowers the students they teach is striking. Sharon McGee calls this the "intrinsic value" the master's degree holds for these graduates, practitioners of English studies who find uses for the knowledge and skills they gain through their programs but that they did not anticipate. Is an "intrinsic value" marketable? If we look at the narratives of Burns, Wells, Thurman, and Hudson in their chapter in this book, the answer is yes, precisely because of the ways in which an MA program can conjoin knowledge and production, critical thought and professional skill, work and socially responsive participation in a community (McGee et al.).

The insistence on a political and social meaning for our work is not new to English studies, and therefore it is no surprise that MA programs in English have been active over the last several decades in producing a vanguard of community college teachers who are deeply engaged in teaching literacy, understanding the challenges of such work, and constructing their labor as a form of empowerment through the social value of literacy. This spirit of social activism and democratic participation has been a mainstay of humanistic inquiry in English studies. The sociopolitical impetus that gives meaning to their work is based on the view that literacy and critical thinking are linchpins of a functioning democratic society and necessary for political enfranchisement. In what ways does literary studies further these aims? MA programs in literature need to make a better case for why and how the MA in literature is a valuable part of this endeavor, particularly in the area of teaching writing. Literary study can indeed prepare the MA graduate to teach in the community college classroom because literary scholars engage in teaching literacy, critical thinking, and writing in effective ways. But literature faculty in

— 72 —

But Can You Teach Composition? The Relevance of Literary Studies

these programs need to articulate how their courses serve their students and make their findings known while moving toward curricular innovation that attends to the question of skill. The MA graduate takes that knowledge to the field, usually as a teacher, so the graduate program classroom is *the* place where what we theoretically envision can be put into practice.

Acknowledgment

I would like to thank research assistant Lauren Van Atta for her work on this chapter.

Notes

1. The ADE Ad Hoc Committee on the Master's Degree also takes up the question of identity more broadly, pointing to such a diffuse curriculum as only one issue to consider; also important are the "disconnect between stated goals for MA programs," which can range from preparing students for entry into a PhD program to working as a technical writer, and "curricular requirements," such as a research methods course, that are aimed primarily at the students who see the MA as a stepping-stone to the PhD but are not geared toward furthering the professional goals of other MA students (9).

2. The ADE report also reveals that this work provides faculty with career employment. The vast majority (78.3 percent) of non-tenure-track full-time positions held by faculty members with an MA have renewable contracts with no restrictions. A smaller number have renewable contracts that are guaranteed for a fixed number of years, while only 5.8 percent hold positions that are not renewable. When we consider that nearly 70.0 percent of faculty at two-year colleges hold full-time non-tenure-track positions, a more complete picture emerges, one that points to the desirability of having a prolonged career as a full-time faculty member at a two-year college.

3. Penrose's survey of MA graduates from North Carolina State University matches national survey data regarding the number who find jobs in a writing profession. The MLA 2009 placement survey of graduates of master's degree programs found that nearly 15.0 percent work in business, government, or not-for-profit organizations, including journalism and publishing. This finding coincides with the 2003 findings of the

National Center for Education Statistics (NCES) that 16.8 percent of MA graduates found work in the category of "artists, broadcasters, editors, entertainers, public relations specialists, writers" (Forrest Cataldi, Fahimi, and Bradburn).

4. Miller and Jackson (683); the authors also point out that in contrast to English programs that offer a PhD, in baccalaureate institutions tenure-line faculty teach 49 percent of first-year writing course (684). Research has yet to be done to determine how programs with an MA as their highest degree might be affected by these numbers.

5. The response rate to the questions concerning the relevance of coursework was lower than the response rate to questions concerning hiring preference. However, the comment rate was somewhat higher. Part of the decline may be due to the position of these questions at the end of a ten-question survey. Four comments reflected difficulty in assessing programs so broadly because respondents were familiar with only a handful of graduate programs, or because their assessment depended greatly on the program. One respondent emphasized again the value of a rhet/comp background in stating that graduate study prepares a student "extremely well if they come from an MA program in composition studies that emphasizes teaching first-year writing, but not well from programs that emphasize literature only."

Works Cited

ADE Ad Hoc Committee on the Master's Degree. "Rethinking the Master's Degree in English for a New Century." *Modern Language Association*. MLA, June 2011. Web. 2 July 2015.

Adkins, Kaye. "From Political Constraints to Program Innovation: Professionalizing the Master's Degree in English." Strain and Potter 79–98.

Ching, Kory Lawson, Tara Lockhart and Mark Roberge. "The Locally Responsive, Socially Productive MA in Composition." Strain and Potter 3–21.

Delbanco, Andrew. *College: What it Was, Is, and Should Be*. Princeton: Princeton UP, 2012. Print.

Desrochers, Donna M., and Steven Hurlburt. *Trends in College Spending 2003–2013: Where Does the Money Come From? Where Does It Go? What Does It Buy?* Washington: Delta Cost Project at American Institutes for Research, Jan. 2016. Web. 15 June 2016.

But Can You Teach Composition? The Relevance of Literary Studies

FitzGerald, William T., and Carol J. Singley. "Crafting a Program That Works (For Us): The Evolving Mission of the Master's in English at Rutgers University-Camden." Strain and Potter 138–56.

Forrest Cataldi, Emily, Mansour Fahimi, and Ellen M. Bradburn. *2004 National Study of Postsecondary Faculty (NSOPF:04) Report on Faculty and Instructional Staff in Fall 2003*. (NCES 2005–172). Washington: National Center for Education Statistics, May 2005. Web. 20 Apr. 2016.

Fox, Steve, and Kim Brian Lovejoy. "Boundary Crossings and Collaboration in a Graduate Certificate in Teaching Writing." Strain and Potter 99–119.

McGee, Sharon James, Rebecca Burns, Kisha Wells, Nancy Thurman Clemens, and Jeff Hudson. Strain and Potter. 234–52.

Miller, Hildy, and Duncan Carter. "'There and Back Again': Programmatic Deliberations and the Creation of an MA Track in Rhetoric and Composition." Strain and Potter 157–75.

Miller, Thomas P., and Brian Jackson. "What Are English Majors For?" *College Composition and Communication* 58.4 (2007): 682–708. Print.

Mossman, Mark. "Academic Capitalism, Student Needs, and the English MA." Strain and Potter 41–58.

Park, Gloria, and Jocelyn R. Amevuvor. "An MATESOL Program Housed in the English Department: Preparing Teacher Scholars to Meet the Demands of a Globalizing World." Strain and Potter 215–33.

Penrose, Ann M. "Student Ambitions and Alumni Career Paths: Expectations of the MA English Degree." Strain and Potter 179–96.

Scheg, Abigail G. "TextSupport: Incorporating Online Pedagogy into MA English Programs." Strain and Potter 120–37.

Strain, Margaret M. "Introduction: Degree of Change." Strain and Potter xi–xxviii.

Strain, Margaret M., and Rebecca C. Potter, eds. *Degree of Change*: *The MA in English Studies*. Urbana: NCTE, 2016. Print.

Teres, Harvey. *The Word on the Street*: *Linking the Academy and the Common Reader*. Ann Arbor: U of Michigan P, 2011. Print.

Vandenberg, Peter, and Jennifer Clary-Lemon. "Advancing by Degree: Placing the MA in Writing Studies." *College Composition and Communication* 62:2 (2010): 257–82. Print.

II

PROGRAMMATIC TRANSFORMATIONS

CHAPTER FIVE

From Political Constraints to Program Innovation: Professionalizing the Master's Degree in English

KAYE ADKINS
Missouri Western State University

In this chapter, I do not address the role of the master's degree as a preparation for doctoral study; faculty in doctoral programs have a better understanding of how the master's correlates to preparation for their degrees. Instead, I focus on graduate programs in which the master's is the highest degree offered. As Michael J. Giordano has noted, our emphasis on the master's only as a step in the earning of a doctorate ignores the value of the master's degree itself; it "cheapens [the master's degree's] value, arouses resentment among students who don't make the grade, and preempts our viewing it as an intrinsically significant accomplishment" (1271).

If the goal of a master's in English is not preparation for doctoral study, what, then, should it look like? For answers about the role of the master's as a terminal degree, I draw on my own situation. I teach at Missouri Western State University, a university that recently began offering master's degrees, a university that will never offer doctoral degrees because of its mission and its situation within Missouri's system of higher education. I also participate in the Master's Degree Consortium of Writing Studies Specialists, a group that brings together programs that offer the master's as the highest degree. Therefore, I am interested in the master's as a terminal degree—in what such a degree should look like and in how such a degree might effectively respond to its political environment and contribute to the economic future of its region, even as it is shaped by that environment. In this discussion, I use Missouri Western's Master of Applied Arts in Written Communication, offered through the Department of English and Modern Languages, as an example of a professional master's in English and as an illustration of how the political and economic environment on and off campus can shape such a degree.

Master's degrees are relatively new to Missouri Western State University. Before 2005, Missouri Western was Missouri Western State College, a four-year school that also offered some certificates and associate's degrees. When the English faculty decided to propose a master's degree, they knew that both external forces and internal limitations would shape it; what they did not realize was that in responding to these forces, the department would be proposing an innovative model for master's programs in English. After a four-year process, in August 2009 Missouri Western enrolled its first students in its Master of Applied Arts (MAA) in Written Communication. Those developing the program proposal recognized that effective master's curricula are closely tied to the communities and regions in which institutions are located. Only after the MAA program proposal was approved did we learn that it meets many of the recommendations of the Council of Graduate Schools (CGS) for professional master's degrees; and when the Association of Departments of English (ADE) Ad Hoc Committee on the Master's Degree report "Rethinking the Master's Degree in English for a New Century" was published in 2011, we saw that we had already implemented many of the recommendations of that report as well.

In their introduction to *Ecologies of Writing Programs*, Mary Jo Reiff, Anis Bawarshi, Michelle Ballif, and Christian Weisser argue that "[undergraduate] writing programs are complex ecological networks," intertwined as they are with "departments, divisions, and colleges; majors, minors, and concentrations; colleagues, organizations, and scholarship; administrators, faculty, and students; proposals, websites, and reports; offices, buildings, and campuses; legislative decisions, budgets, state mandates, and accreditation requirements" (5–6). Graduate degree programs are no different; they are located in, influenced by, and must respond to all of these environmental factors. Kay J. Kohl points out that "there is a growing recognition that higher education institutions cannot exist in a vacuum. The kind of postbaccalaureate learning that a university develops and the way it delivers curricula will be influenced by outside groups—employers, government, or professional societies" (11). The ADE Ad Hoc Committee on the Master's Degree also recognizes environmental influences when they observe that "[m]aster's degree programs vary according to local and regional imperatives, to the interests of participating faculty members, or to the diverse clienteles they serve" (5). These diverse clienteles can affect the content, form, and delivery of curricula, and therefore they affect the content, structure, and style of program proposals. Clientele for master's degrees include not only students and employers, but also the faculty and support staff necessary to create and maintain quality graduate programs. Writers of program proposals must also remember their off-campus stakeholders—governing boards, state legislatures, alumni, and major donors. When I have met with other graduate directors of master's programs—at conferences, at the Master's Consortium, or at ADE Summer Seminars—it becomes clear that while master's programs share many of the same concerns and challenges, each must also take into account its unique situation.

The ability to respond to unique local circumstances is a strength to which terminal master's programs can look, a circumstance recognized by both the ADE Committee and the Council of Graduate Schools. As CGS notes, "The creation of innovative Master's programs has been a primary strategy by which colleges and universities have responded to the needs of the communities and the region" (10). The history of Missouri Western's degree proposal and the curriculum of the MAA in Written Communication illustrate the influence of Missouri Western's environment, the ecological network that shapes all of Missouri Western's graduate programs.

Missouri Western's Graduate Program

Missouri Western was founded in 1915 as Saint Joseph Junior College, and its roots in the community remain strong. In 1969 it became a four-year college, and in 1977 it joined the state's regional university system as Missouri Western State College. Many of Missouri Western's students are first-generation or nontraditional students from working-class backgrounds, and as part of its mission to these students and to the region, Missouri Western emphasizes applied learning through undergraduate research opportunities, study away programs, and internships and practica. Throughout its history, the university has had strong local support, but it often has not received strong support at the state level. For example, per-student allocations of funds have consistently remained the lowest in the state (Myers).

As part of a bid to improve Missouri Western's standing in the state, to attract more students, and to create more revenue, the administration asked the faculty senate to begin planning for graduate programs, even as the proposal for university status was working its way through the legislature. In fact, this was one of the key reasons for seeking university status. When Missouri Western began this process, members of the campus and city communities correctly assumed they would face opposition because of the university's perceived low status among state legislators and because of strongly competing interests with other state universities in Missouri. While much resistance was presented as a concern that new programs would compete with existing programs in the state, it was clear that some state legislators did not want Missouri Western, and other regional state colleges, to be allowed to offer graduate programs, either because they did not see the need for more graduate programs in the state or because they did not feel that open admission institutions "deserved" to offer graduate programs.

In addition, not all Missouri Western faculty were happy about achieving university status or about offering graduate programs. Some had joined Missouri Western specifically because of its status as an undergraduate, open admission institution. Others were concerned about increased expectations for promotion and tenure (with no decrease in expectations for teaching and service). Still other faculty did not want their strong undergraduate programs to be weakened by a shift in faculty attention to graduate students. Undergraduates in departments such as biology have opportunities, such as advanced lab experience and participation in grant-funded research, that are unavailable to undergraduates

From Political Constraints to Program Innovation

on many larger campuses; faculty in those departments did not want to be pressured to offer those experiences to graduate students instead.

In 2005, after much discussion and compromise, Missouri Western State College became Missouri Western State University; Missouri Western was to begin offering master's degrees by August 2007. An ad hoc campus committee was charged with developing curriculum guidelines that would set Missouri Western's graduate degrees apart from other graduate programs in the state and create degrees that met the specific needs of Missouri Western's students and of northwest Missouri employers. The state had two requirements. First, Missouri Western's master's degrees would have to accept the same curricular constraints as other graduate degrees in the state, namely that at least 50 percent of the courses in any program had to be at the 600 level. (Missouri Western's undergraduate courses range from the 100 level through the 400 level.) Second, Missouri Western's master's degrees could not compete with any other degrees in the state (Cronk). This second requirement is common in many states, but because of the political atmosphere surrounding Missouri Western's university status, the committee was concerned that the noncompete compliance would be interpreted narrowly for the new programs at Missouri Western and that the university's program proposals would be subjected to much greater scrutiny than graduate program proposals at other state institutions had historically experienced.

The committee that developed the first degree program created a set of internal guidelines that would help Missouri Western's programs meet these criteria. First, the committee decided that the programs should support the applied learning mission of the institution; that is, they would be "applied" master's degrees, requiring internships, research, and practica similar to those in Missouri Western's undergraduate degrees. To help distinguish its graduate degrees from others in the state, Missouri Western's master's degrees were to be "terminal" degrees, specifically designed *not* to prepare students for doctoral study. This was a different approach to graduate study than that of most master of arts and master of science degrees in the state. Second, since budgets were tightening and the resources originally promised

– 83 –

for the development of master's degrees were no longer available, programs were to be developed with as few new resources as possible. In particular, this meant creating 500-level courses and pairing them with existing 400-level courses when feasible. For our new programs, this was a particular challenge because this requirement was in direct conflict with the state requirement that at least half of the credits be at the 600 level.

To help solve this problem, the first master's program, a master of applied science (MAS), developed a shared interdisciplinary core of courses at the 600 level, with options made up primarily of 500-level courses that were cross-listed with existing 400-level undergraduate courses. This MAS included options such as information technology management, human factors and usability, engineering technology, and chemical safety. No department would be required to participate in a graduate program, but all programs that did participate were to be represented in all decisions about the delivery of graduate education at Missouri Western through membership on the new Graduate Council. The MAS became the model for future degrees, establishing additional internal curriculum constraints: Missouri Western's graduate degrees would include an interdisciplinary core, as well as multiple options (Baker). So, in sum, all master's degrees were not to duplicate other degrees in the state, at least half of their courses must be offered at the 600 level, they must be "applied," they must include an interdisciplinary core, they must include at least two options, and they must make as much use of existing or shared courses as possible.

The Master of Applied Arts in Written Communication

As we prepared a proposal for a master's degree housed in the English department, we married the requirements of Western's "applied" master's degrees with our own research on best practices and model programs. The result was the Master of Applied Arts in Written Communication with options in technical communication and writing studies. Because of noncompete concerns, we would not be able to offer a traditional master of arts in English, so we focused on a graduate program in writing. Writing is a strength in our department; all of our faculty teach composition, and we offer undergraduate concentrations in professional writing. Several full-time faculty are writing specialists, with doctorates in composition and rhetoric and expertise in writing pedagogy; in addition, one faculty member has an undergraduate degree and workplace experience in technical communication. Others have professional experience in advertising, proposal and grant writing, and general business. Some of them have built on expertise, such as one faculty member, a specialist in computers and writing, who enriched her knowledge of usability testing and taught herself help-authoring and Web design tools that are in demand by area employers. Each of these faculty members contributed to the design and delivery of the MAA. We knew that the proposed master's program must appeal to local students, many of whom had been Missouri Western undergraduates (but not necessarily English undergraduates). And it must appeal to area employers, meeting needs ranging from education to industrial training to software and hardware documentation. So, following the model of the new Master of Applied Science, we proposed a Master of Applied Arts in Written Communication with an interdisciplinary core and two concentrations: technical communication, since we have an undergraduate technical communication program, and writing studies, designed as a content area specialization for local teachers.

The applied nature of the MAA means that students graduate with a practical degree that enhances their ability to advance their careers. The core was designed to prepare students for supervisory or administrative work, as well as to build a foundation for applied research and practice in the general field of written communication. Students have the option of creating either a professional portfolio or an "applied thesis." The portfolios, much like those created by undergraduates in technical communication and English education, are strongly recommended for students whose undergraduate programs did not include a portfolio. The applied thesis includes workplace or classroom research. For example, one student evaluated new training materials created for a local company and submitted an evaluation report to his client, the company's human resources director. His thesis consisted of the report and an accompanying scholarly literature review of materials that framed his study. Another student studied student use of blogs in her developmental writing classes.[1] Even the more theoretical projects, closer in style and scope to a traditional thesis, have an applied component, such as that of the student who wanted to improve the grant proposals she wrote for her employer, a regional nonprofit. She studied the use of Plain Language in successful grant proposals.

The concentration areas of the MAA in Written Communication also address the most obvious fields for professional preparation for English majors in our region—teaching and technical or professional writing. The Writing Studies option was originally designed for high school teachers who were seeking a master's in a content area. We have found, however, that many of the students in this option are not currently teaching at the secondary level. Instead, they are interested in community college teaching or in full-time non-tenure-track positions at universities. The Technical Communication option was designed to be open to students from any undergraduate background. It prepares students with no background in the field for technical communication careers, or it can enhance their current careers by improving their writing. Students who are currently employed as technical communicators can leave the program prepared to move into supervisory roles such as project management.

Rethinking the English Master's as a Professional Master's

The MAA in Written Communication was approved by the state's Department of Higher Education in spring of 2009, and it began admitting students immediately (Adkins and Frick). It became apparent that we were taking a fresh look at the master's degree at the same time as other institutions and organizations, and asking many of the same questions that they had: What should be the goals of a master's degree? How should theory and practice be balanced in a master's program? What does it mean when we speak of a "terminal" master's degree? As the academic job market has changed, with fewer tenure-track positions available, attitudes toward the role of the master's have begun to shift.

– 86 –

From Political Constraints to Program Innovation

Increasingly, scholars, faculty, and students have begun to view the master's degree as a pathway to multiple career options. Partly in response to these attitudes, the Master's Degree Consortium was organized and the ADE convened an Ad Hoc Committee on the Master's Degree.

In fact, the ADE Committee report questions how the degree can prepare students for professional work inside and outside of academia:

- How might MA exit requirements or the traditional MA exam be reconceived as a bridge between the classroom and a profession?

- For MA programs based on the study of literature . . . would a skills-based curriculum that focuses primarily on critical analysis and pedagogy be more valuable?

- How could teaching or publishing internships be incorporated into MA curricula?

- What models exist for developing career workshops for students and faculty advisers in terminal MA programs? (2)

Especially notable is the emphasis on the "practical" nature of the master's. The ADE Committee report also notes that while "the study of literature continues to dominate the MA in English and to define it, the expansion of other possibilities for study raises interesting questions about the identity of the MA in English as well as about its purposes, outcomes, and place in the university" (8). The ADE Committee report suggests that, in response to the tightening academic job market, we must design master's degrees that will enhance students' nonacademic careers.

The Ad Hoc Committee report identifies two closely related themes echoed by other researchers—the need to prepare students to succeed in a profession and the need to match graduates' skills with the economic needs of the region in which the institution is located. The report expresses concern that "many MA programs have curricula that are not well adapted to the realities of the current academic workforce and may not be serving adequately the needs of this generation of graduate students" (13). These concerns are echoed by Kay Kohl as she identifies the issues forcing institutions to rethink graduate education, especially as preparation for the twenty-first-century economy:

- The aging workforce
- The increased importance of technology in all jobs, especially digital communication
- The move from production to office and management jobs
- The need for constant retraining and moving from one employer to another.
- Increased individual responsibility for developing and maintaining job skills (12–13)

These concerns—a need to look beyond local environment to larger systems and the global economy—drove much of Missouri Western's curriculum development. They are also addressed in line with the Council of Graduate Schools' policy statement *Master's Education: A Guide for Faculty and Administrators*. Missouri Western's MAA in Written Communication includes the following elements of the CGS's recommendations for professional master's programs:

- *Interdisciplinarity*—All students in the program are required to take courses in organizational communication or management. They may also take courses offered in the Assessment, Human Factors, and Digital Media programs.
- It includes *employment-related courses* that explore current issues and best practices in English education and in workplace communication.
- Courses include individual or teamwork on *real-world projects* such as proposals and documentation projects for clients.
- All of the courses emphasize *communication skills for professional development*, including writing to specifications and presenting projects and research orally, with appropriate graphics and video.
- It includes *supervised practica and internships* in the classroom or in the workplace.

From Political Constraints to Program Innovation

As both the CGS recommendations and the ADE Committee report make clear, the emphasis on the master's degree as professional preparation is part of a general trend toward terminal master's degrees that emphasize nonacademic careers. One study found that 85 percent of master's degrees are practical, professional degrees that students seek in order to advance their careers (LaPidus 6). In her discussion of postbaccalaureate education, Kohl connects the value of interdisciplinary degrees to the "job churning" that most employees face as job requirements change and people move from one career to the next (24). Jules B. LaPidus also emphasizes the value of the master's degree in the twenty-first-century job churning economy when he argues that the master's should give students the knowledge and time to take a broader view of their professional fields, an opportunity they probably do not have in their day-to-day work life. Interdisciplinary master's degrees can prepare students for their careers by encouraging them to see connections across borders (or in business terms, to break down silo walls). Students in the programs learn to apply what they have learned in one discipline to other disciplines and contexts, a skill that will help them adapt to changes in the workplace and in employment. LaPidus suggests that this approach benefits MA students and prospective employers alike:

> Not only can this lead to changes in the nature of practice, but it also serves to prepare students to be leaders and change agents in their professions. Those programs recognized as being the best in their fields transcend professional competency and foster professional leadership. (6)

These are the kinds of arguments that the Council of Graduate Schools had in mind as it prepared its policy statement. CGS noted that these practitioner- and career-focused programs are "designed to prepare students primarily to apply newly-developing or existing knowledge of a discipline to specific social or public/private needs" (7). This concern is at the core of the master of applied arts.

While this practical focus may seem a natural fit for traditionally professional master's degrees (in business, technology, and applied sciences), some MA programs in English departments also have a long history of preparing students explicitly for careers. The profession we have most often associated with English graduate study has been teaching. Since preparation for teaching is addressed elsewhere in this collection, I only briefly describe the Writing Studies option of the MAA at Missouri Western. About half of the students in our master's program enroll in this writing pedagogy option, and about half of those students are currently teaching at the K–12 level. These students generally seek additional professional development for promotion, salary increase, or to fill gaps in their own background as they take on new class responsibilities. The other students in the writing studies option are interested in teaching at the postsecondary level either at community colleges or in full-time non-tenure-track positions. Because some of the students are interested in writing program administration work, we developed internships and assistantships that offer this kind of experience. Students might work with the director of composition or the director of developmental writing; they might also work with the director of the campus tutoring center.

Technical and professional communication master's programs in English departments have also clearly provided career preparation for students, an emphasis that has sometimes made them an uncomfortable fit in traditional, literature-focused English departments; however, the number of programs in the field is growing. In her survey of master's programs in technical communication, Lisa Meloncon identified forty-eight programs that offered a degree or an option in technical communication, an increase of 31 percent over a ten-year period (138). This growth is in direct response to demand in the field of technical communication.

The job opportunities for technical communicators are rapidly increasing in the knowledge economy, as "technical communication has become a key commodity, a fact the field has exploited in the development of its academic programs" (Johnson-Eilola and Selber 406). Surveys of technical and professional writing programs often seek to understand how such programs are balancing theory and practice, humanism and technology, the classroom and the workplace (Allen and Benninghoff; Harner and Rich). At the same time, programs are looking to industry to see how trends such as modular writing can be integrated into

From Political Constraints to Program Innovation

the curriculum (Robidoux), how to make internships more valuable to all participants (Munger), or even to ask "Do Curricula Correspond to Managerial Expectations?" (Rainey, Turner, and Dayton). In fact, professional and technical communication programs may be so focused on professionalization that faculty must make a conscious effort to introduce theoretical and humanistic concerns into the curriculum.

The Technical Communication option of the MAA at Missouri Western shares many of these characterisitics. The program was designed to meet the needs of students who have no undergraduate coursework in technical communication as well as of those who have degrees and practical experience in the field. About two-thirds of the students in the program have no undergraduate coursework in technical communication, although many are currently working in the field. Students have come to the program with undergraduate degrees in literature, communication, business, history, and education. All students in the program are required to participate in an internship, and we find internships that best meet each student's career goals. Students in this option have continued or started careers in government, industry, and nonprofit organizations.

Most of the options I have discussed seem to build on degrees in composition and rhetoric or technical and professional writing, but are these the only options for master's students? Are there options for students in a more traditional English MA that includes literature and language study? Again the ADE Committee report points to important considerations, arguing that we need to be aware that a significant number of English MA graduates also work in professional settings such as "business, government, or not-for-profit organizations, including such fields as philanthropy, journalism, and publishing" (6). In fact, the ADE study found that 51.3 percent "consider preparing students for writing or editing positions as important or very important for the MA in English" and an important career option for the twenty-first century (9). And we must not forget that not all students enroll in MA programs simply for career advancement. Dalbey reminds us that, while many of our students seek professional credentials, others seek personal fulfillment. She reports that "a surprising number—are those first-generation students . . . who have become excited about English, about what they envision as academic life, who want more but don't quite know what that is" (18). A master's program can be designed for professional development but should also address students' intellectual interests.

Locating a Program within Its Ecological Network

If you pay attention to news about the job market, you can't miss the constant stream of stories about prospects for employment in the twenty-first century. The "job churning" Kohl and LaPidus mention is corroborated in surveys that suggest that not only do people change jobs every few years, but also that they will change careers multiple times. But that is just one part of the picture. The in-demand careers of the next decade don't exist now, just as many careers that are growing now (e.g., social media director) didn't exist ten years ago. Changes in technology, work processes, and employers mean that nothing is fixed. We read that employees must be nimble, adaptive, and constantly learning. The information economy, with its emphasis on symbolic-analytic work, will continue to characterize much of the professional career growth in the decades ahead (Johnson-Eilola). As students graduate with bachelor's degrees and move into the workplace, they often find themselves unprepared for or unable to find good-paying, full-time employment. Even if they do find a suitable full-time job, they may feel they don't have the skills to move to the next level. Often their answer for this is to pursue a master's degree. The question then is how can we design an MA program in English that prepares students for the changing workplace, and especially for knowledge work. The answer can be found in the ecological networks of our own programs.

One way we can prepare students for the information economy is through interdisciplinary programs that provide students the ability to work with and in a variety of fields and industries. As the nature of the information economy is constantly changing, English MA programs can benefit from working with other graduate programs. The CGS guide argues that "[m]ultidisciplinary or interdisciplinary graduate degree programs are at the forefront of new developments in Master's education" (44). As

From Political Constraints to Program Innovation

one of these interdisciplinary degrees, Missouri Western's Written Communication program includes courses in management, organizational communication, and digital media. Obviously, English departments can contribute to these interdisciplinary endeavors, offering students the professional communication skills that the CGS sees as essential to professional and applied master's degrees, a role played by Missouri Western's Writing for Management and Supervision course, an elective for students in chemistry, information technology management, industrial life science, and human factors. Interdisciplinarity may exist within one department, or it may be found in departments of modern languages and literature that include linguistics or cultural studies courses, an increasing trend as budget cuts lead to the combination of departments (Miller and Jackson 684).

The second element in helping to prepare students is career-focused courses and activities, especially individual and collaborative teamwork on projects for real clients, clients we can find in our ecological networks. This is a feature of many of the courses in Missouri Western's MAA. For example, students in the Proposal and Grant Writing course work with clients from the community throughout the semester, preparing proposals that the clients submit to granting agencies. Other courses include shorter projects that ask students to work individually and in teams for clients on and off campus, creating reports, policy guides, websites, brochures, and other publications. Some of the courses in the writing studies option help students prepare materials for their own classrooms. Local and regional organizations offer many possible projects for master's students in English programs. The network of organizations surrounding the MAA at Missouri Western includes alumni and local nonprofit organizations where our faculty are active. We often ask students to find their own clients—and students have access to numerous connections through their own work and volunteerism. Students have found clients in local museums, social service groups, and schools where they teach or where their children are enrolled.

Finally, MA programs that consider professionalization their primary goal should have at their core the philosophy that theory and practice must be balanced, each informing the other reciprocally and reflexively. An obvious way to achieve this is through supervised internships and practica that place students in the workplace environment.[2] Missouri Western's program includes a teaching option and a technical communication option, so a teaching practicum and internships in business and industry make sense. But this philosophy underlies the entire curriculum, as our graduate students learn to apply theory to practical problems, to research current issues in their fields, and to communicate the results of their research to interested audiences. An example of this is the Technical Communication Theory and Practice course, a requirement for all students in the Technical Communication option of the MAA and an elective for students in the writing studies option and for students in many of the other master's programs at Missouri Western. It is designed for students who have no background in technical communication, but it also has value for those who have some work experience or even an undergraduate degree in technical communication. Students work on two major projects throughout the semester. One is an instructional user's guide, one of the most common genres for technical communicators. Students develop the guide in stages, collaborating on content and design while learning the various software tools that are common in industry. They publish the final project to multiple platforms (print, PDF, website, help files, and ebook), which reflects current and future publication practices and helps students gain experience with software used by employers in the area. The other project asks students to analyze a workplace document through a theoretical lens, applying theory to practice. They share their results in a paper, a presentation, a poster, and sometimes in a blog or even a 140-character message suitable for tweeting. This assignment gives students practice with the kind of research practitioners do and the multiple ways that practitioners share their research.

How, then, do we help students find related jobs? Internships are one obvious way. Another is through networking with area industry and nonprofits. Missouri Western's graduate program continues to build a strong network of alumni and employers through social media, professional organizations, and reputation. Major employers in the Kansas City area are already familiar with our undergraduates and have been pleased to welcome our graduate students as new employees. Our master's graduates have not

From Political Constraints to Program Innovation

needed much help with placement, perhaps because they already have experience seeking out clients for class projects, or because of the confidence they gain from the program, or because they start the program motivated to improve their employability. All of this requires that we design programs that fit into our local environments, using our resources to understand and reach out to area organizations.

While the details of developing a master's program in English as professional preparation depend on an institution's specific environment, Missouri Western's experience can serve as a model. We began by surveying ourselves—identifying the resources at hand. We had existing undergraduate programs in English education and technical communication, staffed by experienced faculty who are active in academic and practitioner organizations. We had an existing network of alumni and employers that help us know what the important trends are in the area. In setting up the master's in written communication, we made use of these resources.[3]

Conclusion

Higher education faces many challenges in the twenty-first century, and humanities programs seem especially challenged to demonstrate their relevance. However, arguments for the value of a humanities education are gaining attention. Kohl argues that graduate study in the humanities may gain importance as employers find that students who have professional undergraduate degrees like business do not have the critical thinking, problem-solving, and self-education skills needed in the modern workplace (23). Increasingly, the master's degree provides the advanced training that employees need to progress in their careers (CGS 51). English, like other master's degrees, can develop in students skills such as critical thinking, analysis, and problem solving, but English departments must develop master's degrees that meet these twenty-first-century needs. As the ADE Committee report observes, "A curriculum out of sync with the world around it risks isolation and irrelevance as well as loss of an opportunity to make the humanities meaningful in the current environment" (10). By drawing on, and locating our programs within, the

– 95 –

ecological networks of our institutions, we can build integrity and appeal into the MA in English degree. Situating this appeal in the professionalization framework suggested by the CGS and modeled by programs like Missouri Western's can not only help to establish master's degrees that will enhance regional economies and individual careers, but also strengthen graduate programs in English departments. In doing this, we can keep the MA in English relevant and increase its value as a terminal degree.

Notes

1. The first student is currently working as an instructional designer; the second is a tenure-track faculty member at a community college.

2. For information about developing internship programs, see especially Sides and Mrvica.

3. A good resource for those interested in starting a technical communication program, either at the undergraduate or the graduate level, is the Council for Programs in Technical and Scientific Communication (CPTSC), www.cptsc.org.

Works Cited

ADE Ad Hoc Committee on the Master's Degree. "Rethinking the Master's Degree in English for a New Century." *Modern Language Association*. MLA, June 2011. Web. 19 May 2012.

Adkins, Kaye, and Jane Frick. "Program Showcase: The Master of Applied Arts in Written Communication at Missouri Western State University." *Programmatic Perspectives* 1.2 (2009): 197–210. Web. 21 June 2012.

Allen, Nancy, and Steven T. Benninghoff. "TPC Program Snapshots: Developing Curricula and Addressing Challenges." *Technical Communication Quarterly* 13.2 (2004): 157–85. Print.

Baker, Jason. "Re: History of Western's Grad Programs." Interview. 23 Apr. 2012. E-mail.

Council of Graduate Schools (CGS). *Master's Education: A Guide for Faculty and Administrators: A Policy Statement*. Washington: Council of Graduate Schools, 2005. Print.

Cronk, Brian. "Re: History of Our Grad Programs." Interview. 22 Apr. 2012. E-mail.

Dalbey, Marcia A. "What Good Is the MA Degree?" *ADE Bulletin* 112 (1995): 17–20. Print.

Giordano, Michael J. "Revaluing the Master's Degree." *PMLA* 115.5 (2000): 1271–73. Web. 20 May 2012.

Harner, Sandi, and Anne Rich. "Trends in Undergraduate Curriculum in Scientific and Technical Communication Programs." *Technical Communication* 52.2 (2005): 209–20. Print.

Johnson-Eilola, Johndan. "Relocating the Value of Work: Technical Communication in a Post-Industrial Age." *Technical Communication Quarterly* 5.3 (1996): 245–70. Print.

Johnson-Eilola, Johndan, and Stuart A. Selber. "Sketching a Framework for Graduate Education in Technical Communication." *Technical Communication Quarterly* 10.4 (2001): 403–37. Print.

Kohl, Kay J. "The Postbaccalaureate Learning Imperative." Kohl and LaPidus 10–30.

Kohl, Kay J., and Jules B. LaPidus, eds. *Postbaccalaureate Futures: New Markets, Resources, Credentials*. Phoenix: Oryx, 2000. Print.

LaPidus, Jules B. "Postbaccalaureate and Graduate Education: A Dynamic Balance." Kohl and LaPidus 3–9.

Master's Degree Consortium of Writing Studies Specialists. Standing Group of the Conference on College Composition and Communication, n.d. Web. 21 June 2012.

Meloncon, Lisa. "Master's Programs in Technical Communication: A Current Overview." *Technical Communication* 56.2 (2009): 137–48. Print.

Miller, Thomas P., and Brian Jackson. "What Are English Majors For?" *College Composition and Communication* 58.4 (2007): 682–708. Print.

Munger, Roger. "Participating in a Technical Communication Internship." *Technical Communication* 53.3 (2006): 326–38. Print.

Myers, Jimmy. "Budget Talks Yield Money for Colleges." *St. Joseph News Press* 9 May 2012. Web. 1 July 2012.

Rainey, Kenneth T., Roy K. Turner, and David Dayton. "Do Curricula Correspond to Managerial Expectations? Core Competencies for Technical Communicators." *Technical Communication* 52.3 (2005): 323–52. Print.

Reiff, Mary Jo, Anis Bawarshi, Michelle Ballif, and Christian Weisser. *Ecologies of Writing Programs: Program Profiles in Context*. Anderson: Parlor, 2015. Print.

Robidoux, Charlotte. "Rhetorically Structured Content: Developing a Collaborative Single-Sourcing Curriculum." *Technical Communication Quarterly* 17.1 (2008): 110–35. Print.

Sides, Charles H., and Ann Mrvica. *Internships: Theory and Practice*. Amityville: Baywood, 2007. Print.

CHAPTER SIX

Boundary Crossings and Collaboration in a Graduate Certificate in Teaching Writing

STEVE FOX AND KIM BRIAN LOVEJOY
Indiana University–Purdue University Indianapolis

The changing demographic in classrooms and the need to honor students' linguistic differences while also teaching Edited American English have posed particular challenges to teachers. Many practicing K–12 teachers and college instructors have never taken a course that focuses on writing pedagogy, much less a range of such courses. At the same time, the incentives for teachers to do graduate work are being undermined by school reform efforts in some states, including Indiana. State policymakers argue that license renewal and pay raises should be more closely tied to student achievement and school improvement goals. Just taking courses or earning graduate degrees is not in itself valuable, such reformers argue. They would rather see professional development provided within a district or school and targeted at "student achievement," and they claim that such professional development will save teachers from paying university tuition.

In their monograph on school reform, Jane David and Larry Cuban note that traditionally, teachers have earned pay raises for years of service and from adding degrees or certifications (41). Efforts to institute performance-based pay have seldom been maintained long enough to see significant results, but recently districts and states have instituted plans to reward teachers primarily for student achievement. However, as in Denver's ProComp program, there can also be pay rewards for "acquiring new skills and knowledge in their teaching field" (44). David and Cuban also write about efforts to reform professional development for teachers. They sum up the efforts this way: "Together, the reform view of professional development focuses the content on what teachers need to know and do and locates the activities in the school where teachers can work together and get help to improve their teaching" (149). This overall approach might diminish the focus on university courses as a means of professional development. But David and Cuban also note a "list of essentials" in effective professional development that includes "a teacher enrolled in redesigned university courses, attending one-week or longer summer institutes, observing master teaching for extended periods of time" (148). It would seem possible, then, for even a reform view of professional development to include room for graduate coursework like that found in certificate programs focused on teaching writing. The question is whether states and districts will encourage or require teachers to do most of their professional development in school-based workshops, learning communities, and mentoring or coaching, or whether they will also see a valuable role for university-based continuing education.

One recent development may complicate this picture further. The Higher Learning Commission[1] that accredits colleges and universities in the North Central region has issued revised guidelines for faculty credentials in higher education, noting that these apply to high school teachers instructing dual credit courses. Dual credit teachers without a master's degree, therefore, will have to earn such a degree or supplement a master's in another area, such as education, with a minimum of 18 graduate credit hours in the content area, such as English. MA and certificate programs may see additional enrollments as a result.

Whatever the flaws or merits in these reforms, laws and policies have been passed that leave teachers unsure about how they will be rewarded and even, in some cases, how they will keep their jobs. Many are still motivated to do graduate work, especially if it helps them to stay intellectually challenged, develop their reading and writing abilities, and improve their classroom teaching. Indeed, teachers may read this set of circumstances as all the more reason to continue their education with a sharper focus on coursework that will positively impact their teaching and their students' learning. Others, disillusioned by the forces that increasingly rob teachers of their professionalism, seek out intellectual spaces in graduate programs to renew and rebuild their knowledge and reboot their pedagogy (and for some, even their self-esteem).

Given these challenges to literacy education—the demand for improved writing instruction at all levels, new approaches to evaluating and rewarding teachers that emphasize standardized test scores, and attempts to reform professional development that affect graduate programs—we want to argue for the value and timeliness of graduate certificate programs in teaching writing, using our program at Indiana University–Purdue University Indianapolis (IUPUI) as an example. A program like IUPUI's provides teachers with the resources to become well-grounded professionals who practice with a heightened awareness of their theoretical principles, who understand the challenges of a diverse and tech-savvy population of students, and who can engage in teacher research within their own classrooms. Such teachers can also critique the "packaged" curricula, superficial school reform efforts, pressures to standardize and narrow assessments, and limited, ahistorical views of literacy that mark today's educational landscape. Moreover, a certificate program in teaching writing can become a site of valuable cross-level and interdisciplinary conversations and collaborations. Such a program can help bridge divides between K–12 education and university education, between English and English education, and between academic disciplines that all have a stake in improved student writing. First, we show the benefits, values, and purposes of such graduate certificate programs in teaching writing; then we explain what our certificate program looks like and how we have begun assessment. Finally, we discuss several tensions we face in the program.

Benefits, Values, and Purposes

We mentioned earlier the most obvious and primary need for a graduate certificate in teaching writing: many K–12 teachers, including English teachers, have had little or no coursework in writing pedagogy. As noted by the National Writing Project (NWP) and Carl Nagin in the 2006 *Because Writing Matters: Improving Student Writing in Our Schools*, "few states require specific coursework in the teaching of writing for certification" (59, citing Sandra Gibbs of NCTE). The requirements for teaching reading are much more rigorous and extensive than those for writing, "[y]et research shows that literacy is reading *and* writing and the two are best learned together" (NWP and Nagin 60). University faculty in education know this is true and certainly believe their undergraduate majors need more courses in writing and teaching writing. We have worked with our own English Education faculty to include as many courses in writing as possible in the English portion of preservice undergraduate students' degrees. Lovejoy developed a course in teaching writing that complements the methods courses taken by undergraduate students in the School of Education. But the demands are many, the credit hours limited. Thus, even with enhanced undergraduate coursework in writing pedagogy, teachers soon realize the need for additional work at the graduate level.

For education majors in other strands, including elementary education, special education, English as a new language, and content areas, there is even less room for courses in writing or writing pedagogy. Yet as NWP and Nagin argue, "We cannot build a nation of educated people who can communicate effectively without teachers and administrators who value, understand, and practice writing themselves" (60). Therefore, districts and schools look to organizations such as NWP and their own inhouse instructional coaches to provide workshops on teaching writing. We would argue, however, that such inhouse professional development would be even more effective with teachers who have taken graduate coursework in composition and rhetoric—teachers with the theoretical background and philosophical understandings to critically assess their new learning. Understanding the relationship between theory and practice is critical in decision making for the classroom teacher, and a graduate certificate can provide the depth and experience that inservice programs cannot. The same can be said of professional development for university writing program faculty, many of whom have degrees that focused primarily on literature or creative writing. Those instructors bring knowledge and experience to the writing classroom, but they still need a deeper grounding in theory, research, and classroom pedagogy.

One powerful benefit of graduate courses in teaching writing

Boundary Crossings and Collaboration

offered in certificate programs is the opportunity for teachers to study, write, and research with teachers from a variety of schools, levels, and subject areas. Our students have included middle and high school teachers of English, social studies, and English language learners, as well as university instructors of writing, literature, creative writing, ESL, Spanish, political science, art, and philosophy. This diversity of backgrounds has always been a hallmark of the NWP Summer Institutes, where teachers from urban, suburban, and rural schools learn about one another's students, classrooms, communities, and constraints. Teachers of English, art, science, history, math, and music talk about the different roles that writing plays in their classrooms but also find many areas of commonality; they quickly realize that a thoughtful writing-based activity or unit from any subject area can be adapted by teachers in other disciplines. We have found this to be true in our certificate program, not only in the Hoosier Writing Project Summer Institute (which is part of the certificate program), but in other courses as well. Cross-disciplinary conversations and collaboration in certificate courses have the potential to promote WAC/WID initiatives in secondary schools and on university campuses. A Spanish instructor in our program used what she was learning to begin planning an advanced course in writing in Spanish, and even imagined a Spanish Writing Center.

Several of our certificate graduates and current students attest to the value of working in a cross-level program like ours. College writing instructors learn from middle and high school teachers what kind of writing instruction their students might have experienced at that level; as one certificate graduate notes, "[G]etting a glimpse into what our students experienced coming to college can be helpful as we develop assignments and as we talk to students about what they're bringing to the classroom" (Donhardt). Another college instructor learned useful approaches from secondary English teachers and was also inspired to continue such collaboration through professional organizations. She stated, "[W]orking with these practitioners made me not only better prepared for the next class I taught at IUPUI (as far as subject matter and teaching strategies that would grab and hold my students' attention), but it also encouraged me to join a couple of professional organizations like NCTE, so that I can start reading articles and posts from other teachers who teach on all grade levels" (Hampton). Building relationships among teachers at different levels is the desired outcome of a program in which students are encouraged to share their ideas in a trusting environment. Class discussions of theory and pedagogy are lively and pointed as teachers work through their prejudices and biases about the "other side."

These examples of collaboration bring up an important purpose of certificate programs in teaching writing: bridging the gap between secondary and college writing instruction. Too often, secondary English teachers are told they must prepare their students for college writing, and increasingly they must teach AP and Early College courses that are supposed to *be* college-level writing, yet they may not fully understand the theory and research underlying college writing instruction. Even though they took writing courses as undergraduates, they did not necessarily explore the theoretical underpinnings of the curriculum. At the same time, college writing instructors may have never taught in a K–12 setting, read the literature about K–12 writing instruction, or understood the real nature of the standardization, accountability, testing, and reform movements that shape what K–12 writing teachers do.

Middle and high school teachers in the program learn from their college-level counterparts what goes on in first-year college writing and how FYW instructors perceive new college students who, a few months before, were high school seniors. A middle school teacher currently in our program notes, "I have always sought ways to stay informed about what high school, college, and university teachers expect and desire of students' skills. Taking classes with these people is a great way to stay informed" (Therber). A high school teacher gained a new perspective on her AP students by talking with first-year college writing instructors: "I realized that my students shared similar writing struggles as basic writers at the college level. . . . This shift in my thinking after discussions with ENG101 instructors yielded huge changes in my expectations, my pace, and my patience" (Gellin).

Teachers in the certificate program learn from those at other levels about the contexts within which they teach. Understanding those contexts helps teachers avoid the blame game (why

Boundary Crossings and Collaboration

didn't the teachers before me teach these students what they need to know?). One of our certificate program graduates, who had taught political science in college, states eloquently what he learned from his fellow students who taught at the middle and high school levels:

> Many of the activities or methods for the teaching of writing that appear to be effective when evaluated in isolation . . . are increasingly challenging or next to impossible to implement in an age of Common Core standards, an attention-deficit disorder approach to class scheduling, authoritarian educational paradigms and the incentivizing of educators to teach for "the Test" instead of investing precious class time on concepts such as Deep Reading and peer-review. Having only taught at the college level, I needed my middle-school and high-school colleagues to remind me that institutions play arguably a larger role than even pedagogy in writing instruction. (Giles)

We would agree with NWP and Nagin that "a distinctive feature of the NWP's approach to instructional improvement has been to address the issue of aligning the K–12 and postsecondary worlds of educators. To date, its summer institutes are one of the few places where teachers, administrators, and university academics join as peers to develop themselves as writers and writing teachers" (64). A 2002 volume edited by Robert Tremmel and William Broz, *Teaching Writing Teachers of High School English and First-Year Composition*, addresses the need for this cross-level dialogue and professional development. In his introduction, Tremmel insists, "Writing teacher education for secondary teachers should not be a completely separate enterprise from writing teacher education for first-year composition" (13). He advocates that English educators and writing program administrators form an alliance to develop writing teacher education as a discipline, seeing this collaboration across educational levels as one of the contact zones that literacy scholars claim to value: "It is honest work, after all, that creates one of the few genuine opportunities for academics to transact business directly in the social, cultural, and community contact zones that we have been telling ourselves for years are important grounds for critically relevant and valuable work" (15).

In our work at IUPUI, we have been developing this kind of collaboration. It has been a career-long concern for us, in fact. We both have been active in the Indiana Teachers of Writing (ITW), a unique statewide organization that brings together teachers of writing at all levels, K–college. ITW launched the *Journal of Teaching Writing (JTW)*, edited by Lovejoy; this journal also spans the teaching of writing from elementary to college levels. Fox directs the NWP site located at our university; like the journal, this site was sponsored by ITW. Lovejoy's long association with the journal and his contributions to a national survey of high school and college teachers on language attitudes affirmed the importance of dialogue across educational levels.[2] Fox has worked in area schools as part of Hoosier Writing Project professional development programs. The kind of certificate program we designed requires such cross-level experience and connections. From the beginning, we did not want this to be a TA program or one focused entirely on secondary school teachers: we wanted to continue the kinds of collaboration that marked our work with ITW, *JTW*, and NWP.

Yet another crucial argument for a graduate certificate program is that it can help teachers see themselves as reflective scholars. In a period in which teachers can be viewed more than ever as merely implementing the curricular packages and directives handed down by administrators, and in a society that has too often swung wildly between putting teachers on a pedestal and seeing them as incompetent timeservers, teachers themselves need to deepen their identities as intellectuals, as disciplinary scholars, as critically informed professionals. High school teacher Sam Scheer quotes John Dewey on the importance of a teacher being an "intellectual leader" (91) and argues that time spent reading the work of pedagogical thinkers such as Dewey, Aristotle, and Rousseau "is worth a week of what passes these days for professional development" (93). Scheer sums up his credo: "For me, teaching is—or at least it should be—the scholar's art" (94). His essay appears in *Burned In: Fueling the Fire to Teach* (Friedman and Reynolds), a collection intended to counter the burnout, alienation, and weariness of many teachers. An excellent certificate program in teaching writing should "fuel the fire to teach," providing opportunity for teachers to see themselves as scholars

– 106 –

Boundary Crossings and Collaboration

or scholarly practitioners of an ancient and honorable profession. The coursework should not consist of endless lectures on theory and research divorced from actual classrooms, nor should it become "strategy-o-rama," giving teachers reams of lesson plans and reproducible units. It should enable teachers to understand theories that undergird their thinking and the practices they enact as teachers of writing. This kind of program must allow teachers to reflect and see their work as action research, as praxis.

Last, but in many ways perhaps most important, a graduate certificate in teaching writing can help equip teachers to question and resist destructive trends in education more broadly, and literacy education in particular. A good undergraduate program in education can and should launch teachers into critical pedagogy, but given the constant drumbeat opposed to critical, reflective teaching, most teachers need further support to stand up against so much that ails our schools and colleges today. Usually, professional development created within or contracted by schools or districts represents a response to such pressures, and if *capitulation* seems too harsh a term, *accommodation* certainly characterizes those programs. Teachers who wish to question these programs and their underlying assumptions need allies; they need conversation partners; they need a diversity of ideas and resources. They can find these things in a graduate certificate program in teaching writing.

The Certificate in Teaching Writing at IUPUI

Why a certificate program instead of a full master's degree? Because current education policy tends toward *not* rewarding teachers for graduate degrees, a certificate program can seem more practical as an initial step for busy teachers. Admission into a certificate program may be less difficult (our program does not require the GRE or recommendation letters, for example). Once teachers begin taking courses in a certificate program, they may realize that such graduate work is rewarding, that it does benefit their teaching and fulfill their curiosity and intellectual drive. In other cases, a teacher may already have a master's degree but would like the certificate in teaching writing to complement that degree and show specialized expertise.

What does such a certificate program look like? No comprehensive survey, database, or account currently exists to answer that question,[3] but we can offer a detailed description of our own program—and based on our limited knowledge of other programs, ours seems fairly representative. First, some background: The English department at IUPUI, a large urban university in the capital city, was approved to offer an MA in about 1998. The program began with offerings primarily in literature and TESOL and has evolved to include writing pedagogy as a third concentration. Two long-standing graduate courses focus on teaching writing, which many of our writing program instructors have taken. When Fox was hired, he developed another course, Introduction to Literacy Studies. Fox also became director of the NWP site at IUPUI, and area teachers could take the Summer Institute for graduate credit in English.

After years of developing our undergraduate concentration in writing and literacy, and recognizing the need to continue strengthening the teaching of writing in Indiana schools, Lovejoy conceived the Graduate Certificate in Teaching Writing. In particular, he knew that teachers were struggling with increasing numbers of students from widely varying social and cultural backgrounds, as well as the added pressure of responding to testing shortfalls. He saw the graduate certificate as one way for teachers to address their questions and improve their effectiveness in the classroom. In consultation with Fox, he developed a proposal for this certificate that was approved in 2009. To increase awareness of the program, we sent announcements to several email lists, including our English graduate program list, the IUPUI graduate student organization list, our writing program faculty list, and the Hoosier Writing Project list. We also emailed teachers who had attended recent conferences of the Indiana Teachers of Writing.

The certificate program has drawn significant interest and participation from area middle and high school English teachers, adjunct college composition faculty, and MA students from a variety of disciplines interested in teaching writing or becoming more informed teachers. The goals of the program are for students to

◆ understand language and literacy from a theoretical and historical basis;

Boundary Crossings and Collaboration

- ◆ acquire a reflective, research-based approach to major issues in teaching writing; and

- ◆ develop and articulate an informed, practical pedagogy for teaching writing.

This 20-hour program of study includes courses that introduce students to theories and methods of teaching writing; the nature of the "writing process" and how it can be effectively taught; understanding linguistic diversity as a means of teaching effective communication; uses of technology in writing as a process and product; social aspects of writing development; nonfiction writing; writing assessment; and teacher research. Students can complete the certificate program on a stand-alone basis, or as part of the MA program; all certificate program credits apply to the MA program. Our MA program has both a thesis and a nonthesis option. Starting in fall 2013, the graduate program also offers a Certificate in Teaching Literature, so someone wanting both teaching certificates can do them within the 40-hour nonthesis program track.

This is not a PhD program in rhetoric and composition, so the courses must be broad in scope and focused on pedagogy, although we do want our certificate students to deepen their understanding of composition scholarship and theory. It is also important that the curriculum not outpace the energy and interests of the faculty (which currently is relatively small) nor proliferate so rapidly that courses will not enroll. Three closely aligned courses are sequenced to provide students with a well-rounded understanding of the theory, application, and practice of teaching writing. W509, Introduction to Writing and Literacy Studies, is one of the gateway courses in the English MA and is the required core course for the Certificate in Teaching Writing. It focuses on the concerns of scholars in rhetoric and composition as well as literacy studies more broadly. Two other courses offered regularly and recommended to students focus on teaching writing: W500, Teaching Writing: Issues and Approaches, emphasizes the practical aspects of teaching writing, while W590, Teaching Writing: Theories and Applications, explores different theories and perspectives and how to apply theory to a classroom setting in a conscious, deliberate way.

– 109 –

PROGRAMMATIC TRANSFORMATIONS

Further helping certificate students connect theory, research, and practice are the National Writing Project Summer Institute and Advanced Institute; students who take these intense workshops find in this teacher-centered experience a set of core principles that transform their view of teaching writing—including the idea that teachers of writing must be writers and that teachers can become authoritative researchers of their own classroom practice. We encourage certificate students to take one writing course, usually W615, Graduate Creative Non-Fiction, or W508, Graduate Creative Writing for Teachers. Other courses draw on our faculty's expertise and the needs of classroom teachers. They include a course on digital literacies in teaching composition; a course on language, dialects, and the teaching of writing; and a course on second language writing. We are also developing ways for graduate students to work in our University Writing Center and learn writing center approaches that can also be adapted to the classroom.

We try to provide teaching experience to certificate students who are interested in college-level writing instruction. Most of our first-year writing courses are taught by full-time and part-time lecturers who already have a graduate degree. So the certificate program is not a way to staff the writing program, although students in the certificate or MA program can apply for TAships, which are rare and coveted, usually one or two per year. But we encourage students in the certificate program who show strong teaching potential to apply for adjunct positions. Graduates of our certificate program who have a master's degree are looked on favorably when applying for adjunct positions and the occasional full-time position that comes open.

The certificate program offers area teachers the perspectives and resources of several strong programs: the First-Year Writing Program, which offers six courses and employs about fifty full-time and part-time faculty; the University Writing Center, where faculty and student consultants work with students from across the campus; the Hoosier Writing Project; and the *Journal of Teaching Writing*, where program students can do internships to learn about the process of producing an academic publication. Our certificate students also benefit from the range of faculty in the program, faculty committed to pedagogy as a theory-based,

— 110 —

Boundary Crossings and Collaboration

classroom-tested enterprise. Currently our faculty include one full professor, one associate professor, two assistant professors, and two senior lecturers in English. The program's growth helps us continue to make the argument for hiring more faculty in composition and rhetoric.

We know from the steady number of applicants and graduates that our program is meeting a need. As of fall 2015, the program had twenty active students; the total number has fluctuated between twenty and thirty-eight as students complete the program and new students are admitted. Since the program began, more than forty-five students have graduated. Certificate courses like ours therefore enable conversations and inquiry across institutions and levels of instruction, across disciplines, and across career backgrounds. They allow teachers to integrate the practice of writing with pedagogical theory and practice, to learn from a diverse set of colleagues, and to prepare for teaching writing in a wide range of settings, not just in the writing program connected to their graduate program.

Assessing Our Program

Recently, certificate faculty have begun assessing more closely the program's effects in the teaching lives of our certificate students and alumni. We started with a survey, administered in April 2012, and have been conducting some exit interviews. The survey asked students about their perceived learning in the three broad outcomes of the program: knowledge about major theories, historical perspectives, pedagogical issues, and philosophical foundations of writing; understanding of writing—its contexts, genres, research, and practical pedagogy; and applications of writing, including thinking critically, arguing persuasively, writing effectively, giving/receiving feedback, and adapting to linguistic and cultural differences. Students were asked to rate their learning progress on a four-point scale. Students reported growth in all three areas, and those who had taken four or more courses in the certificate program reported gains of two or more levels and saw themselves as strong or very strong in these outcomes. Obviously we would like to develop additional assessments, including evaluation of

— 111 —

representative student work and surveys of graduates' employers. Those who interview applicants for part-time positions in our writing program have begun to notice that applicants from our certificate program demonstrate impressive knowledge and thoughtful ideas about composition pedagogy. Data from our assessment will help us in planning, revising the program as needed, and demonstrating its value to our colleagues, our dean, and potential students.

Tensions and Challenges for Certificate Programs

Our certificate program, and others like ours, exist with certain tensions—potentially productive tensions, but they need to be acknowledged and examined. One such tension has already been cited as a strength of these programs: the mix of middle school, high school, and college teacher participants. We would not want to have a less diversified program, but certainly the needs of each group differ. College composition teachers, for example, often teach only composition, not the full range of English studies that most middle and high school English teachers are responsible for. College teachers sometimes know little about the conditions under which secondary teachers work. Middle school teachers often work in teams, collaborating with other disciplinary teachers and perhaps working with a small cohort of students, while high school English teachers often work in large departments, teach five to seven classes a day, and have little opportunity for interdisciplinary teaching. College instructors in our courses are often adjunct faculty who may teach at two or more institutions; some of our certificate students have not yet taught a college course but hope to do so after taking some of our courses or earning their certificate. The resulting "tensions" are not necessarily uncomfortable, but they require careful consideration of texts, assignments, and goals as well as skillful facilitation of discussion so that people do not make unwarranted assumptions about teaching at other levels, or try to focus the class exclusively on their particular concerns. When teaching a course in composition theory or practice, we cannot just assign the usual textbooks and articles about first-year composition. (In fact, it is difficult to find

— 112 —

Boundary Crossings and Collaboration

a good writing pedagogy textbook that bridges these different levels, and most journal articles are also focused on one level only.[4])

Another tension, between applied pedagogy and research or theory, appears in any teaching-focused curriculum, and it has created problems in our field. Yet this tension, while arising even in composition/rhetoric MA or PhD programs, can be especially acute in a Certificate in Teaching Writing program. The phrase "teaching writing" might suggest to some students that the courses are all about how to design syllabi and units, how to create good assignments, how to evaluate student writing, how to motivate student writers, and how to teach revision or style or grammar. The word *certificate* also tends to suggest a professional, applied focus. We do want those connotations, and we strive to make every course in our certificate program help teachers do their jobs better. That means including teaching demonstrations and activities, reading pedagogical articles and books, and asking of any research or theory, "What does this mean for teachers and their students?" But we also want teachers to realize that everyone has a theory or theories of teaching and learning and that examining those theories helps us become more thoughtful, consistent—or purposefully inconsistent!—teachers. And we want students not only to read research and theory, but also to begin doing research and theory themselves. In the core course we begin by asking students to think about the kinds of research done in this field and then invite them to step into the research waters by writing a research proposal or doing a small-scale research project—say, examining the way "writing" is talked about in university documents. In the National Writing Project Summer Institute, we introduce teachers to classroom research, ask them to develop a small-scale, focused teacher research proposal, and urge them to implement the proposal in their classrooms that fall.

As noted in the introduction, another challenge lies in the changing educational landscape for teacher licensing and pay. School reform organizations have been critical of state policies that reward teachers for earning advanced degrees. Students First, a school reform organization founded by Michelle Rhee, controversial former superintendent of Washington, DC, has as one of its objectives under Elevate Teaching to "Reform Salary Schedules. Ensure that the attainment of advanced degrees and/or education credits are not the primary factors used to provide pay increases to teachers." They give a report card for all fifty states, and only four states (Indiana is one) currently have the highest score, a 4, based on prohibiting districts from "implementing compensation systems that provide salary increases based only on the attainment of advanced degrees or additional education credits." The National Council on Teacher Quality, in its 2010 report, cites meta-analysis of research showing little to no connection between advanced degrees and student achievement (based on standardized test scores). The Council recommends that states eliminate

> regulations requiring master's degrees and other non-specific graduate coursework requirements for obtaining permanent and advanced licensure status. . . . Requiring teachers to get additional training in their teaching area certainly has the potential to be meaningful. However, these requirements are usually vague, allowing teachers to fulfill coursework requirements with little consideration for relevance to instruction. In circumstances where more coursework should improve a teacher's performance, the reward should be directed at improved results in the classroom, not the coursework itself. (8)

Our own state of Indiana has been a center of such reform efforts in recent years. For example, Indiana Code states that no more than 33 percent of a teacher's pay raise shall be based on a combination of years of experience and attainment of additional university degrees (Indiana General Assembly). Given such new policies, schools of education are noticing enrollment declines in graduate programs (Richards and Thomas). Whether graduate programs located in English, focusing on improved pedagogy, might experience a similar decline remains to be seen. A new task for administrators and faculty of such programs will be to demonstrate the effect of their programs on improved teaching and learning and to lobby with state policymakers, as well as to convince teachers that investing in such a program will benefit them professionally.

Another area of tension or concern is the employment situation for college-level instructors of writing. While we designed the certificate program with middle and high school teachers in mind, we recognized that university-level instructors might find the program appealing, especially adjunct faculty and non-tenure-track lecturers. We have seen growing numbers of such instructors enter our certificate program, as well as graduate students who are hoping to teach at the college level. Like all graduate programs in the humanities, we must be honest with our students about the currently bleak labor market for teachers of writing, especially those with only master's degrees who teach primarily in first-year writing programs. We don't want to offer the Graduate Certificate in Teaching Writing as a reliable gateway into full-time university teaching positions. Certainly adding one of these certificates to an MA in English should make someone more attractive to hiring committees, but the competition for positions is intense. Many university writing programs advertise for non-tenure-track positions saying that a PhD in composition/rhetoric is preferred or even required. Therefore, recruiting students for a certificate in teaching writing poses challenges. As noted earlier, K–12 teachers are not always encouraged to do graduate study, and while university instructors must have a graduate degree, their job prospects are worse than those of K–12 teachers.

We have also encountered the programmatic tension of students wanting courses outside of our writing pedagogy concentration to count toward the certificate. What about courses in pedagogy developed by other areas of English or offered by the School of Education? We have only 20 hours (five courses, at 4 credits each) and want a student earning our certificate to have sufficient breadth and depth within the field of writing studies. When developing the program, we also had to consider potential overlap with graduate programs in education and have that faculty review our proposal. We have not felt that our certificate program was in competition with master's degree programs in education, but it is important to keep open the lines of communication. Faculty in education have referred some of their students to our courses, and several doctoral students from education have done a writing minor that involved taking some of our courses, though not the whole certificate. This is an area of institutional boundary drawing and crossing that must be negotiated a bit differently at each university. Given the current political climate surrounding education reform, we want to be careful not to play

– 115 –

into the hands of some policymakers who want to pit content areas against schools of education.

The certificate program has also been generative in the sense that literature is now on board with a teaching certificate; when combined, the two certificate programs amount to a full 40-credit-hour MA without a thesis. Our department expects that many teachers will wish to get both of these certificates. Another option is to combine our department's TESOL certificate with the Certificate in Teaching Writing—an indication that our respective fields are now closely aligned given demographic changes, and a hopeful sign for more collaboration between our first-year writing program and our English for Academic Purposes (formerly ESL) program. Although some faculty may worry about the move away from requiring a thesis, certificate programs are demonstrating their value in recruiting new students, many of whom go on to complete the full MA, and making our graduate program distinctive.

In a difficult economy, and with forces suspicious of higher education often gaining the upper hand, teachers might be hesitant to commit to a master's degree program. An MA is not required for K–12 teaching and is not sufficient for tenure-track college positions. We think that certificate programs in writing pedagogy offer a reasonable and attractive entry into graduate English education for many teachers and thus may help keep MA programs alive and well.

Certificate programs are valuable components of an MA program, not just because they recruit students who might continue on into the MA program, but also because they help the program reimagine itself. As William FitzGerald and Carol Singley note elsewhere in this volume, stand-alone MA programs face challenges to justify their continued existence and to rethink their character in the midst of local, national, and global changes in the profession and in higher education. FitzGerald and Singley note the opportunities for an MA program to see itself as providing professional education and as furthering an urban university's commitment to civic engagement. At IUPUI, an urban university with many professional schools, our Certificate in Teaching Writing (along with our Certificate in Teaching Literature and our TESOL Certificate, soon to become part of an MA in TESOL) helps to mark our MA as a professional degree in its own right, and one that serves the local community. Our certificate's focus on language diversity in writing, complemented by the Certificate in Teaching Literature and the TESOL Certificate's focus on cultural and linguistic diversity, positions our MA to move toward global relevance and confront the issues challenging graduate education in the new demographic era of majority minority populations. Certificate programs can open the door and even provide a path for English MA programs to apply the humanities to contemporary problems.

Our own program shows how certificate programs in teaching writing might foster partnerships between higher education and K–12 education, between schools of education and English departments, and even between different disciplines. Those are ambitious goals. But keeping MA programs running is not an end in itself; such programs require meaningful goals that fulfill important human needs. We believe that our schools and their students benefit when teachers are scholars, inspired and informed, eager to take an inquiry stance in their professional lives, and able to take on retrograde and harmful trends in literacy instruction. Certificate programs in teaching writing can be sites for such scholarship, the kind of scholarship that nurtures praxis and thus helps teachers become the primary agents of long-lasting, humane educational reform.

Notes

1. Formerly the North Central Association of Colleges and Schools.

2. The *Language Knowledge and Awareness Survey* final research report, submitted by the CCCC Language Policy Committee to NCTE, January 2000, is available at http://www.ncte.org/library/NCTEFiles/Groups/ CCCC/Committees/langsurvey.pdf. For a discussion of the survey results, see Elaine Richardson's "Race, Class(es), Gender, and Age: The Making of Knowledge about Language Diversity" in *Language Diversity in the Classroom: From Intention to Practice*, edited by Geneva Smitherman and Victor Villanueva (Carbondale: Southern Illinois UP, 2003, 40–66).

3. From a quick Web search of about twenty such programs, we can offer some initial impressions. These programs usually require about half the time of a full master's program—in other words, four to six courses, 12

to 20 credit hours. Some programs are connected to an NWP site and therefore include as required or optional the NWP Summer Institute. Most courses within the programs emphasize pedagogy, but courses in writing itself, whether professional, technical, creative, or scholarly, are sometimes included in the mix offered to students. Those who complete these certificate programs can often count the credits toward a master's degree at that same institution, though they may have a separate application to the master's degree program.

4. For example, courses for writing program TAs might include Erika Lindemann's *A Rhetoric for Writing Teachers*, Duane Roen et al.'s *Strategies for Teaching First-Year Composition*, or Victor Villanueva's *Cross-Talk in Comp Theory*. A course focused entirely on teaching writing in middle and high school could use texts such as Nancie Atwell's *In the Middle* or Kelly Gallagher's *Teaching Adolescent Writers*. In our core course, we have used Villanueva and more recently Susan Miller's *The Norton Book of Composition Studies*. But we have also used a variety of articles drawn from different journals, ranging from *English Journal* to *College Composition and Communication*. Some instructors also offer students an opportunity to choose a book related to their own interests to read and review. Whatever texts are chosen, the challenge is to help everyone draw on ideas that can be adapted to their particular instructional setting.

Works Cited

Atwell, Nancie. *In the Middle: Writing, Reading, and Learning with Adolescents*. Upper Montclair: Boynton/Cook, 1987. Print.

David, Jane L., and Larry Cuban. *Cutting through the Hype: The Essential Guide to School Reform*. Cambridge: Harvard Education, 2010. Print.

Donhardt, Tracy. "Re: Question about Certificate Program." Message to Steve Fox. 24 Aug. 2013. Email.

Friedman, Audrey A., and Luke Reynolds, eds. *Burned In: Fueling the Fire to Teach*. New York: Teachers College, 2011. Print.

Gallagher, Kelly. *Teaching Adolescent Writers*. Portland: Stenhouse, 2006. Print.

Gellin, Laura. "Re: Question about Certificate Program." Message to Steve Fox. 23 Aug. 2013. Email.

Giles, Clark. "Re: Question about Certificate Program." Message to Steve Fox. 26 Aug. 2013. Email.

Boundary Crossings and Collaboration

Hampton, Johnna. "Re: Question about Cross-Level Collaboration." Message to Steve Fox. 25 Aug. 2013. Email.

Higher Learning Commission. *Determining Qualified Faculty through HLC's Criteria for Accreditation and Assumed Practices.* Mar. 2016. Web. 20 June 2016.

Indiana General Assembly. Indiana Code 20-28-9-1.5. "Teacher's Minimum Salary; Basis." Archived Indiana Code. 2014. Web. 3 July 2015.

Lindemann, Erika. *A Rhetoric for Writing Teachers.* New York: Oxford UP, 1987. Print.

Miller, Susan. *The Norton Book of Composition Studies.* New York: Norton, 2009. Print.

National Council on Teacher Quality. *Restructuring Teacher Pay to Reward Excellence.* Dec. 2010. Web. 3 July 2015.

National Writing Project, and Carl Nagin. *Because Writing Matters: Improving Student Writing in Our Schools.* San Francisco: Jossey-Bass, 2006. Rev. ed. Print.

Richards, Erin, and Arthur Thomas. "Loss of Master's Degree Pay Bump Has Impact on Teachers, Grad Schools." *Milwaukee Journal Sentinel Online* 1 Sept. 2012. Web. 21 June 2016.

Roen, Duane, Veronica Pantoja, Lauren Yena, Susan K. Miller, and Eric Waggoner, eds. *Strategies for Teaching First-Year Composition.* Urbana: NCTE, 2002. Print.

Scheer, Sam. "The High School Teacher as Scholar?" Friedman and Reynolds 90–94.

Students First. "Policy Agenda." State Policy Report Card 2014. Web. 3 July 2015

Therber, Angie. "Re: Question about Cross-Level Collaboration." Message to Steve Fox. 23 Aug. 2013. Email.

Tremmel, Robert. "Introduction: Striking a Balance—Seeking a Discipline." *Teaching Writing Teachers of High School English and First-Year Composition.* Ed. Robert Tremmel and William Broz. Portsmouth: Boynton/Cook, 2002. 1–16. Print.

Villanueva, Victor. *Cross-Talk in Comp Theory: A Reader.* Urbana: NCTE, 1997. Print.

CHAPTER SEVEN

TextSupport: Incorporating Online Pedagogy into MA English Programs

ABIGAIL G. SCHEG
Western Governors University

When embarking on my research into technology use in MA programs, I was distressed by the terms used to describe this degree: *stepping-stone, way station, test, jack-of-all-trades, undefined, road to a PhD,* and many more. All of these terms in some way reference the MA as a semiprofessional degree, lost between a BA and a PhD. I earned my MA degree knowing that I wanted to pursue a PhD in English, but I never considered letting that discredit the time, learning, and effort I put into my program. My MA program was what opened my eyes to all that English studies could include (the track I pursued was in traditional literature), and it afforded me the curiosity to consider how far I could stretch the boundaries of interdisciplinarity.

During my tenure as an MA student, I struggled with medieval literature, reveled in twentieth-century American literature, learned about the hierarchy of English studies and argued for my position in that hierarchy, fell in love with creative nonfiction, and learned the pedagogy of syllabi and rubrics. Although my foci were vast, I tend to agree with Erika Wright's claim that the *strength* of an MA program is that it must "serve students with a far broader range of goals and abilities" (30; Dalbey 17). Many of my colleagues in the program were elementary and high school teachers taking their mandatory graduate-level courses, but I always looked up to them for their hard work and meticulous readings of our texts. Everyone in my program seemed to come at our work from a different angle, which made our discussions

TextSupport: Incorporating Online Pedagogy into MA English Programs

lively, fluid, and full of possibility. I never viewed varied perspectives as a challenge of the program, but rather an opportunity.

When I graduated, I was on top of the world with my accomplishment and began to share my CV with potential employers. My unspoken goal was to earn an online teaching position and move to somewhere fabulous, perhaps tropical, and never actually set foot inside of a physical classroom. Almost immediately after graduating, I became an adjunct instructor for the University of Phoenix and learned two very hard lessons:

1. Despite the wide range of topics covered by my MA program, we never even discussed teaching online and, therefore, I knew nothing about it.

2. None of the face-to-face (F2F) skills that I did learn in my MA program were directly transferrable to the online environment.

This is not to say that the skills and training I earned in my courses were irrelevant, only that there are significant differences between *teaching* online and F2F. Always being a fast learner, I researched learning management systems (LMSs) and quickly studied up on online accreditation and how adjuncts are often used prolifically for online courses. I learned about establishing learning communities in the online setting. I learned about early and significant preparation necessary for online classes and that technological errors have the potential to ruin the entire course.

Fast-forward to my entry into a doctoral program, where I became *the* technology person in the program in a roundabout way. I was admitted into the program with an inclination toward writing center pedagogy (based on my experience as a graduate assistant in my MA program), but I immediately dropped that interest when I took the Technology and Literacy course and learned all about the gadgets, gizmos, programs, and opportunities that technology affords writing. Though that class was largely experimental, it led me to backtrack into the realm of computers and composition, a field well established but entirely new to me. I longed for more time, more classes, more experimentation, more reading in the field and eventually found all of that by focusing my dissertation on online pedagogy and online teacher training. After becoming the graduate assistant of the Technology and

Literacy course professor, I assisted him with projects and was asked to participate in technology training programs hosted by the university.

Perhaps it was my novice approach to teaching online, but my initial experience as an online instructor sparked a passion for researching and arguing for online teacher training. I spoke to many other online and F2F instructors, leading the conversation into the differences between these teaching environments, and everyone shared the same commiseration: no one was trained to teach online, but almost everyone was expected to do it. My colleagues navigated through it in the same manner I did: trial and error. Eventually, somehow, someway, we began to feel as comfortable in the online realm as we do in front of a F2F classroom. Although we managed to figure this out, trial and error is not the best approach when training could be done in terminal MA programs. This chapter examines how MA programs may or may not be adequately preparing their graduates to teach content (writing, literature, or other subjects) in online environments. I discuss how MA programs might incorporate the theoretical and practical preparation for using technology, if only at a minimal level. As I have argued elsewhere (Scheg), we need to increase the development of degree programs in online pedagogy, as well as integrate these practices with various subject areas. Acknowledging the challenges involved in the complete overhaul of degree programs, this chapter also makes recommendations and suggestions for incorporating a single course in online pedagogy into MA programs. In offering one course, the stepping-stones toward building up online pedagogy would be small and, therefore, more manageable for programs, departments, and institutions.

Current MA Programs in the United States

To understand the variety of MA English programs in US higher education, let me take time to examine some of the possible choices. In an attempt to view potential graduate programs in English like a prospective student, I visited GradSchools.com. There are 872 institutions in the United States offering the MA in English degree ("English Graduate Programs"). This is an overwhelming

TextSupport: Incorporating Online Pedagogy into MA English Programs

number of programs that students presumably narrow by price, geographical location, possible online offerings, and other known information about the program such as faculty or reputation. It is no wonder, then, that these program offerings are general: they need to suit the needs of a varied student demographic. According to Vandenberg and Clary-Lemon, MA programs are far more diverse in population than PhD programs insofar as "the percentage of students of color pursuing MA degrees is approximately 23 percent" (266). Likewise, "sixty percent of master's students are women, 70 percent are enrolled part-time, and 54 percent are an 'employee enrolled in school'" (Brown 5). Once these diverse MA students graduate from their programs, they will seek employment down a number of avenues. Arguably, the most sought-out career path for an advanced degree in English is teaching.

Although there are limited opportunities for full-time online English instructors, it is very possible that a recent MA graduate could earn an online adjunct position or an instructor-level position at an F2F institution, many of which come with the added responsibility of teaching online courses. According to Steve Kolowich in the *Chronicle of Higher Education*, more than seven million students participate in online courses, and this number continues to rise. With this rapid increase in students taking online courses comes a concomitant increase in the number of online instructors, particularly (and unfortunately) adjuncts. According to a study by Dunn and Mueller (2013), graduates of English MA programs rank "community college instructor" and "further graduate study: doctoral study" in writing studies as the top two career goals (16). Because many community colleges are now being asked to provide distance education for their students (and to appeal to a larger variety of students), instructors who desire a career teaching English at the community college level should have experience with distance education and online pedagogy in order to make them desirable candidates for such positions. With doctoral study (presumably, but not always, to achieve a teaching position) and teaching at the community college level as the number one and two outcome goals of MA English graduates, it begs the question: does the traditional MA English program adequately prepare instructors for the online teaching they are likely to do?

In my research for this chapter and other projects, I have discussed this question with a number of individuals who earned their MA-level degrees, not just in the United States but also throughout the world. Some note that technology and distance education were discussed consistently throughout their programs. Others had similar experiences to my own, citing only traditional reading and writing assignments with little regard for transitioning to online education. What is interesting, though, is that everyone regrets that they were not trained to *teach online*. Rather, we have taken what we learned as appropriate to the F2F classroom, combined with our own knowledge and experience of distance education, and tested it out on our unsuspecting students. The more work, time, research, and experimentation put into distance education the better the results—sometimes outstanding results—but unfortunately this has yet to become the norm for graduate-level teacher preparation in the United States.

Indiana University of Pennsylvania, one of the Pennsylvania State System of Higher Education (PASSHE) universities, offers an MA generalist degree, as well as other MA degrees with varying foci, such as TESOL. The MA generalist program offers students a chance to

> take courses from across the field of English Studies—literature, composition, teaching English as a second language, and teacher preparation—giving you the opportunity to explore the range of possibilities for focus and career preparation. But, as you find your passion, you'll have the opportunity to specialize in that area and to really prepare yourself for particular educational or career paths. This program is perfect for the student who loves English but doesn't quite know what it might mean to be a professional in the field. (Indiana University of Pennsylvania)

However, even that description does not encourage well-rounded views of the MA program. Rather, it encourages students to learn more about these learning opportunities in order to claim a specialization in a particular vein of English studies (and possibly continue that into a doctoral program). While the breadth of a terminal MA is, as I see it, a strength of the program, some

– 124 –

TextSupport: Incorporating Online Pedagogy into MA English Programs

programs may need to reexamine the phrasing or emphases offered within the program and consider incorporating courses in technology and online pedagogy to better support their current students. Perhaps one of the major challenges of a terminal MA in English studies is balancing the traditional requirements, which include literature, traditional pedagogy, and some research and theory, while still remaining cutting-edge in the areas of educational technology and distance education. While it can seem like an insurmountable amount of information to navigate in a limited-term MA program, the pedagogy of teaching with technology can be incorporated in ways to support, not work against, the program's current curriculum.

In recent years, many programs have been or are in the midst of reevaluating the influence of technology on the traditional MA. Knievel and Sheridan-Rabideaux at the University of Wyoming have considered remaking the MA in composition and rhetoric for the electronic age with three tracks examining digital spaces, globalization, and public audiences (Vandenberg and Clary-Lemon 270). Beard examines the MA offerings at the University of Minnesota Duluth, which include a WRIT4250 course, New Media Writing, as well as JOUR3700, Media Laws and Ethics, and WRIT1506, Literacy, Technology and Society (2). Although these are great strides in the right direction, moving the terminal MA forward, these courses still lack the inherent connection between teaching and technology, which is an inescapable direction of higher education. In other words, current MA English students need preparation in online pedagogy to be strong job candidates postgraduation.

Understanding Terminology

Understanding some of the terminology associated with technology in English programs is a necessary step in recognizing the direction and goal of an MA program with a technology focus. *Digital humanities* is a current buzzword in the humanities and education that roughly translates as "the intersection of humanities and technology." Some graduate-level programs have adopted the concepts of digital humanities as an addition, extension, or

— 125 —

distant relation to their traditional English departments. However, it is important to understand the concepts discussed and used within such programs in order to glean suggestions for improving technology in traditional MA programs.

Michigan State University offers an undergraduate degree with a specialization in digital humanities. The coursework requirements are a unique blend of traditional and modern, visually based courses. Michigan State's program strives to "provide students an opportunity to engage with technology in classrooms and in professional environments while focusing on how technology has and is changing humanist thought and work" (par. "College of Arts and Letters"). The University of Virginia offers an MA in digital humanities that includes a core requirement of Teaching Media Studies[1] (Institute for Advanced Technology in the Humanities). This is a F2F course that affords MA students the opportunity to learn theoretical practices necessary for success in teaching with technology and also a sound environment in which to utilize these pedagogical tools.

Loyola University Chicago is among the many universities offering an MA in digital humanities. This degree program "combines theoretical and practical courses, but its aims are ultimately practical and professional, training new digital specialists for the growing knowledge and information economy and today's research in humanities disciplines." I am especially intrigued by the burgeoning field of digital humanities because of its vast potential for interdisciplinarity. However, as indicated by the Loyola University Chicago program description, teaching is not always at the forefront of digital humanities. Digital humanities has been adopted by many educators and integrated into major discussions at conferences such as the Conference on College Composition and Communication and Computers and Writing, but its foundations belong in training and securing new digital researchers and specialists. Also, as indicated by the BA program at Michigan State, bringing traditional written texts into the realm of digital exploration is a focus that may or may not have a place in the classroom. Digital humanities, then, represents a number of concepts depending on author, audience, student, and conversation; however, in the relation between traditional English studies and technology, digital humanities plays a significant role.

— 126 —

TextSupport: Incorporating Online Pedagogy into MA English Programs

Online pedagogy is another term worthy of exploration for the purposes of this research. According to Rafi Nachmias:

> To look at the impact of these developments within the context of higher education implies, in fact, to examine the ways they challenge the 2500-year-old Socratic, face-to-face, lecturing, and discussion modes characterizing most of college and university teaching. (214)

Understanding how online pedagogy differs from traditional pedagogy is key to effectively training teachers to teach online, and therefore it needs to be incorporated into programs such as traditional MA English programs.

According to my research, only a handful of programs in the United States offer MA-level programs in online pedagogy, one of which is the University of Maryland University College (UMUC). UMUC currently has four master's level degree options in its Distance Education program, including three MDEs (master of distance education) in distance education policy and management, training specialization, and technology specialization. UMUC also offers an MS in technology management for distance education (Grant 49; UMUC Graduate Programs). However, as previously stated, these are *not* MA programs, or even English programs, but rather MS or MDE programs that focus entirely on the area of distance education.

Likewise, the University of Michigan-Flint offers an MA in technology in education, which is designed for "[t]eachers, administrators, educational specialists in business or community organizations, and others who seek relevant, practical grounding in tools and concepts related to the use of technology in educational settings." Unfortunately, the MA in technology in education is not offered as a dual enrollment degree with their MA in English or any other content area of study. Therefore, individuals pursuing sufficient training to teach English courses online would need to hold two degrees: the MA in English for content area and the MA in technology in education for the aspects of online pedagogy. While I certainly encourage individuals to participate in additional degree programs in their field or areas of interest, I also feel that it is unrealistic at this point to expect every online

– 127 –

adjunct in the United States to hold at least *two* graduate-level degrees before teaching online courses. Therefore, terminal MA programs should address the needs of their students by incorporating online pedagogy into their curricula. This is especially relevant in MA in English programs whose graduates will go on to be English instructors at varying levels. As writing is becoming an increasingly multimodal form of communication, to best prepare our writing students we (the instructors) need to be prepared to educate through and communicate with technology, as well as instruct students in teaching with technology.

Adjusting the MA to Meet Technological Demands of Online Education

This collection and other texts have called attention to the struggles and debates within the realm of English studies. Change is not new. As Hawisher, LeBlanc, Moran, and Selfe identified in *Computers and the Teaching of Writing in American Higher Education*, "English studies has never been quick to adopt new technologies and computers did not change old habits" (32). McComiskey's *English Studies* discusses the dangers of hyper-specialization and calls us to "*re*imagine ourselves as members of a larger community of English studies disciplines" (41). Mc-Comiskey calls us to be aware of and acknowledge the social context of our areas of specialization as a point that will draw all of English studies back together. Perhaps technology can be the key, the challenge, to bringing the unique but related disciplines together. We all share technological challenges and reconceptualizations of our subject areas brought on by paradigm shifts of online and technological pedagogy.

Undoubtedly, technology has drastically changed the social context of writing and literature classrooms, not to mention the classroom landscape and possibilities. Technology is being introduced into institutions, departments, and courses for various reasons, but the training that precedes its implementation is worth questioning. It is necessary to mention that teacher resistance to online education and, in some cases, lack of experience provide a unique challenge to individuals and institutions. In fact, the Online

Learning Consortium (formerly Sloan Consortium) report found that less than one-third of college-level chief academic officers believe their faculty have accepted online education as valuable and legitimate (Allen and Seaman). Although online education is increasingly in demand in higher education, there are still few individuals in the country with expertise in the field of online pedagogy. Therefore, individual institutions may actually have no one on the faculty with expertise in the field, thus increasing the level of resistance to the online transition. This cyclical problem must end; individuals in graduate programs must be sufficiently trained to become online educators, not only for preparedness in their careers, but also for the further development of the field.

In the previous section, I examined MA programs that consider the integration of technology into traditional pedagogy and challenged that tradition with the introduction of the concept of online pedagogy. Next I consider why change is necessary and what types of change are necessary for current MA degrees to fulfill the needs of terminal MA holders.

Starting Small: Guidebooks

Until online pedagogy grows to fill a more profound place in formal academic training, one of the major places one can learn about the challenges and opportunities associated with online teaching is through guidebooks. Guidebooks have been at the forefront of the development of online teaching and online pedagogy, typically stemming from instructors' personal dissatisfaction with their own online training and teaching experiences. Such texts provide introductory information for instructors transitioning (or being thrust into) online teaching in terms of technology, pedagogy, and expectations.

Myers-Wylie, Mangieri, and Hardy's *The In's and Out's of Online Instruction* is founded in the traditional thought of Vygotsky and Piaget, extending their theories of proximal development to the realm of online education. This text begins with the understanding that instructors are typically ill-equipped and ill-prepared to teach online courses. These and many other authors of guidebooks strive to make connections between the

PROGRAMMATIC TRANSFORMATIONS

F2F and the online classroom as a way to make the unfamiliar familiar by relating online content to content presentation in the F2F classroom. Though this is not always the most effective way to teach about online training, for those who have been unable to learn about it in their formal educations, the guidebooks are an invaluable tool for teacher preparation.

Ko and Rossen's *Teaching Online: A Practical Guide* explains the phenomenon of online education and what its many changes mean for us:

> In 1993, if you had written a book about teaching, you would not have needed to describe the basic tools of the trade—the classroom, the rows of seats, the blackboard, the chalk. These were taken for granted; they never changed.
>
> Today, you must describe how the virtual and real worlds intertwine in a process known as teaching online. You must talk about discussion boards, streaming media, asynchronous environments, real-time chat, instant messaging, as well as social networking, and the many collaborative and interactive tools collectively known as Web 2.0. (xvii)

These significant changes have transformed what it means to be a teacher. Therefore, teacher training for educational venues must also change to meet these transitional times. In particular, the terminal MA serves as a jumping-off point for many who go on to be instructors. Lacking the skills, pedagogical knowledge, and experience to teach online will not only negatively impact institutions, but it will also do a disservice to populations of online students and negatively impact a graduate's success in landing a job.

Another major argument of the Ko and Rossen text is that online pedagogy is *not* interchangeable with F2F, traditional pedagogy. Though many individuals and institutions feel that if you can teach F2F you should be able to teach online, this is not the case. Many institutions require no training to prepare their instructors for online teaching; some require only a working knowledge of an LMS/CMS (course management system) such as Blackboard, Moodle, Desire2Learn (D2L), or eCollege. Having *just* a working knowledge of a CMS is similar to having the working knowledge to open a textbook; it is certainly an

— 130 —

TextSupport: Incorporating Online Pedagogy into MA English Programs

important facet of the educational process, but it is not the only or most important aspect of teaching. Although Ko and Rossen use F2F pedagogy as a starting point, they do not rely on a direct transition from F2F to online pedagogy. The authors emphasize that "the online environment is so different from what most instructors have encountered before" (3) and proceed to present a unique and comprehensive view of online pedagogy.

Still, relying solely on guidebooks to do the transitioning of teacher training from F2F to online pedagogy for MA students is insufficient preparation. There are other places and platforms where these conversations can take place, such as in our MA classrooms. Formal education, like that offered in our terminal MA programs, is necessary as part of the curriculum to expand the learning experiences of potential teachers and prepare them for their inevitable teaching assignment: online education. Although it will be a slow transition to the incorporation of online pedagogy, this is a necessary transformation that should take place in terminal MA programs, which are producing so many of our current and future online educators. Even making small changes to programs can have a significant positive impact on students.

Proposed Curriculum for Terminal MA Programs

An essential curriculum for online pedagogy should be added to terminal MA programs to facilitate discussions, experiences, and practice for potential online instructors. For MA students to have the most fulfilling learning experience regarding online pedagogy, their coursework on this subject should blend pedagogical and practical tips of online education (Grant).[2] This means that online teacher training programs should not rely solely on practical training such as platform training—a foundational, pedagogical knowledge of online teaching needs to be established before students get into the details. In the same vein, simply learning online pedagogy without the opportunity to practice the skills discussed would be a disservice to potential online instructors.

Online teacher training cannot rely solely on the technological skills required to operate a CMS, nor can the training be intended for F2F instructors. As previously discussed, we cannot rely on

— 131 —

traditional F2F teacher training or methodology to prepare our future instructors for their online teaching responsibilities. Many current online instructors have taken part in training that is too heavily focused on acquisition of technological skill (i.e., platform training) and feel they are ill-equipped for the online classroom (Barrett; Boise State University; Clark-Ibáñez and Scott; Delfino and Persico; Hampel; Orleans). Some instructors have taken part in training that is too heavily focused on learning pedagogical skills (most likely F2F pedagogy, as online pedagogy is only a recent development), which is equally problematic for effective online classroom management (Boettcher and Conrad; Kennedy; Littlejohn, Falconer, and Mcgill; Savenye, Olina, and Niemczyk). While the ratio of pedagogy to practice depends on the subject of the course, the integration of both is important to program or course design (Grant).

A single course could be implemented in terminal MA English programs to afford these students the opportunity to learn about and practice teaching online, an experience many of them will have one way or another in their career. Perhaps a program has a place and need for an introduction to online pedagogy course, but the processes for new course design and integration are nearly impossible to navigate through the university. In that case, online pedagogy could be incorporated into a course that already discusses pedagogy, course design, syllabi, and practical teaching techniques. Perhaps students could have the opportunity to choose their focus in that type of course: online or F2F pedagogy and practice. Perhaps students could use the opportunity to learn more about both aspects of teaching so that they have introductory discussions and materials prepared for any teaching assignment that may come their way as they begin their career. The possibilities of how online pedagogy could be incorporated into an MA program are many; as with all courses and programs, one size or type of course will not fit all.

For instance, in both my MA and doctoral programs, I took courses that gave me the opportunity to prepare syllabi, teach lessons, conduct presentations, create handouts, and much more. Although there was no discussion about or opportunity to consider online courses, these practical courses provide a wonderful opportunity to introduce online pedagogy as a form of teaching

TextSupport: Incorporating Online Pedagogy into MA English Programs

distinct from its F2F counterpart. Discussing differences between F2F and online teaching environments, differences in communicative styles (email/posts versus speaking aloud), and student/teacher expectations in the classroom are places to begin a conversation about online pedagogy.

To provide a brief outline of the possibilities, I offer some proposed outcomes for a course in online pedagogy. The following is a brief course design for online pedagogy that could be modified to suit the needs of any terminal MA program. Likewise, any and all of these objectives could be adapted to fit within the parameters of a currently existing MA English course so that program changes to accommodate online pedagogy would not be too great (Scheg).

An introductory course in online pedagogy should target instructors who want to teach online and, ideally, those who have not yet taught online. Such a course should discuss the balance of technological acquisition and pedagogical learning necessary for online instructors to be successful in their courses. More specifically, at the end of the course, potential online instructors should understand and be able to explain the unique type of instruction necessary to successfully facilitate online learning and be able to differentiate between online and F2F learning. Potential online instructors should also be able to differentiate between the theory necessary to understand the components of an online classroom and the technology necessary to put those theories into action. On a practical note, potential online instructors should be able to produce educational material on online pedagogy suitable for an entry-level online instructor (Grant 108). In this way, students in a traditional MA program can have the same exposure to their subject areas, but assignments, discussions, and assessments can include elements of online pedagogy to support currently existing pedagogies. This structure has many strengths. In particular, it is extremely flexible, allowing for discussions, adaptations, or complete changes based on the needs, interests, and career directions of MA English students. The interests and goals of the students should lead the conversation in an organic manner so that students discover their questions and answers, preparing them to be effective and knowledgeable online instructors.

Incorporating an introduction to online pedagogy does not have to be an extremely time-consuming or challenging task for an MA program. It is a change that will better prepare our future online writing instructors teaching in online environments. Programs can take small steps at first, such as adding a section on online pedagogy to a preexisting course. Then they might add an entire course in online pedagogy. Making this transition slowly will allow universities with terminal MA English programs to seek out the online training needs of their faculty members to determine the best path for program development.

As the number of institutions offering online courses continues to grow, so will the number of students and potential instructors. Terminal MA English programs play a vital role in the preparation of both full-time and adjunct instructors who will eventually have an opportunity to teach online courses. Although higher education is moving in the direction of recognizing online pedagogy as a unique and important field of study, this is not happening fast enough given the number of online courses being offered. MA English programs provide a wonderful opportunity for potential online instructors to begin learning about, discussing, and practicing the challenges and nuances of online teaching. The strength of a terminal MA program is its flexibility to allow a number of students with varying career goals to learn more about teaching, research, and a particular subject area. Small steps toward incorporating online pedagogy make for significant learning opportunities for potential teachers, who may not get this experience any other place. The possibilities for the terminal MA English degree are endless but do need to include sufficient recognition of the burgeoning field of online pedagogy.

Notes

1. According to the University of Virginia website, the course description reads: "This workshop provides training in pedagogy for students serving as teaching assistants in MDST 110: Information Technology and Digital Media. Issues of pedagogy and the use of information technology in the teaching environment will be addressed."

TextSupport: Incorporating Online Pedagogy into MA English Programs

2. For additional information regarding acquisition of technological skills and learning online pedagogy, see my dissertation, *Reforming Teacher Education for Online Pedagogy Development*. This section is a shortened version of the dissertation material that discusses program design based on accreditation standards and typical university guidelines.

Works Cited

Allen, I. Elaine, and Jeff Seaman. *Learning on Demand: Online Education in the United States, 2009*. Newburyport: Sloan Consortium, 2010. Print.

Barrett, Bob. "Virtual Teaching and Strategies: Transitioning from Teaching Traditional Classes to Online Classes." *Contemporary Issues in Education Research* 3.12 (2010): 17–20. Print.

Beard, David. "The Case for a Major in Writing Studies: The University of Minnesota Duluth." *Composition Forum* 21 (2010): n. pag. Web. 21 June 2016.

Boettcher, Judith V., and Rita-Marie Conrad. *The Online Teaching Survival Guide: Simple and Practical Pedagogical Tips*. San Francisco: Jossey-Bass, 2010. Print.

Boise State University. "Academic Technologies Homepage." *BoiseState.edu*, n.d. Web. 20 June 2012.

Brown, Heath. "Data Sources." *CGS Communicator* 39.6 (2006): 5–6. Print.

Clark-Ibáñez, Marisol, and Linda Scott. "Learning to Teach Online." *Teaching Sociology* 36.1 (2008): 34–41. Print.

Dalbey, Marcia A. "What Good Is the MA Degree?" *ADE Bulletin* 112 (1995): 17–20. Print.

Delfino, Manuela, and Donatella Persico. "Online or Face-to-Face? Experimenting with Different Techniques in Teacher Training." *Journal of Computer Assisted Learning* 23.5 (2007): 351–65. Print.

Dunn, John S., Jr., and Derek N. Mueller. *Report on the 2012 Survey of Programs*. Master's Degree Consortium of Writing Studies Specialists, 20 Feb. 2013. Web. 22 June 2016.

"English Graduate Programs." *GradSchools.com*. Education Dynamics, n.d. Web. 20 May 2012.

Grant, Abigail A. *Distinguishing Online and Face-to-Face Learning: Acquisition, Learning, and Online Pedagogy*. Diss. Indiana U of Pennsylvania, 2012. Ann Arbor: ProQuest Dissertation. Web. 22 June 2016.

Hampel, Regine. "Training Teachers for the Multimedia Age: Developing Teacher Expertise to Enhance Online Learner Interaction and Collaboration." *Innovation in Language Learning and Teaching* 3.1 (2009): 35–50. Print.

Hawisher, Gail E., Paul LeBlanc, Charles Moran, and Cynthia L. Selfe. *Computers and the Teaching of Writing in American Higher Education, 1979–1994: A History*. Norwood: Ablex, 1996. Print.

Indiana University of Pennsylvania. "M.A. in English: Generalist." Indiana University of Pennsylvania, 2012. Web. 1 June 2012.

Institute for Advanced Technology in the Humanities. "Master's Degree in Digital Humanities Media Studies Program University of Virginia." University of Virginia, 2012. Web. 21 May 2012.

Kennedy, David M. "Standards for Online Teaching: Lessons from the Education, Health, and IT Sectors." *Nurse Education Today* 25.1 (2005): 23–30. Print.

Ko, Susan, and Steve Rossen. *Teaching Online: A Practical Guide*. 3rd ed. New York: Routledge, 2010. Print.

Kolowich, Steve. "Exactly How Many Students Take Online Courses?" *Chronicle of Higher Education* 16 Jan. 2014. Web. 8 July 2016.

Littlejohn, Allison, Isobel Falconer, and Lou Mcgill. "Characterizing Effective eLearning Resources." *Computers and Education* 50.3 (2008): 757–71. Print.

Loyola University Chicago. "MA in Digital Humanities." Loyola University Chicago, 2012. Web. 21 May 2012.

McComiskey, Bruce. *English Studies: An Introduction to the Discipline(s)*. Urbana: NCTE, 2006. Print.

Michigan State University Undergraduate Specialization. "Undergraduate Specialization—Specialization in Digital Humanities." Michigan State University, 2012. Web. 25 July 2012.

Myers-Wylie, Danan, Jackie Mangieri, and Donna Hardy. *The In's and Out's of Online Instruction: Transitioning from Brick and Mortar to Online Teaching*. Denver: Outskirts, 2009. Print.

TextSupport: Incorporating Online Pedagogy into MA English Programs

Nachmias, Rafi. "A Research Framework for the Study of a Campus-Wide Web-Based Academic Instruction Project." *Internet and Higher Education* 5.3 (2002): 213–29. Print.

Orleans, Antriman V. "Enhancing Teacher Competence through Online Training." *Asia-Pacific Education Researcher* 19.3 (2010): 371–86. Print.

Savenye, Wilhelmina C., Zane Olina, and Mary Niemczyk. "So You Are Going to be an Online Writing Instructor: Issues in Designing, Developing, and Delivering an Online Course." *Computers and Composition* 18.4 (2001): 371–85. Print.

Scheg, Abigail G. *Reforming Teacher Education for Online Pedagogy Development*. Hershey: IGI Global, 2014. Print.

University of Maryland University College (UMUC) Graduate Programs. "Distance Education Teaching and Training (DETT) Specialization Description." University of Maryland University College (UMUC) Graduate Programs, 2012. Web. 21 May 2012.

University of Michigan-Flint. "What Sets UM-Flint's Technology in Education (MA) Program Apart?" University of Michigan-Flint, 2012. Web. 22 May 2012.

Vandenberg, Peter, and Jennifer Clary-Lemon. "Advancing by Degree: Placing the MA in Writing Studies." *College Composition and Communication* 62.2 (2010): 257–82. Print.

Wright, Erika. "Graduate Degree on the Margins: Educational and Professional Concerns of the MA Student." *Journal of the Midwest Modern Language Association* 37.2 (2004): 30–36. Print.

CHAPTER EIGHT

Crafting a Program That Works (for Us): The Evolving Mission of the Master's in English at Rutgers University–Camden

WILLIAM T. FITZGERALD AND CAROL J. SINGLEY
Rutgers University–Camden

Like other entities, academic institutions evolve over time and at variable rates of speed. One might think of such change in terms of punctuated equilibrium, that notion in evolutionary biology in which eras of gradual change are interrupted by bursts of rapid transformation in response to ecological factors. Or one might think in terms of variable currents, as when water appears to be quite placid, yet swifter currents flow just below the surface. Perhaps geology provides a better metaphor still in the gradual build-up of seismic forces along tectonic plates; their collision eventually results in eruption and upheaval, remaking the landscape in the process.

In this chapter, we consider forces of change impacting the master's program in English at Rutgers University–Camden, the smallest and southernmost campus of Rutgers, the State University of New Jersey. We do so with an eye toward the multiple factors that contribute to institutional and curricular change, if not on a geologic scale then on a human scale of decades. Our master's program is recognizably in a state of flux after a long period of stability. Indeed, we experienced as timely a 2011 MLA report, "Rethinking the Master's Degree in English for a New Century," prepared by the Association of Departments of English (ADE) Ad Hoc Committee on the Master's Degree. This report details many concerns we encounter in maintaining the MA in English

Crafting a Program That Works (for Us)

as a relevant and productive degree for us and for our students. Foremost among these concerns is the growing "gap between students' aspirations and employment outcomes on the one hand and MA programs' stated goals and curricular requirements on the other" (1). Here, we point to internal and external forces that prompt a frank assessment of where we stand and conclude that this is a critical moment to consider the evolution of our MA program. We have yet to travel far along a road of change, so options are open.

It should be stated up front that a spirit of tradition more than innovation, and a preference for gradual over radical change, are central to our departmental ethos. We contend with change more than we celebrate it, even when this change is self-initiated. In this, we do not find ourselves alone. Indeed, a similar spirit informs many stand-alone MA programs (i.e., not linked to a PhD) at institutions large and small, public and private. Looking beyond our walls, we see the MA in English undergoing increasing specialization as traditional programs in literature rub shoulders with programs in rhetoric and composition, professional and technical writing, TESOL and other fields. Programs like ours, behind the leading edge, also have stories to tell. Here we account for our master's at a time when similar programs are wrestling with dynamic forces impacting higher education.

Locating Our MA in English

What happened at Rutgers–Camden was this: After many years as a vibrant part of a more comprehensive MA in English, an emphasis in creative writing became, in 2009, a master of fine arts (MFA) in its own right. Where there was once a single MA with several tracks (literature, creative writing, composition), now there were two programs, with the MFA recognized as a terminal degree. The creation of an MFA program was rightly celebrated as a major step for our department and our campus, and we point to our MFA's fast rise to prominence with pride. However, such developments are not without growing pains, including ramifications to our existing MA. Dividing a single program into two brings with it shifts in enrollment, selectivity, and allocation of resources. It can also initiate a discernment process to better understand and articulate objectives for the MA in English.

In one version of this account, we could offer insider baseball on relations between two master's programs in one department. In another version, parochial matters such as these can be read as symptomatic of broader issues impacting higher education, including the general viability of master's degrees in the humanities. The latter account is a far more interesting tale. Its overarching insight is that *our* MA in English must be retooled to meet the needs of stakeholders—in the profession, on our campus, and in the South Jersey region. Indeed, matters of location (location, location) are paramount in determining our future direction.

We offer some background on our program to inform this narrative. Rutgers–Camden can be understood largely by tensions inherent in its name. On the one hand, *Rutgers*–Camden is a unit of Rutgers, the State University of New Jersey. A colonial and later land grant college, once-private Rutgers only became a public university in 1956. Today ranked among the nation's top research universities, Rutgers is by any measure a major player in higher education. On the other hand, Rutgers–*Camden* is the quintessential regional campus in a state that, while small geographically, is sharply divided culturally and politically between North and South Jersey. Indeed, many who live in New Jersey are unaware that Rutgers *has* a campus in Camden, directly opposite central Philadelphia.

This contrast in size and scope between Rutgers–Camden and Rutgers–New Brunswick is never far from mind for us on the Camden campus. Whereas Rutgers–New Brunswick exceeds 50,000 students across more than two dozen schools, colleges, and institutes, Rutgers–Camden has roughly 6,500 students in four units: a law school, a business school, a school of nursing, and the Camden College of Arts and Sciences. Rutgers–Camden is also quite young, only becoming part of Rutgers in the 1950s. Even today, Rutgers–Camden is only half as large as its regional counterpart in Rutgers–Newark, the second campus of three in the Rutgers system.

Beyond matters of size and lineage, Rutgers-Camden has for much of its history functioned as an island of relative privilege in a poor and beleaguered city whose once robust industries, includ-

Crafting a Program That Works (for Us)

ing the fabled Campbell Soup Company, have since moved or struggle. Despite its proximity to the cultural and economic riches of Philadelphia, the city of Camden is known today more for its violence than for its most famous resident, Walt Whitman, whose statue graces our campus quad. To understand Rutgers–Camden, it is necessary to understand its place in an academic institution and in a particular city.

To understand the role of the master's programs at Rutgers–Camden, one must also understand the relationship between degrees offered and the Rutgers organizational system. All three campuses of Rutgers constitute a single research university with respect to tenure and promotion, a centrally administered process. However, Rutgers-Camden is predominantly a master's-granting institution. Only in 2013 did the campus award its first PhD, in childhood studies. A culture of stand-alone master's education has thus long been integral to our identity. Only Rutgers-New Brunswick offers a PhD in English. A lack of doctoral programs at Rutgers-Camden and (to a lesser extent) Rutgers-Newark contributes to a mistaken sense that only New Brunswick is a *real* research university. Consequently, MA programs at Rutgers-Camden are defined against a backdrop of absent PhD programs, with an accompanying loss of prestige. The MA in English has functioned historically as a mini-PhD in terms of perceived benefits to faculty: namely, graduate students and teaching assistantships.

Of course, MA programs *are* distinct from doctoral programs in multiple ways, and we recognize the value of MA programs in addressing specific needs and populations. A distinguishing feature of our program, like many, is that it serves a largely local population from South Jersey. Upon earning their degrees, most remain in the region, finding or returning to jobs in teaching or in writing-related fields. Few students begin or complete our program intending to go on to a PhD, though some do, including those who establish successful academic careers.

This issue of demographics in relation to location, both geographically and in terms of an academic pecking order, is of obvious significance to us. "Who are our students?" is arguably *the* question in charting a future course. Do we strive to meet the needs of our current population, or reshape our applicant pool through a different approach to master's education? To answer this question, we need to better understand the education we do provide.

Our MA Curriculum

Within the Camden College of Arts and Sciences, English is the largest department in terms of faculty, if not majors. Besides an undergraduate major and several minors, our department houses a two-semester writing program for first-year students and, as noted, two graduate programs. The relationship between our undergraduate writing program and graduate programs is symbiotic. Between our two master's programs, eleven teaching assistantships support the writing program. With this robust level of support, fully two-thirds of first-year writing courses are staffed by graduate students completing either an MA or MFA, all of whom take a composition practicum with our writing program director, who, unconventionally, may be a scholar in literature, not composition. The opportunity to gain teaching experience and receive funding is among our program's top draws. (In addition to tuition remission, a teaching assistantship carries a stipend exceeding $25,000.) Students who do not receive full funding have opportunities to teach at area community colleges.

Like our undergraduate curriculum, the MA program is centered on literary studies and reflects a traditional approach to English. Such traditionalism extends to the composition of our department's twenty tenured or tenure-track faculty: thirteen in literature, four in creative writing, two in rhetoric, and one in linguistics. Two non-tenure-track positions, in journalism and writing, complete the roster of full-time faculty. With rare exceptions, only tenured or tenure-track faculty teach graduate courses, generally one course per year. In a given semester, six to eight graduate courses are offered and are open to both MA and MFA students. Our MA program offers three tracks: literature, writing studies, and literature and culture of childhood. MFA students take at least three "literature" courses (including offerings in linguistics and rhetoric/writing studies). MA students may, with permission of the MFA director, enroll in craft courses in creative writing. In addition to Introduction to Graduate Literary Study,

Crafting a Program That Works (for Us)

MA students in literature take two pre-1800 courses, one course in American literature, and one course in linguistics or rhetoric/writing studies to satisfy a "philology" requirement. Those in the writing studies and literature and culture of childhood tracks meet the same requirements except they take only one pre-1800 lit course and four courses related to their area of study.

Beyond coursework (30 credits), MA students sit exams in two subject areas, chosen from five options: medieval–Renaissance (to c. 1640); transatlantic British and American (c.1640–c.1800); nineteenth century (Romantic, Victorian, and American); twentieth century–present (Modernist and postcolonial); and specialized studies (focused on such areas as criticism and critical theory, rhetoric, media studies, linguistics, childhood studies, etc.). With the exception of Specialized Studies, whose lists are developed by students in consultation with a faculty advisor, exams are based on fixed lists, revised in 2012 after extensive review of the exam structure. A change in nomenclature from "comprehensive" to "candidacy" exam reflects a subtle shift of perspective. Our MA students may choose a thesis in lieu of one exam—about one-quarter do so. Most students interested in rhetoric or writing studies choose the thesis option.

As noted, our MA reflects a conservative approach to English grounded in, and largely synonymous with, literary studies. Our highly productive research faculty have particular strengths in, among other areas, American literature, children's literature and culture, and the early modern period. However, a single line in rhetoric/writing studies is not sufficient to complement literary studies. Absent from our curriculum is a focus on English education (which is handled through the teacher preparation program). Also missing are courses in professional or technical writing, editing, and media studies offered by more comprehensive or specialized programs. In our region, Saint Joseph's University's Department of English offers an MA in writing studies, as does Rowan University's Department of Writing Arts. These local variants underscore emerging diversity in MA programs in contrast to the staying power of traditional programs like ours at neighboring Villanova, Arcadia, and West Chester Universities.

Despite modest tinkering, our recently revised exam reflects an "if it's not broken, don't fix it" perspective toward the aims

– 143 –

and methods of our MA. For instance, we did not undertake a more radical change in our capstone requirement, say, moving from an exam (or exam/thesis) requirement to a portfolio option as some institutions have done, either to replace or supplement a comprehensive exam. We are not unique in maintaining traditions in our curriculum and structure. At the same time, we ask, what alternatives *might* we consider? And what is required to realize those options?

In our department and across our campus, we are pondering such questions in light of institutional dynamics that signal a period of accelerated change. The university and the Camden campus have turned to acts of self-definition in the form of strategic plans for undergraduate, graduate, and professional education. Coupled with more public discussions, the close work of limning program-specific learning goals has become more substantive of late with an increased focus on assessment and a major revision of general education requirements for undergraduates. Assessment plans for the MA and MFA were recently revised to incorporate data on student satisfaction to be gathered from exit interviews and follow-up surveys; these data should yield insights into the program's evolving mission.

The most significant change impacting master's education at Rutgers–Camden is arguably a concerted effort to think *beyond the master's* with the introduction of new PhD programs in childhood studies, computational and integrative biology, and public affairs and community development. Other interdisciplinary programs in humanities, social sciences, and STEM fields are in discussion, with a goal to make Rutgers–Camden a doctoral degree–granting institution by Carnegie standards sometime in the next decade. In 2013 the campus awarded its first three PhDs in childhood studies—the first program of its kind in the nation.

This shift toward doctoral education has opened up current and future master's programs to scrutiny. At Rutgers–Camden, a certain ambivalence attends the evolving character of master's level education, which must now contend with PhD programs in advancing the profile of the institution. Given that PhD programs are a means to enhanced status, what role do master's programs play? Might they serve to subsidize expensive doctoral programs? Do departments offering the PhD outrank those offering only a

Crafting a Program That Works (for Us)

master's? Rutgers–Camden has concluded that growth in size and prestige is essential and will be achieved, in part, through new graduate programs, especially those that award the highest degree in a field, but missional tensions between master's and doctoral degree programs remain.

We do not wish to seem pessimistic in observing that a rising tide does not lift all academic boats. Master's programs address different needs, attract different students, and realize different visions of the academy (as a site of cultural capital or engine of economic development) than their doctoral counterparts. Master's programs are more situated in a local environment of campus and community, more responsive to local conditions for their forms of life. A master's program that meets the needs of the wider community by contributing to a more literate workforce or, especially in the case of English, by serving as a training ground for educators is not necessarily a program that functions as an incubator for developing scholars. Occupying the middle tier in an academic hierarchy, master's programs are at once a completion of the intellectual formation of an undergraduate degree and a site of professionalization with respect to a body of knowledge. This "in between" status is sufficient to raise questions about value.

Because a sharp divide can exist between the demands of scholarship and the imperative to prepare graduates for a range of careers, master's programs often seek to split the difference through a curriculum that readies *some* students for advanced study while promising others a plausible career path. Our MA underscores just this flexibility:

> The program is designed for students who seek qualification for admission to a doctoral program in English; for those who desire increased competence in English preparatory or supplementary to teaching in that field on the secondary school or community college level; for those who desire to hone professional writing skills; and for those who wish to pursue a liberal arts education at an advanced level. (Rutgers University–Camden)

Like others, our program aspires to meet multiple objectives in light of multiple motives for graduate study. Such statements as ours assume that these objectives are reconcilable at a curricular level—in other words, that the same program can serve these diverse ends. It assumes, reasonably enough, that students will position themselves variously with respect to the profession of English. Most will conclude that going beyond the master's is not for them, perhaps leveraging their degree to obtain a position in teaching or communications. Others, confirmed in their progress (and undeterred by dire prospects), will pursue further studies in literature or in rhetoric in the hopes of becoming part of the professoriate. Still others, in completing the degree, will have scratched an intellectual itch or achieved a personal milestone. Of course, we observe an implicit hierarchy in our text, one that begins with preparing students for doctoral programs, even though this is the least common outcome. (On average, one master's student a year advances to a doctoral program.)

Notwithstanding a record of success in meeting diverse objectives, the time is ripe to consider paths through the profession of English not taken by our MA program. Such exploration, we underscore, is informed as much by institutional as disciplinary concerns. We recognize a busy crossroads between motives for offering an MA and motives for obtaining one. Indeed, we acknowledge the challenge of hitting that sweet spot where our students' aspirations align with those of our program. The obligation to assess a program's mission and effectiveness is a perennial one, but especially so when contending with forces of change.

We return, then, to a watershed moment in 2009 when our MA program gave birth to our MFA program. As positive as this step was for us, our MFA in creative writing ushered in tensions and exposed fault lines not otherwise evident. Most immediately and tangibly, the English department's long established bank of nine teaching assistantships (in the only master's program on campus to offer assistantships) would now be shared between two programs; the new MFA did not come with additional faculty or TA lines. To no surprise, differences of opinion arose about how to allocate valuable resources. After an initial fifty-fifty split, with a line alternating between programs each year, it was decided that five assistantships would go to the MFA and four to the MA program. This unequal split acknowledged the importance of recruiting for the MFA at a national level. It also reflected a new policy that assistantships go only to terminal degree

Crafting a Program That Works (for Us)

programs. From the first, the goal was to sustain two strong, complementary programs.

Five years on, each program continues to evolve along diverging paths. Currently, our MFA program has about 35 students enrolled, having admitted 17 students in fall 2013. Our MA program also has about 35 students, a number down from a high of 57 students two years before. In spring 2013, we graduated 17 MA and 14 MFA students. Not surprisingly, the MFA draws many more students from out of state: in 2013, 19 versus 7 students. A major contrast between the two programs is that the MFA is intentionally small and selective. The MA, while reasonably selective, would welcome a return to enrollment levels of 50 to 60 students.

In 2012, two additional teaching assistantships were assigned to the MFA (for a total of seven) and one graduate assistantship to either the MA or the MFA program (for a potential total of five), or twelve assistantships in all. The GA position supports a newly established Teaching Matters and Assessment Center, directed by one of this essay's authors (FitzGerald). These new lines recognize a need to maintain recruiting strength for each program. Even so, both programs have had to be resourceful to support and attract students, including, in some cases, offering one-year TA positions with or without a second year of adjunct teaching. As a result, about eighteen students are fully supported for either one or two years. Beyond these measures, some students receive modest stipends or credit-bearing internships to serve as TAs in large literature classes.

Despite an enviable level of support, however, a period of expansion for terminal degree programs and our recent enrollment trends raise questions about our MA in English long term. With only two or three assistantships to distribute each year, we lose some of our strongest applicants to better funded or more prestigious programs, including programs that also offer a PhD. In this we are hardly unique, of course. As a terminal master's program, we are not in a position to compete with doctoral programs. Nonetheless, we strive to meet our objectives in a landscape that has grown sufficiently complex and challenging to make us wonder about doing the MA in English differently. We conclude this chapter by exploring some alternatives and by recognizing constraints to implementing change.

A Future for the MA in English at Rutgers–Camden

Any future MA will reflect the imperative to fulfill the mission of a research university. What remains to be seen is to what extent our program's mission will be informed by our identity as an *urban* research university, in a particular city and region, and to what extent it responds to evolving paradigms in the profession of English as a whole. These are not necessarily opposing forces, of course. One need only observe the academic job market in English to realize that disciplinary developments are in dynamic relation with local conditions. How will those relations play out for us at Rutgers–Camden? At issue, for us, is the extent to which a traditional master's centered on literary studies can respond to shifting currents in professional education (beyond undergraduate studies) with an MA recognized as relevant to stakeholders and potential students in the region or beyond.

In reflecting on this challenge, we have yet to note the significance of a campus culture increasingly marked by a commitment to civic engagement. In 2010, the Office for Civic Engagement was established at Rutgers–Camden with a mission of outreach and collaboration with community partners, particularly in the context of our urban setting. In a short period, this mission has found expression in virtually every school and department, including English. (In 2015, Rutgers–Camden achieved classification for community engagement by the Carnegie Foundation for the Advancement of Teaching.) The Office for Civic Engagement currently sponsors annual cohorts of student scholars, faculty fellows, and graduate students. (Each of us has participated in the program.) How might this focus on civic engagement contribute to master's education in English? What forms might that engagement take?

Without thinking civic engagement to be "the answer" for us, or any institution, we recognize the sea change represented by this development and the attraction that engaged learning holds for institutions and for students. It is especially fitting that an

Crafting a Program That Works (for Us)

urban university like ours realize the dictum to "think globally but act locally" by demonstrating the relevance of our academic programs to the challenges facing the communities where we work and live. In many respects, graduate education is "the next frontier of the service-learning and civic engagement movements" (O'Meara). An MA that works *for* us may also be one that works *with* community partners to advance common goals.

Civic engagement can take the form of efforts to extend the work of our classrooms, studying literature and language, by forging links to area schools and other centers of literacy and culture. A number of our graduate students are already engaged in bringing creative writing to nearby elementary schools. Increasingly, our department is in dialogue with area schools and educators, including current and former MA students, as we realize there is much to learn from one another. This fostering of "town–gown" relations is a win-win for us and for our students. When we further the aspirations of our students to make a difference in their communities by integrating intellectual with civic formation, we bring the interests of our students and those of our institution into alignment.

How are such aspirations realized at a curricular level? At one level, a focus on civic engagement runs counter to conventions of literary studies, at least those manifested at the research university. The times may be a-changin', but long established divides in academic culture between theory and practice or between scholarship and pedagogy remain hurdles to be cleared. One risks appearing too "applied" if focused on preprofessional training. A focus on civic engagement runs similar risks insofar as efforts in *service* learning are conceived as extraneous, or orthogonal, to scholarship in the humanities, which concerns itself with critical inquiry rather than experience or practice. At the same time, a shift toward civic engagement provides opportunities to reconsider the binary of theory and practice, especially in literary studies.

Of course, growth in recent decades of programs or tracks in rhetoric and composition itself marks a shift toward the practical and the engaged. A deepening of our departmental bench in rhetoric, writing, and media studies (our Digital Studies Center was founded in 2014) is an obvious direction for change, one that many other institutions have taken. Such fields are underrepresented in our department given current trends in English studies. However, any expansion of our English curriculum much beyond literary studies is for us a major crossroads. Expansion signals a change of mission and departmental culture, one whose effects are not easily predicted.

Sometimes, of course, impetus for change comes from without. The effort to create the Digital Studies Center at Rutgers-Camden resulted in a new hire in English (in rhetoric) in 2014. Already, this shift in institutional dynamics has led to new conversations about the intersections between literary studies, technology, and pedagogy. In the next year or two, we will likely have an opportunity to hire again. To what extent we use that opportunity to develop in one or more nonliterary fields remains to be seen. It is reasonable to predict that future hires in English will overlap with digital studies initiatives and that such hires will shape a future MA in English.

While we can predict that English will contribute to new interdisciplinary master's or doctoral programs, it less likely that our department will offer a second MA in English any time soon. More likely is further differentiation within our existing MA as a complement to literary studies. Here we can look to developments nationally and within the region. Beyond the aforementioned master's programs in writing studies offered by Rowan and Saint Joseph's Universities, La Salle University, also in Philadelphia, offers an MA in English with distinct tracks in literary and cultural studies and in English for educators, the latter designed for licensed elementary and secondary school teachers. This is a realistic possibility for us as part of a broader mission to support K–16 education in the region. Indeed, such a move could integrate literary, writing, and digital studies under a pedagogical umbrella and perhaps lead to literacy studies as an expression of a commitment to civic engagement. While Rutgers–Camden has no school of education, it serves as a gravitational center for teacher formation in South Jersey. Recently, our Department of Foreign Languages began to offer a master of arts in teaching (Spanish), a curricular move that suggests a possible path for us.

Another possible path is the flip side of the Rutgers motto, "Jersey Roots. Global Reach." The prospect of going global has

Crafting a Program That Works (for Us)

generated much buzz in our department, particularly around the emergence of world literature as a field to which our program might contribute. Rutgers–Camden has long required a course titled World Masterpieces of its undergraduates, a requirement recently broadened into a heritages and civilizations category for general education, to be satisfied through select courses in literature, philosophy, history, and the arts. Under a heading of "World Literature," we imagine, broadly, the production, circulation, reception, and translation of texts in various genres within increasingly global contexts (Damrosch).

This expanded approach to what was formerly identified as comparative literature is attractive to us in its potential for innovative, interdisciplinary curricula at undergraduate and graduate levels, gathering elements of our curriculum (e.g., translation studies, international studies, film studies) into a greater whole. Above all, we recognize the promise and the necessity of educating for *global* citizenship as a vital complement to civic engagement at the local level. Recognizing the complementarity of local and global concerns is conceivably a productive path, but there is no single way to realize this vision. Ours would certainly not be the first program or track in world literature, but one of a growing number of variations on a theme at institutions such as North Carolina State and Case Western in the United States and at Warwick and Oxford Universities in the United Kingdom. Discussing our MA in the context of "the global future of English studies," to cite the title of a recent book (2012) by James F. English, furnishes us with means to imagine and negotiate change. English argues that the future of English studies on a global scale is bright. We believe the future of our MA program is likewise bright if we appropriately localize the value of English studies as a global phenomenon of twenty-first-century education through efforts to integrate literary studies with literacy studies. This sketch of possible avenues for our MA program imagines a range of options as well as their responsiveness to parochial and professional concerns. We can remain circumspect for another year or two, but the opportunity to put a distinctive stamp on our program is a window open only so long.

All the while, the ground is shifting below our feet. Indeed, we've barely begun to address how technology is reshaping higher education and, in particular, what effect distance learning will have on curricula and demographics. We speak of our students, but increasingly we must allow for possibilities of reaching students beyond our immediate region and traditional applicant pool. A fully online master's degree in English, such as those currently offered by Morehead State University in Minnesota or Bowling Green State University in Ohio, is not something we are prepared to offer. However, some combination of online courses in addition to face-to-face instruction—hybrid courses—seems increasingly likely to constitute the new normal for professional education at the master's level. In the past two years, our department has seen an explosion of online courses in both literature and writing at the undergraduate level, going from zero to nearly two dozen. How such trends shuffle the deck of who gets an MA, and from where, remains to be seen. Nonetheless, we can anticipate that the traditional graduate seminar meeting in a brick-and-mortar setting must yield at some level to the virtual. Perhaps such settings will include recent MOOC (massive open online course) formats that attract students from multiple institutions or no institution at all. Perhaps in the not-too-distant future, master's programs will be engaged in vetting coursework taken online, at various places, through a portfolio process that finishes work begun elsewhere.

Online education is but one of many factors contributing to an evolving landscape for the MA in English. The most significant factor, we believe, is shifting expectations for the degree itself. This shift reflects inherent tensions in the degree's character as at once academic *and* professional. At Rutgers–Camden, as in the profession at large, the MA in English is conceived in largely *academic* terms—the middle term in a BA-MA-PhD hierarchy. Most important, the MA is defined by what it is *not* (i.e., a doctoral degree), the entry-level qualification for most academic positions in higher education. However, for the vast majority of students who earn a master's, this degree *is* a professional credential, one that signals mastery of subject matter and, therefore, the qualifications to teach that subject. The MA in English has long been accepted as a qualification to teach college-level courses at two-year and four-year institutions, even if the degree is deemed insufficient for tenure-track positions at four-year institutions.

Crafting a Program That Works (for Us)

Moreover, the MA serves as both a capstone and a credential-izing degree for many secondary school teachers who return to school after years in the field to refresh and refine their skills. In effect, a two-tier system exists in which the MA is accepted as a professional degree *but only up to a point.*

In observing here what is widely known, we think it useful to consider what bearing this situation should have on master's education, considering that relatively few who obtain the MA go on to earn a doctorate. For most, the MA in English *is* a terminal degree—and a mark of their professionalization. This is especially the case in specialized fields such as TESOL, professional and technical writing, and English education, each with specified ca-reer paths connecting formal study and future employment. We therefore ask, what does it mean to conceive of the MA in English in broad terms as a *professional* degree as well as an academic one? What hallmarks of professional education should define the degree? These questions lie at the center of any retooling of our MA in English. Although the answers are not clear, our predominantly literature-based, theory-trained faculty are well equipped to probe the relationship between academic and profes-sional training; to interrogate critically the ways in which these modes of learning are not only complementary but also mutually reinforcing; and to bridge divisions between the two. The chal-lenge before us is one of translation; that is, how to translate the skills, methodologies, and insights related to literary studies to an evolving twenty-first-century society and workplace.

Increasingly, it is clear that rather than conceiving our cur-riculum in terms of content or areas of specialization, we must embrace an activity-based model of professionalization—what we characterize as experiential learning in our undergraduate curriculum. Two of our faculty are involved in major scholarly editorial projects; the decisions and practices required to perform this kind of textual editing can easily involve graduate students, affording them internship-like experience while they earn the MA degree, and can provide a basis for developing courses or even a track in editing and publishing. Here, however, we do not see greater specialization or a proliferation of tracks as the move for us. Instead, we look to incorporate experiences long integral to specialized fields of English studies into a generalist model still

— 153 —

largely centered on literary studies, though one responsive to the needs of the students and the community we serve.

Along this path, we must locate fruitful points of intersection between our master's academic and professional character. Locating such points involves connecting the classroom with the work of English beyond it. We bristle at *preprofessional*, a term that suggests being ever preparatory and reductive in its aims. But we welcome *professional* as a term that signifies a quality of engagement in which MA students assume apprenticeship roles and maintain a focus on practice, applying what they learn in specific contexts. These contexts include involving MA students in editorial and archival projects, in teacher research, and in outreach to area schools and community centers—developments in the past year or two that concretely manifest a turn toward professionalizing our master's program. We also look to deepen our students' training in pedagogy with new courses in the teaching of literature (as a complement to our practicum in composition) and in professional writing (e.g., grant writing).

In an increasing emphasis on professionalism, one that builds on our now annual, daylong professionalization conference, two elements stand out. The first is a new course in revising manuscripts for publication taught by the current director of the MA program. The second is a major literary project that affords multiple opportunities in editing and publishing to MA students. As the general editor of the twenty-nine-volume Complete Works of Edith Wharton (CWEW) published by Oxford University Press, Carol Singley is bringing together a traditional field of literary scholarship—textual editing—with tools of the new digital era. Wharton's texts will be presented in traditional print (hardbound volumes purchased by college and university libraries; hefty, durable, tangible, linear); in the Oxford Scholarly Editions Online (by paid subscription; searchable and easily revised, with reader-friendly navigation of explanatory and textual notes); and through Digital Wharton (a free, interactive, open-access site that maps Wharton's texts and writing processes). Singley has applied for a three-year $300,000 NEH grant to support construction of both the print and Digital Wharton components of CWEW.

Meanwhile, a grant Singley received from the Digital Studies Center at Rutgers–Camden will provide training workshops in

– 154 –

Crafting a Program That Works (for Us)

Scalar and ArcGIS in the fall of 2016. These workshops will be open to the public, with graduate students invited to attend. In the fall of 2017, Singley will introduce and teach a graduate course titled Publishing and Editing Online and in Print that will allow MA students to develop textual and digital editing skills. Work on the Digital Wharton project will also be accomplished through trained undergraduate assistants in our Writing and Design Lab, a new writing center housed in the English department. Finally, MA students can explore an aspect of Wharton's writing and publication through the independent study option.

As we take what for us are still early, tentative steps, we do so mindful of the imperative to develop in concert with our students, graduates and undergraduates alike, to professionalize *ourselves* as a faculty in ways we delineate in this chapter. As we incorporate technology into our classrooms or design new internship programs or build courses around local service learning opportunities or international travel experiences, all things our English faculty increasingly do, we discover ways to link our own development as scholars with the professional development of our students. For our master's program, this means anticipating and articulating—and, of course, providing—pathways through the MA that enable students to see a next chapter in their lives for which further study serves as a springboard, whether that chapter involves teaching language arts at the secondary or community college level or a position in the for-profit or nonprofit sector in which intellectual skills intrinsic to English studies—critical textual analysis, research, and writing—may be applied. And for a few students, that next chapter will involve going beyond the master's into a doctoral program in literature or rhetoric and composition.

In this period of transition at Rutgers–Camden, we remain hopeful that the MA, and in particular *our* MA, is still relevant, that students continue to recognize the value of the intellectual formation and professionalization that the master's in English can provide. But we are not blind to the forces in higher education that demand that the case for relevance be made. We conclude that what matters most is the development of a particular vision of English as a site of professional education, one that invites students to understand themselves as working professionals in training, including in the work of humanistic and engaged scholarship—the intellectual and civic value of which is no less important now than in times past.

Works Cited

ADE Ad Hoc Committee on the Master's Degree. "Rethinking the Master's Degree in English for a New Century." *Modern Language Association*. MLA, June 2011. Web. 2 July 2015.

Damrosch, David. *What is World Literature? (Translation/Transnation)*. Princeton: Princeton UP, 2003. Print.

English, James F. *The Global Future of English Studies*. Hoboken: Wiley-Blackwell, 2012. Print.

O'Meara, Kerry Ann. *Brief 20: Graduate Education and Civic Engagement*. Paper 44. Boston: New England Resource Center for Higher Education, 1 Feb. 2007. Print.

Rutgers University-Camden. "M.A. in English." Rutgers University, 10 Dec. 2014. Web. 2 July 2015.

CHAPTER NINE

"There and Back Again": Programmatic Deliberations and the Creation of an MA Track in Rhetoric and Composition

HILDY MILLER AND DUNCAN CARTER
Portland State University

Last year we began pondering whether the time was right to propose a rhetoric and composition emphasis at the MA level. For us, it was a logical step, following four years of developing and delivering an enhanced rhetoric curriculum, tracking increasing enrollments, and gauging growing student interest. The process so far has proved to be a surprisingly multilayered and complicated rhetorical problem, forcing us to consider a range of issues to do with identity—those of our faculty, our department, our institution, the discipline of rhetoric and composition and of English studies, and our students. In this chapter, we recount our process, structuring the chapter by five guiding questions and the issues that provoked the most thought and debate for us. These questions are a heuristic, if you will:

- How do faculty's particular strengths and interests shape the program?
- How will the new program mesh with disciplinary concerns within rhetoric and composition and English studies?
- How does the program fit with department mission and identity?
- How does the program fit with departmental curricula and institutional goals?

- ◆ How will the program meet students' professional needs in our local context?

We, like many faculty considering a programmatic change, initially thought that the main issue was simply what form the program should take: track or stand-alone MA. In a process that might accurately be described as "there and back again," we found that the journey was seldom straightforward, often filled with detours and occasional setbacks. But we made our way through, and we offer the following advice to anyone considering a programmatic change: plan for a period of sustained critical reflection on these larger, more complex, and varied disciplinary and contextual issues.

How Do Faculty's Particular Strengths and Interests Shape the Program?

MA programs in rhetoric and composition studies have, in recent years, increasingly taken on an identity of their own. No longer just a stepping-stone to a PhD or an add-on to a literature degree, they have become a vital topic of discussion in the field. Their similarities and differences are what create much of this excitement, and, in turn, these differences seem driven by different faculty interests.

Our first step in exploring possible shapes for our rhetoric and composition offerings was to examine other contemporary models. Graduate curricula, as we know, have changed and grown as the field has developed. For sample programs, the website of the Master's Degree Consortium of Writing Studies Specialists proved to be an invaluable resource in helping us to identify a variety of MAs to examine. The rhetoric and composition graduate configurations we modeled most closely included those at Washington State University (which also offers a PhD) and Oregon State University. In them we saw curricula that grew out of the unique scholarly interests of their faculty: Washington State offered emphases in, among other things, digital technology and culture, and paired rhetoric with professional writing;

Oregon State offered emphases in either literature and culture or rhetoric, writing, and culture. Unlike the MAs of a decade ago, which seemed to focus on only a limited number of core courses, these two contained a rich and varied number of courses that fully introduced students to the field. Our curricula already included a variety of such courses—digital rhetoric, theories of style, composition and postmodernism, and more—arising from our varied interests. In fact, we came to see that our faculty were well positioned to deliver such an updated track precisely because all of us had such a broad set of scholarly interests. This we could do.

Nowadays, MA programs are starting to look more like PhD offerings than ever before. What differs is perhaps the scholarly range of the individual faculty who deliver the courses; unlike those in PhD programs, who generally teach only in their specialized areas, in newer MA programs, faculty must be versatile in covering a broad range of specialized areas. In this context, breadth is a strength. In fact, breadth is essential given the often small number of rhetoric and composition faculty, particularly in departments without PhDs.

As with many programs (Carlo and Enos), we started taking stock of several core graduate and undergraduate courses already in place: Contemporary Composition Studies, an overview of the last forty years of research and scholarship; History of Rhetoric, a survey of major historical figures; Research Methods in Rhetoric and Composition, a methods course focusing on both secondary research and primary historical and contemporary qualitative and quantitative research; and, finally, Teaching and Tutoring Writing, a practical applications course.

To this list we added a rotating Topics in Rhetoric course, which offered such topics as composition studies and postmodernism; style; digital rhetoric; gender, sexuality, and rhetoric; and nineteenth-century women's rhetoric. All were "split" courses, jointly taken by both upper-division undergraduates and graduate students. Realizing that we also needed a rhetoric course for juniors, we developed Introduction to Rhetoric and Composition Studies. And, finally, since the majority of our offerings were in history, theory, and scholarship, we opened up some writing courses beyond the standard service ones. These courses, titled

Topics in Composition, covered specialized areas such as writing and healing and writing and the environment and were offered at the lower-division, upper-division, and graduate levels. So far so good. To those offerings we added a discussion group, which met once every two weeks. Students enrolled in it for a credit or just sat in for the intellectual stimulation it provided. Topics were selected by the group and included everything from the rhetoric of quilts to digital rhetoric, along with dry runs for conference presentations and the like. A website detailing all we were doing was added to the departmental site, and we developed pamphlets explaining who we were and what we had available. This preparatory work allowed us to avoid the pitfall of what Margaret Strain calls an "If we build it, they will come" approach to starting a graduate program. We were already well on our way.

How Will the New Program Mesh with Disciplinary Concerns within Rhetoric and Composition and English Studies?

When we began to think about what shape our program should take, we realized that, perhaps unconsciously, we were already oriented in a definite direction. It was clear that our courses were long on theory, history, scholarship, and teaching applications but decidedly short on writing itself. After examining other programs, we saw that some MAs and MA tracks leaned more toward literature and some toward creative, nonfiction, and professional writing. Which way should we lean—and which way was the field leaning?

Strange Bedfellows: Writing or Literature

If we developed a track or area of emphasis, should it be in the existing MA in English or the MA in writing? There were pros and cons either way. To test out the track options, we developed sample tracks in each, largely by examining tracks of other institutions, which varied considerably depending on what the local connection was between "composition" and "writing." Schools such as Rowan University with its MA in writing, including tracks in composition studies, creative writing/journalism, and new media, suggested a clear and comfortable connection between composition proper, creative writing, professional writing, and nonfiction writing. Those programs seemed to de-emphasize the sorts of theory, history, scholarship, and teaching applications that we offered. Composition seemed to fit naturally there, fitting in with and overlapping the actual writing courses. Its purpose was clearly to produce competent writers who could prepare for the array of writing jobs where, by many accounts, 50 percent of English graduates are employed.

Uniting with the other writing areas initially made sense to us as a possible way to proceed. Hildy in particular had long puzzled over the divide between composition and creative writing, how it had occurred and why it persisted. As far back as graduate school in the 1980s, she recalled reading the work of Ann E. Berthoff, who famously declared, "[A]ll writing courses are creative writing courses," an assertion with which Hildy intuitively agreed (69). Of course, there are several accepted narratives of rhetoric and composition's development (Berlin, *Rhetoric and Reality;* Connors; Crowley; Nystrand, Greene, and Wiemelt) and the development of creative writing (Moxley; Myers). These historical studies generally explain how the subfields emerged in the context of English studies, with the implication that the differences among them developed rather fortuitously over time. In contrast, Wendy Bishop focuses specifically on the cultural differences between creative writing and rhetoric and composition; as someone trained in both subfields, she is uniquely positioned to comment on both ("Places"; *Released*). At the crux of her analysis is the idea that creative writing looks for already talented writers, whereas rhetoric and composition works with anyone and everyone and holds that most writers can become at least proficient. Therefore, the two subfields serve two different audiences, as it were. The profound differences between composition and creative writing make collaboration difficult, yet some departments had clearly found a way to mitigate these differences and work together.

But was that programmatic connection with writing possible in our program? At an administrative level, it did not look promising. The creative and nonfiction writers had left the old MA in writing, developed in 1998, which once aligned them with professional writing and, later, the MA in publishing. By 2008 the creative and nonfiction writers struck out on their own. They began an MFA, and with that shift in degrees, their outlook understandably changed considerably. Now they focused on working only with the most talented and promising writers, on sustaining a rigor consistent with the best MFA programs in the country, on enhancing their reputation, and on linking their graduates with both teaching and nonteaching jobs. What was left in the old MA in writing was essentially just professional writing and publishing. If we joined them, what would our track look like and what purpose and student population would it serve?

The sample track we developed attempted to address these questions; it consisted of offerings in the topics in composition course, along with a theory course or two, and courses from other writing areas. We imagined an audience of students who wanted to do what the old MA in writing once did—practice writing of all sorts and get a credential for it. However, we were not sure what our identity would be and what we would really have to add to that program. Wouldn't our students just crowd into the creative and nonfiction writing classes right when those faculty were trying to be more selective? At one time, back during the 1990s, it seemed for a while as though the field of rhetoric and composition might house such newly developing writing areas as nonfiction and travel writing. Though this absorption appeared to have occurred in some individual departments, for the most part, nationally, nonfiction and travel writing migrated elsewhere, aligning themselves with creative writing (Bishop, "Suddenly Sexy"). Composition, then, was restricted to focusing primarily on academic writing, particularly disciplinary writing both within the academy and beyond. Such a focus on academic writing did not seem viable. We could not imagine enough students electing to take the courses to warrant a composition track.

There was, however, definitely an audience of students in English who wished to practice writing but who did not fit the mold of the new MFA. That is, they did not wish to be certified as creative or nonfiction writers. These students appeared in courses such as Writing Process and Response, in which anyone

"There and Back Again"

could work on whatever he or she wished—try their hand at fiction or write chapters of a nonfiction book in a supportive atmosphere with plenty of thoughtful feedback from the instructor and other students. They also turned up in Hildy's American Gothic Literature course, in which nearly all students opted to write their own Gothic fiction rather than traditional academic papers. Duncan reports that some of these students even turned up in his History of Rhetoric course, all ready to take the dialogue assignment and turn it into a screenplay. Though it seemed that none of the subfields of English, at least in our department, was addressing these students' needs, we wondered if we should be the ones to do so. Would that not make us a shadow field of creative writing? After many discussions, we concluded that, given our rhetoric and composition faculty's background and inclinations, we simply did not fit there either.

Leaning toward Literature: A Surprising Fit

Instead, a track within the MA in English that aligned us with literature seemed an obvious—yet somewhat surprising—choice. The rhetoric and composition curricula we had developed over the years emphasized history, research, and scholarship. And, in this respect, we were perhaps unconsciously guided by the direction the field had taken over the last twenty years, with its wholehearted embrace of critical theory and cultural studies. It has become a commonplace to say that, for better or for worse, the field took on a scholarly identity that was very like that of the literature subfield. Had we lost sight of writers and writing? When had they moved to the periphery of our scholarly and teaching lives? We began speculating that perhaps the field itself had lost sight of them somehow all those years ago around the time of the social turn (Salvatori and Donahue). Matters to do with writers and writing were perhaps also associated with what were considered outmoded expressivist and process approaches and, like them, began fading from view. Added to that was the early marginalization of style and grammar, perhaps, historically speaking, a defensive reaction to centuries of equating rhetoric with only style and grammar. This kind of speculation helped us

– 163 –

to understand why, at least in this department with the orientation our rhetoric and composition faculty had—indeed, reflecting that of the field in many ways—we were far more comfortable aligned with our literature colleagues.

How Does the Program Fit with Department Mission and Identity?

What was surprising about our decision to align with literary studies is that our relationship with the literature faculty has never been particularly easy. A number of them understand and support what we are doing. However, some younger faculty, keenly aware of the loss of prestige attached to literature, coupled with the drastic changes in the academy generally, have struck a rather defensive ideological stance. The steady erosion of literature jobs and enrollments, the general decline in respect for the humanities, and the sudden competition from other emerging subfields in English all contributed to their feeling of being both embattled and devalued. Symptomatic of these changes, during this period membership in the Modern Language Association (MLA) shrank while that of the Conference on College Composition and Communication (CCCC) flourished and grew. The literature faculty's position seemed much like the reactionary stance described by Marc Bousquet as a longing for a return to the 1960s—to some real or imagined time when what they most cared about seemed to matter (120). They were not so much opposed to rhetoric and composition; indeed, they were never quite sure what it was. Rather, they wished to make literature front and center in the department, to make it virtually synonymous with English. To that end, some faculty had recently spearheaded a revision of the English MA that obscured our burgeoning rhetoric and composition curriculum. What had been a growing interest and expanding enrollment in rhetoric and composition courses suddenly reversed itself under the revised MA, with enrollments falling off and our publicity efforts squelched. Given the tensions between the two subfields, then, joining with them was going to be challenging. Perhaps it was because we all had a scholarly interest in rhetorical history that we felt an affinity with the values and methods of literary research. Or perhaps it was the training we had all received, emphasizing both literature and rhetoric and composition, that seemed to exert a lasting influence on us. Much as Peter Elbow once observed of himself, our professional identities sometimes oscillated between the two subfields, half identified with each. No wonder we were more comfortable positioning ourselves within the MA in English rather than within the MA in writing.

The sample track we developed in the English MA simply made sense to us. We imagined a track in literature and a track in rhetoric and composition, with students free to select from both for the majority of the 44 required graduate credits. Those opting for rhetoric and composition would take 16 of the credits from our core courses and special topics courses. As a nod to what we realized was a lack of emphasis on actual writing courses, we would allow—even encourage—students to take one or more graduate writing courses. Those in our track would be required to take our methods course; other courses, such as one required critical theory class, would be common to both tracks since both sets of faculty view it as an important common core course. Otherwise, we would encourage students to take additional courses in literature, critical theory, and cultural studies in consultation with their faculty advisors. Those on the rhetoric and composition track could choose a portfolio for their exam option; generally speaking, we had discovered that, at least in our department, literature colleagues were less inclined to understand or fully approve of the portfolio as a method of examination. So in their track it would not be an option. Part of the appeal, then, of the tracks as a way to structure our curriculum is that it allows the two subfields, literature and rhetoric and composition, to disagree amicably—such as on the efficacy of the portfolio—leaving no one forced to engage in a practice that does not fit with their cultural norms and preferences.

Theoretical Grounding for a Rhetoric Track

One needn't look far to find a theoretical basis for the inclusion of a rhetoric track within what was a literature-dominant MA.

Gerald Graff noted that English was a growth industry from the end of World War II up to the late eighties. One consequence was that when a new specialty emerged—Marxism, say, or feminist criticism—departments would respond by adding a person who could "cover" that. As long as departments were adding faculty, they didn't have to stop to rethink what they were doing, how one specialty related to another or how either contributed to the mission of the department as a whole. Departments became fragmented; there was little to no communication between literature and rhetoric, American and British literature, creative writing, composition or professional writing, and so on. With the budget cuts of the 1980s and 1990s, this situation changed. As departments shrank, faculty suddenly found themselves unable to afford the luxury of isolation and fragmentation. They had to think more carefully about how the various pieces fit together, which in turn meant they had to think anew about the nature of English studies and what that meant for the department's mission (Graff).

Integration became the goal. This took various forms. For James Berlin, it involved rhetoric, poetics, and culture (Berlin, *Rhetorics*). For us, Bruce McComiskey's vision of English studies as consisting of equally valuable subfields was of more direct use: it gave us the authorization we needed to put rhetoric and composition forward as co-equal to literature and creative writing. Our department, influenced by Graff's thinking (in spite of the fact, as Christy Friend has pointed out, that he excluded rhetoric and composition from his theory), has generated two long-range plans since 1997, ultimately settling on language, culture, and historicity as the main components of its mission. Not only are these components envisioned as being of equal importance, but they also interact with one another. Therefore, it is reasonable— even desirable—to include literature and rhetoric in a single MA because it serves the goal of integration. Interestingly, it was our current chair who wrote the most recent planning document. So, fortunately, he both understands and supports our proposal; it fits the local context well. However, it remains to be seen how the theoretical underpinnings of the department will jibe with the desire of some faculty to continue having literature as the dominant subfield when we propose our track.

How Does the Program Fit with Departmental Curricula and Institutional Goals?

Effect on Our Undergraduate Curriculum

In a sense, we were going about this backwards, in that we were putting together a graduate track in rhetoric and composition before establishing a coherent undergraduate curriculum (such as a minor or track) to feed into it. In this matter, though, we were closer to being typical than anomalous, because so many rhetoric and composition programs around the country have also developed "backwards." Perhaps it is the complexity and maturity necessary to an MA—or doctoral—program that positions an institution to go on to develop an undergraduate program later, rather than the other way around. In our case, we started with the MA partly because, of the varied students we serve, only a few were coming to us by way of our own undergraduate curriculum. There's a discontinuity here: undergraduates often hear about rhetoric for the first time only when they enroll in the split (undergraduate–graduate) courses—*if* they enroll in those courses. As it stands now, many of our MA students have never heard of rhetoric and have to discover it by accident; most tellingly, that group includes even the new teaching assistants.

To alleviate this problem, it would obviously be desirable to develop our undergraduate curriculum and articulate it with the MA track. We have already made some moves in that direction, moves warranted by increased undergraduate interest. The most important of these was the development of a new course at the junior level, Introduction to Rhetoric and Composition Studies, which regularly enrolls approximately thirty students. Therefore, our program could be termed *vertical* in the sense that it bridges the gap between undergraduate and graduate studies.

This introductory course is at the junior level because that tends to be when our students come to Portland State. As an urban university, we have more juniors than first-years. It is so common, in fact, for students in the split courses to have no background whatsoever in this area that we have resorted to providing overviews of the field before we even begin to introduce the actual content of the course. Duncan routinely begins some courses with Mike Rose's *Lives on the Boundary*; not only is it about composition, but it also conveys what it would be like to have a life in composition. And students can relate directly to some of Rose's early difficulties with school. Hildy jokes that she covers the 2,500-year history of rhetoric in a ten-minute synopsis on the first day of every course. In any case, undergraduates also benefit from our steady expansion of offerings at this level.

Paradoxically, we offer an array of writing courses, although the university as a whole has no writing requirement (some individual departments and other units still require various writing courses). To meet our English department requirements, students have some thirty-six courses to choose from (including creative writing, professional writing, and publishing). So the requirement, which gives us a curricular toehold and degree of visibility, along with the number of rhetoric and writing courses we already offer, means the pieces are in place for us to develop a minor or track. As we move to a more coherent rhetoric and composition curriculum at the undergraduate level, our challenge will be to bring the writing courses into meaningful relation with our rhetoric and composition courses.

Effect on Professional Development and Community Outreach

Our proposed MA track will be supported by a variety of training programs now in place, most of which involve community outreach. As an urban university, Portland State sees community engagement as part of its mission. The sign on a bridge in the center of campus reads, "Let Knowledge Serve the City." It is only natural, then, that our Teaching and Tutoring Writing course involves a practicum component. Students taking this course want to learn something about teaching writing, and this is virtually the only course in which non-teaching assistants can get some teaching experience to put on their résumés. They are wise to do so, as 30 percent of the jobs advertised in the most recent MLA Job Information List are in rhetoric and composition. Many of the students hope to get teaching positions in area community colleges or other institutions, though, of course, others plan to teach at the secondary level. The course meets their expectation

– 168 –

"There and Back Again"

of teaching experience, based as it is on the premise that when it comes to teaching writing, theoretical work simply has to be complemented by direct contact with students who are trying to learn to write.

So we have generated a list of some twenty institutions that host our students for practica, generally either in a writing center or as a teacher's writing assistant. Two of these placements are on the Portland State campus (writing center and athletic department). Eight others involve writing centers at area colleges or community colleges. The remaining ten are in high school settings, some in their writing centers and a number assisting high school teachers teaching college-level courses through our dual credit Challenge Program. Students are expected to devote three hours a week to their practica. These practica are like other community-based courses in many respects; that is, students adopt their roles with something approaching missionary zeal, eager to impart what they know to students hungry for knowledge.

How Will the Program Meet Students' Professional Needs in Our Local Context?

Although faculty interests were critical, throughout our discussions we repeatedly returned to the question of how our ideas and identifications fit with the needs and identifications of the students we serve.[1]

Students Using the MA as a Stepping-Stone to a PhD

Prospective students in the track would, we imagined, look like those we attract to date. Many come from either Portland itself or from elsewhere in the Pacific Northwest. As the second largest city in the region, Portland is often a magnet for young people. Others come from outside the region. However, as often happens with schools in major metropolitan areas, many students elect to remain here after graduation. Either they like the place too much to leave or they have personal reasons for staying on. Of the students who choose to focus on rhetoric and composition, some will simply find themselves more at home in our subfield

– 169 –

than in others, much as most of our faculty did back when we were students; they will want to pursue this interest in more depth, many with the intention of later entering PhD programs. So this group of students will match up with the more traditional function of MA programs—namely, serving as a stepping-stone to a PhD.

Using the MA to Teach in Community Colleges

A second group will primarily be interested in using their MAs to teach locally. Portland is a large, sprawling metropolitan area on the border of Oregon and Washington that hosts several community colleges, numerous small private colleges, and two other universities. Outlying small towns beyond the metro area also have numerous schools. The rhetoric and composition courses the students take will give them—were they later to apply for adjunct work—a credential that qualifies them well for what continues to be a competitive adjunct market. Though we had qualms about preparing one subset of students for adjunct work given the ongoing discussions of the problems of contingent faculty, we came to see a variety of positive outcomes to local adjunct employment (Robertson, Crowley, and Lentricchia; Schell). For many students in our current program, adjunct work is a stepping-stone to their next career move. In fact, we have come to refer to it as spending a "gap year"—or two. Some of our graduates working as adjuncts were eventually promoted internally into permanent tenure-track positions. Others taught only until they had plotted out their next career move: a PhD program, a graduate education degree, an MA in publishing, or other further form of education.

Using the MA for Writing Careers and Alternative Lifestyles

A third group will eventually move on from adjunct work to writing jobs of all sorts, sometimes on a full-time basis, sometimes combining adjunct work with other kinds of employment, with some, of course, bypassing the adjunct gap years and simply moving directly into non-teaching-writing-related jobs. Portland has a large population of people under the age of thirty-five whose community values often include atypical career paths that consist

"There and Back Again"

of, for example, communal housing, food co-ops, growing their own food, bicycling, and living and working in the same neighborhood, with time to pursue their own creative, social justice, or environmental concerns. Part-time teaching plus writing-rhetoric-communication jobs fit their lifestyle needs nicely. Whereas MA programs traditionally tend to see it as their responsibility to prepare students for full-time competitive careers, we recognize that a portion of our clientele really wants to mix and match their way to individually crafted career alternatives.

Full-time nonteaching jobs are also somewhat plentiful in this community where urban myth has it that nearly every resident has a book chapter under his or her arm. Large technical writing companies, a fairly robust corporate and government sector, and multiple schools, all with their variety of jobs, are among the career possibilities. Furthermore, with present-day technical innovations, many writing jobs are available outside the metro area, allowing graduates to live in Portland but work elsewhere, providing them what amounts to access to a global market. In preparing students for nonteaching jobs, we realized that we were resisting the pervasive myth in which all English majors or MAs are preparing for teaching jobs. At the undergraduate level, we offer a special writing course called Writing Careers for English Majors, which introduces students to a wide range of career possibilities and the research skills they need to discover job titles and possibilities they do not even realize exist.

Using the MA for Secondary Teaching

And, finally, a fourth group will use their interest in rhetoric and composition through their MA to help them in careers as high school teachers. Though this direction may at first seem to serve students taking a traditional career path with an English MA, the situation in Oregon is more complicated than this. The metro area has two graduate education programs for teachers, including one at Portland State, with a job market that, like so many today, is up and down with the changing economy. Years ago the state revised its credentialing of teachers to require a master's in education rather than a disciplinary MA. That change might suggest a reduced need for MAs in English, much less those with a rhetoric and composition focus. However, this is where the situation gets complicated. Many teachers go on to teach in neighboring Washington State or elsewhere where the credentialing is different. Yet, here in Oregon, right at a time when English teachers are less likely to have the preparation in rhetoric and composition to teach writing, much less to oversee curricular changes to improve student writing, we find ourselves struggling at the secondary level to improve writing. The latest round of state-level test scores showed only 67 percent of Oregon high school juniors passing the accepted measure of writing abilities (Hammond). So we foresee that a credential in rhetoric and composition such as the one we will offer will become increasingly important for teachers in the competitive local job market.

Already we have seen a decided uptick in secondary schools interested in participating in the Challenge Program, a dual credit program in which students can take a college-level lower-division writing course in high school. The teachers in the program must have an MA in English or comparable experience, with a minimum of two designated rhetoric and composition courses, in order to teach college-level writing. So our graduates are potentially well qualified to compete for these jobs. Currently, we are working with several local schools not only to teach college-level writing courses, but also to develop high school–level courses devoted to writing—not typical English courses in which writing is simply folded in—and to institute WAC programs. These innovations have been long needed to bridge what often seems to be a paradigmatic gap between the way writing is taught in colleges and in secondary schools both in Oregon and perhaps nationally.

Conclusions

In the end, we've learned that creating an MA track is about more than just choosing a practical form. Indeed, it is almost axiomatic that any program must fit its local context: one size doesn't fit all. It is instead about recognizing this choice as a rhetorical problem, as a process in which we must reflect deeply on the many layers of faculty's disciplinary identities: what we can offer

— 172 —

given the collective results of our individual scholarly interests; how our identities mesh with the identity of our department and institutional patterns and plans; where we stand in the ongoing conversations about disciplinary identity both within rhetoric and composition and in English studies. It's about pondering too the identities of our audience, the students whose needs we serve. How can who we are mesh programmatically with who they are? How can we prepare them for the myriad possible careers they choose?

In our own case, whether our planning will succeed, given the complex departmental relationship between composition and literature, remains to be seen. As we mentioned, the various disciplinary identifications of our faculty left us inclined to lean toward literature; simply put, we want rhetoric and composition students to have background in literature, critical theory, and cultural studies—far more than we can provide. We believe that, at least here at Portland State, literary studies and rhetoric and composition can inform and enrich each other, creating a synergy that is productive and beneficial to all. We are pleased with the solution we have settled on and hope that it will meet our students' needs—and our own.

Note

1. For a thorough account of how students might use their graduate degrees to make themselves marketable in a variety of careers, see Moore and Miller.

Works Cited

Berlin, James A. *Rhetoric and Reality: Writing Instruction in American Colleges, 1900–1985.* Carbondale: Southern Illinois UP, 1987. Print.

———. *Rhetorics, Poetics, and Cultures: Refiguring College English Studies.* Urbana: NCTE, 1996. Print.

Berthoff, Ann E. "Learning the Uses of Chaos." *The Making of Meaning: Metaphors, Models, and Maxims for Writing Teachers.* Montclair: Boynton/Cook, 1981. 68–72. Print.

Bishop, Wendy. "Places to Stand: The Reflective Writer-Teacher-Writer in Composition." *College Composition and Communication* 51.1 (1999): 9–31. Print.

———. *Released into Language: Options for Teaching Creative Writing*. Urbana: NCTE, 1990. Print.

———. "Suddenly Sexy: Creative Nonfiction Rear-Ends Composition." *College English* 65.3 (2002): 257–75. Print.

Bousquet, Marc. "The Figure of Writing and the Future of English Studies." *Pedagogy* 10.1 (2010): 117–29. Web. 18 June 2015.

Carlo, Rosanne, and Theresa Jarnagin Enos. "Back-Tracking and Forward Gazing: Marking the Dimensions of Graduate Core Curricula in Rhetoric and Composition." *Rhetoric Review* 30.2 (2011): 208–27. Web. 18 June 2015.

Connors, Robert J. *Composition-Rhetoric: Backgrounds, Theory, and Pedagogy*. Pittsburgh: U of Pittsburgh P, 1997. Print.

Crowley, Sharon. *Composition in the University: Historical and Polemical Essays*. Pittsburgh: U of Pittsburgh P, 1998. Print.

Elbow, Peter. "Opinion: The Cultures of Literature and Composition: What Could Each Learn from the Other?" *College English* 64.5 (2002): 533–46. Print.

Friend, Christy. "The Excluded Conflict: The Marginalization of Composition and Rhetoric Studies in Graff's *Professing Literature*." *College English* 54.3 (1992): 276–86. Print.

Graff, Gerald. *Professing Literature: An Institutional History*. Chicago: U of Chicago P, 1987. Print.

Hammond, Betsy. "Test Scores Show Oregon High Schoolers Lost Ground in Writing, Math and Science." *OregonLive* [*Oregonian*]. Oregon Live, 12 Sept. 2012. Web. 18 June 2015.

McComiskey, Bruce. *English Studies: An Introduction to the Discipline(s)*. Urbana: NCTE, 2006. Print.

Moore, Cindy, and Hildy Miller. *A Guide to Professional Development for Graduate Students in English*. Urbana: NCTE, 2006. Print.

Moxley, Joseph M., ed. *Creative Writing in America: Theory and Pedagogy*. Urbana: NCTE, 1989. Print.

"There and Back Again"

Myers, David Gershom. *The Elephants Teach: Creative Writing Since 1880*. Chicago: U of Chicago P, 2006. Print.

Nystrand, Martin, Stuart Greene, and Jeffrey Wiemelt. "Where Did Composition Studies Come From? An Intellectual History." *Written Communication* 10.3 (1993): 267–333. Web. 18 June 2015.

Robertson, Linda R., Sharon Crowley, and Frank Lentricchia. "Opinion: The Wyoming Conference Resolution Opposing Unfair Salaries and Working Conditions for Post-Secondary Teachers of Writing." *College English* 49.3 (1987): 274–80. Print.

Rose, Mike. *Lives on the Boundary: The Struggles and Achievements of America's Underprepared*. New York: Free, 1989. Print.

Salvatori, Mariolina Rizzi, and Patricia Donahue. "Disappearing Acts: The Problem of the Student in Composition Studies." *Pedagogy* 10.1 (2010): 25–33. Web.

Schell, Eileen E. "Part-Time/Adjunct Issues: Working toward Change." *The Writing Program Administrator's Resource: A Guide to Reflective Institutional Practice*. Ed. Stuart C. Brown and Theresa Enos. Mahwah: Erlbaum, 2002. 181–201. Print.

Strain, Margaret M. Phone Interview. 14 Jan. 2012.

III

CHANGING STUDENT POPULATIONS

CHAPTER TEN

Student Ambitions and Alumni Career Paths: Expectations of the MA English Degree

ANN M. PENROSE
North Carolina State University

Three weeks into my new position as director of graduate programs in English, I receive the annual request from the dean's office for enrollment targets. It's a simple bureaucratic task. Consulting with our MFA and MS directors, I learn that the process is straightforward. The MFA program has funding for twelve teaching assistantships and will only admit students they can support. From the 200-plus applications they receive, the creative writing faculty select the six most promising fiction writers and six finest poets and call it a day. The enrollment planning spreadsheet also generates little angst for the director of our MS in technical communication. This nationally recognized degree is well established in the regional economy, which funnels a small but steady stream of working professionals to the program, often paying their way, and also directs recent college graduates to our door, eager for a professional credential. With little need to provide funding and a clear career path for graduates, the MS faculty admit as many qualified students as they can teach.

But the MA in English? I ask my department head what principles govern the size of the program and the selection of applicants. Ever sensible, he advises me to review the figures from previous years and stay the course. Other DGPs in the college advise me to aim low. (It's good to exceed enrollment targets, bad to fall short.) I average over the past five years, round down, and submit the spreadsheet, buying myself a year to figure out

– 179 –

why we do what we do. What is our admissions philosophy and how does it square with our program goals? And what are those?

We've offered the MA in English in my department for some thirty years. It is one of the few issues we do not fight over. My colleagues and I enjoy teaching graduate courses in our specialties (literature, linguistics, film, rhetoric and composition), and each of these concentrations attracts students who are bright, motivated, and fun to have around. Things are going well. And yet every topic on the English Graduate Committee's monthly agenda leaves this congenial body mired in existential reflection, not unlike the profession at large.

> We discuss admissions: Should we offer our fifteen teaching assistantships to the strongest MA applicants, prepare them well for doctoral study or teaching careers, and turn the rest away? Or should we admit all forty to fifty applicants who are qualified, trusting that the degree they seek will be its own reward? Or should we recruit more widely and "grow" the program, as our dean's office urges?

> We step back: What are our goals for the MA English degree? Are we offering adequate support for students going on for the PhD? (Is it ethical to encourage students in that direction?) Should the MA function as a teaching credential? (Where are those jobs and what are they like? How well do we prepare graduates for those positions?) Where else can the degree lead? Must it lead anywhere?

> We quickly realize that we know little about why students enroll in our programs, about the careers they pursue when they graduate, or about how their degrees support their personal and professional growth.

Converging with this collection's call to assess the state and future of the English MA, our Graduate Committee shifted its focus to information gathering. Our goal was to learn more about the students who seek out this degree at our institution. To this end, we began by conducting two parallel surveys that form the basis of this chapter. The first, administered to our MA students,[1]

Student Ambitions and Alumni Career Paths

was designed to address our questions about why students seek an MA in English and how they expect to benefit from the degree. We asked students directly: Why are you pursuing a master's degree? What career or profession or line of work do you hope to pursue? How does (or doesn't) your master's degree figure into your career aspirations? Analyzing students' replies to these questions has helped us to identify common assumptions about the MA degree's purpose and value and to examine the range of ambitions students bring to such a program.

The second survey, administered to alumni from the previous five years,[2] was intended to help us see how students' expectations played out in real life. We asked respondents to identify the profession or line of work in which they were employed or seeking employment, to indicate whether they had pursued another graduate degree, and to comment on how their master's degrees had intersected with their career paths.

These local data enable us to go beyond our personal impressions and anecdotal reports to gain a grounded understanding of the North Carolina State University English master's student population and these students' personal and professional aspirations. Situated as we are—a mid-sized master's program at a land grant university in a fast-growing metropolitan region—our explorations shed light on a range of motives for pursuing the MA in English. As the national discussion of our disciplinary goals for graduate education continues, these data provide an opportunity to represent students' goals and expectations in this conversation. In this chapter, I describe students' ambitions when embarking on their MA degrees, report on the career paths of recent graduates, and examine how the MA English degree mediates between these expectations and outcomes.

Student Ambitions

While faculty may be ambivalent about whether the MA English degree should lead somewhere, our surveys reveal that students are not ambivalent at all. In describing their motives for pursuing a master's degree, all respondents to the survey of current MA students indicated that they expect their degrees to help them in the job market. Their professional goals fall into three predictable categories, with many respondents listing multiple career options (Table 10.1). As Table 10.1 indicates, 70 percent of respondents are pursuing the MA in order to enter the teaching profession or, less often, to advance in their current teaching positions. (Only five respondents mentioned intending to continue in a current teaching position, three at the secondary level and two postsecondary.) The majority of these responses indicate that students believe the degree will qualify them for teaching positions in community colleges, private high schools, and other educational settings—an assumption shared by master's degree seekers nationally, according to ADE's Ad Hoc Committee on the Master's Degree.

An overlapping 54 percent of respondents seek the master's degree at our institution to prepare themselves for doctoral work. This ambition varied somewhat across programmatic concentrations, appearing with higher frequency in responses from students in linguistics and film studies than from those in literature or rhetoric and composition, though it must be noted that these subgroups are quite small. Some students stated that they're not sure whether they will go on for a PhD, but they see the MA degree as an opportunity to explore this option. Overall, responses indicate that students understand the PhD as necessary if they aim to teach or conduct research at the university level.

Last, roughly one-fourth of respondents are hoping for careers in writing and editing, explicitly mentioning the domains of book

TABLE 10.1. MA Student Career Goals

Responses from 37 enrolled MA students		
Career Path	Number of Respondents	Percent of Respondents*
Teaching, total	26	70%
Enter profession	(21)	
Enhance credential	(5)	
Doctoral preparation/exploration	20	54%
Writing/editing/publishing	9	24%

*Exceeds 100%; respondents could list multiple goals.

publishing, magazine writing, film criticism, nonprofit communications, translating, corporate communications, Web work, and technical communications. These respondents described writing/editing as their primary goal or as one of two or more equally interesting possibilities. Students from all four concentrations identified writing/editing/publishing as a potential career interest, including one-third of respondents from the rhetoric/composition concentration and just under one-quarter of those specializing in literature. One respondent indicated that he or she was already pursuing a writing career before entering the master's program; two stated they had positions in "the professional world" or "the corporate world" but were hoping to advance by developing their professional communication or editing skills. Comments from the majority of respondents indicated that they thought the MA degree would provide an entrée to writing/editing as a profession.

In addition to these professional aspirations, 38 percent of respondents mentioned the inherent value of graduate study when asked to explain why they are pursuing a master's degree. Some emphasized the broader value of critical reading and writing skills; others highlighted their appreciation of literature or a simple love of reading. But it is significant that in addition to these personal or intellectual benefits, all respondents specified one or more career goals toward which they expect the degree to help them advance, as the following examples illustrate:

Why are you pursuing a master's degree?

I want to become a better writer. I also want the credential so that more short-term teaching and writing opportunities will be open to me.

To teach English to illiterate adults/at risk youths, and because I love to read.

I need a higher degree to get a decent job, of course. The other reason is more personal: literature and writing criticism is an essential part of my life. In fact, I wouldn't feel fully human without constantly reading and critiquing what I read.

Judging from their remarks, many MA students are looking for intellectual challenge and the opportunity to engage deeply with literature; but none of our students have the luxury of pursuing graduate education solely for their own knowledge or enrichment.

Alumni Career Paths

Given the prevailing assumption among students that their MA degree will help them obtain meaningful work, the career paths of our alumni represent a logical point of comparison. We were pleased to find that 80 percent of the thirty-nine alumni respondents feel they are on satisfactory career paths: 44 percent report they are employed in the profession in which they hope to spend their careers and another 31 percent are pursuing further education toward that end; two respondents (5 percent) had opted out of the job market to stay home with children. The remaining 20 percent are less content. Seven of these eight respondents report they are employed but not in the field in which they hope to build a career, and one was looking for work at the time of the survey.

As to which career paths they've followed, Table 10.2 summarizes the proportion of alumni currently employed in the three domains targeted by current students. The proportion of respondents currently employed in teaching (38 percent) mirrors a nationwide pattern reported by MLA's Office of Research. In MLA's 2009 survey of program directors, an average of 40 percent of MA English graduates were reported to be employed in teaching positions at the secondary or postsecondary level (ADE Ad Hoc Committee 32). Our data from graduates themselves provide a useful complement to these administrative estimates, which the authors note may be incomplete (6). Most respondents in this category identified their profession simply as "teaching" or "education." Those who specified further listed such positions as college English instructor, adjunct English instructor at a community college, adjunct instructor in English at two community colleges, VISTA volunteer, full-time lecturer in English (3-yr. cap), assistant professor of English, high school English teacher.

Student Ambitions and Alumni Career Paths

TABLE 10.2. MA Alumni Employment

Responses from 39 MA graduates		
Current Occupation	Number of Respondents	Percent of Respondents*
Teaching	15	38%
Further education	14**	36%
Writing/editing/publishing	6	15%
Other	5	13%
Not employed	3	8%

*Exceeds 100%; some graduates are pursuing further education while working.
**Includes one alum who had completed a PhD by the time of the survey.

A comparable proportion of respondents, 36 percent, report that they are pursuing further education. This figure is somewhat lower than in the MLA survey, where program directors indicated that 44 percent of graduates went on for doctoral or professional degrees (ADE Ad Hoc Committee 32). Not surprisingly, the national survey reports different rates of further study among graduates of MA programs in institutions with and without their own PhD programs (55 percent vs. 31 percent). Our own figure perhaps reflects the fact that although we offer a cross-disciplinary PhD in communication, rhetoric and digital media in conjunction with our Department of Communication, that program is not formally aligned with our MA English degree, in which half of students concentrate in literary study. Of the fourteen alumni respondents pursuing advanced degrees, thirteen are enrolled in or have completed PhD programs in English, literature, education, linguistics, American studies, or rhetoric; one respondent is pursuing another master's degree in archival management.

Only 15 percent of respondents specifically identified positions involving writing, editing, or publishing, though some of the jobs classified as "Other" in Table 10.2 may well involve that type of work: public relations, biotechnology, government, library, museum. Both categories are pertinent to the MLA survey finding that 15 percent of MA graduates were employed in business, government, or not-for-profit organizations, a category that includes "such fields as philanthropy, journalism, and publishing" (ADE Ad Hoc Committee 6).

Expectations vs. Outcomes

Comparing current MA students' expressed goals with what former students have done with their degrees allows us to gauge how realistic those initial expectations are. A comparison of Tables 10.1 and 10.2 suggests the outcomes are mixed. While the alumni data show us that MA graduates do find employment in the three areas that MA students hope to enter, the distribution of career paths is other than might be expected. Notably, 70 percent of current MA students aspire to careers in teaching, but only 38 percent of alumni respondents are now employed as teachers—though more will presumably enter the profession when they complete their doctoral degrees. But the position titles listed earlier suggest that the percentage of graduates employed in full-time professional teaching positions is considerably lower. Indeed, two of those employed as teachers note that they are actively looking for more long-term teaching positions. Three additional respondents (two employed as "other" and one unemployed) report that they have been unable to find teaching positions.

In the other domains of interest, 54 percent of current students are considering doctoral work, and 36 percent of recent graduates report they have pursued that path. Twenty-four percent of current MA students hope to find positions as writers or editors, and 15 percent of graduates have found work that they characterize in those terms. Though the data from this local sample correspond neatly with the national trends reported by MLA's ADE Ad Hoc Committee on the Master's Degree, we should interpret these patterns with caution. The survey data cannot tell us whether the disparities between student goals and alumni outcomes reflect changing ambitions, the state of the academic market, the depressed economy in general, or a mismatch between what students want to do, what the MA degree can prepare them to do, and what the job market has on offer. It's also important to recall that 80 percent of alumni respondents seem satisfied with their basic career trajectories. Additionally, when asked in a separate item to assess the value of their master's degree experience, 92 percent of respondents chose the top rating: "quite valuable." The high approval ratings are supported

Student Ambitions and Alumni Career Paths

by responses throughout the surveys, especially the enthusiastic praise respondents offered for individual faculty and courses when asked what they had found most engaging or valuable in their degree program. With few exceptions, alumni seem proud and happy to have earned their MA English degrees, regardless of career direction or employment status.

The specific benefits they perceive vary interestingly across respondents. When asked to describe the role of their master's degree in career development, some respondents emphasized the opportunity for personal and academic growth:

> My experience at NC State—the amazing courses I took by incredible professors and the teaching experience I gained along the way—prepared me not only for a career in teaching but helped me become a more critical thinker. I am extremely happy that I chose to pursue my MA at NCSU and am confident that I am well qualified for positions both within and outside the classroom.

> I wouldn't have continued . . . if I hadn't enjoyed it at NC State. The professors and opportunities I had there were vital to my decision to pursue further education. I have a much better idea of what I want to do with my life thanks to the support of my professors at NCSU and the learning experiences I had there.

> Getting my master's degree was one of the best decisions I have ever made. Going through the program made me a better person. Not only did I learn more about writing and communication, but I also became more independent. Getting my master's really gave me a sense of accomplishment and showed me that I can do anything I set my mind to. The program taught me about meeting deadlines, balancing life and school, how to collaborate with others, etc. My time at NCSU was truly a life-changing experience that I will always remember and be thankful for.

Others highlighted specific types of knowledge and skill they developed:

> As an English teacher I frequently use the information garnered from my time at NC State to supplement my lesson plans. I teach many of the works that I studied while working on my MA and find that I am able to push my students to deeper levels of understanding in our classroom discussions.

My studies toward the MA allowed me to learn how to conduct advanced research in my field. . . .

Developed useful research, writing, and presentation skills that fit in nicely with my other education and current career [in library/museum].

My master's degree was something I pursued in the hopes that I would become more marketable in multiple fields. I wasn't sure if I wanted to pursue a Doctorate and chose not to for now. I am really struggling to find direction but I don't blame my master's. I feel that I learned how to be an excellent writer, editor, and researcher through my master's degree.

A third group focused on the credentialing value of the degree:

I would not be able to teach curriculum English [at a community college] without my Master's degree.

Simple. Without the master's, I would not be teaching at a CC.

My role [in tech media publishing] requires close reading and professional writing skills. I can now compete for jobs that require an MA.

The focus in this third category on credentialing over content—that is, on the degree itself as the outcome rather than the knowledge and skills accrued—could give us pause, for it raises the question of how well students understand the nature of these professions and the expertise they require. We've all encountered students, for example, who believe they need nothing more than an aptitude for writing or a love of literature to teach in either domain. In a useful recent critique, Moore profiles several common misunderstandings of academic life and work, including the student who wants to teach at the college level but has no sense of the labor conditions that prevail in the academic market, the student who wants to teach Shakespeare but doesn't realize how few faculty have the luxury of so specializing, and the student who believes a teaching career will allow plenty of time to pursue her

— 188 —

Student Ambitions and Alumni Career Paths

real interests as a writer (162–63). Each of these naïve assumptions surfaced in our survey data, underscoring Moore's point that students need help understanding the nature and demands of the professional careers they aspire to. But it is clear from comments throughout the surveys that many students do indeed recognize the need for specialized preparation as teachers. Half of the alumni respondents had held teaching assistantships while enrolled, and many in this group cited this teaching experience when asked what they had found most valuable in their degree program. In addition, several respondents who had not been TAs expressed appreciation for the opportunity to learn about writing pedagogy through their coursework. Two alumni recommended offering a course on methods for teaching literature, an indication that at least some students recognize the need for discipline-specific teaching expertise. Comments indicate that those who had had the TA experience consider themselves not just certified but prepared to teach college-level writing.

Similarly, though I still occasionally meet grad students who expect to find work as technical writers even though they've had neither coursework nor practical experience in that domain, many survey respondents clearly understand that such careers also require specialized expertise. Alumni in particular seem to recognize that professional writing careers are not simply theirs for the asking. When asked what would have enhanced their experience in the MA program, alumni responses include the following recommendations:[3]

More professional development opportunities for students planning to work outside of academia

More practical applications of English language skills for the workforce . . .

More work in digital humanities . . . would be useful for a career in or outside the academy

Some sort of required internship that partners with area businesses; need real work experience and networking . . .

More discussion of career development or planning . . .

CHANGING STUDENT POPULATIONS

Among current students, three respondents recommended offering more practical coursework in professional writing. All were students in the rhetoric/composition concentration who had taken elective courses in Web design, digital media theory, professional writing research, or science journalism and were looking for more courses of this sort. In sum, despite the many personal and intellectual benefits derived from their MA coursework, these students and alumni understand that writing for academic courses is not sufficient preparation for writing in the nonacademic settings in which some of them hope to build careers. Indeed, an ample body of research demonstrates that the English major's transition from school to workplace is not a simple matter at all. Case studies of undergraduate interns and recent English graduates have documented their frustration and disorientation as they attempt to apply their well-honed academic writing skills to the unfamiliar purposes and genres of corporate, nonprofit, and governmental workplaces (Beaufort, *College Writing*, "Writing," *Writing*; Anson and Forsberg). Our respondents' requests for more "real-world" experience before they leave the academy suggest that the English graduate student population is coming to appreciate these complexities.

Aspirations for the MA English Degree

As we too come to understand these complexities, we must acknowledge the discontinuities between the paths we followed as faculty and the paths our students are tracing. Only a handful of faculty in my department have taught in secondary schools or community colleges, and even fewer have experience writing in nonacademic settings. Of the three basic career trajectories in our survey data, results indicate that we are very good at mentoring students for doctoral study (the one-third who take the path we took ourselves). We are also good at mentoring aspiring teachers through our assistantship program, but we can offer this experience to only one-third of our students while more than two-thirds have this goal. Our efforts in this area are also limited in scope in that the pedagogical training we offer is focused primarily on first-year college composition, not the broader range of educational

— 190 —

Student Ambitions and Alumni Career Paths

settings our alumni have entered. Last, we've only just begun to offer support to students who want to be writers and editors (through a new internship course), and few of us feel competent to advise students exploring that direction.

Our situation offers a local illustration of the disconnect between goals and curriculum that MLA's ADE Ad Hoc Committee observed across MA programs nationally. In the 2009 survey, at least half of responding institutions rated the preparation of postsecondary teachers, preparation of secondary teachers, and preparation for writing and editing positions as important to their missions, but program materials revealed little emphasis in curriculum to support these goals (9). The committee points out, for example, that the most common requirement in MA programs continues to be a research methods course, while courses in pedagogy and requirements pertinent to technology or globalization tend to be required of only some students or not at all (10). The committee concludes that "many MA programs have curricula that are not well adapted to the realities of the current academic workforce and may not be serving adequately the needs of this generation of graduate students" (13).

These trends, local and national, raise the critical question of how we are to shape curriculum and mentor students for professions we know little about. It seems obvious that we must first redefine our role as faculty and our relationship with graduate students. Others have noted that the conventional master–apprentice model of graduate education makes little sense if we do not expect these student apprentices to ultimately join our profession (Bérubé; Bieber and Worley). Broadening the professional development goals we aim to support means we can no longer view graduate education through this traditional lens. With the majority of MA graduates entering professions in which we faculty do not consider ourselves "masters," we will need to understand and embrace a different mentor identity, a more collaborative relationship in which we and our students aim to learn more about the applied practices and professions that consider our discipline foundational. Cindy Moore argues that a responsible MA program faculty will learn enough about academic and nonacademic work to help students explore options and to support their professional development in multiple directions. Cindy Moore and Hildy Miller's *A Guide to Professional Development for Graduate Students in English* advises students on ways to prepare themselves for productive careers after graduate school, and in so doing models some of the roles we can learn to play as informed faculty mentors. Under this conception, our value as mentors lies in our support for students' individual career explorations and our willingness to learn from their experience.

In the domain of education, for example, even our limited survey data offer rich insight into the teaching professions MA students are entering. While many of our students aspire to teach college composition in programs similar to our ENG 101, others want to teach adult literacy, at-risk youth, or English as a second language. Graduates have found jobs in community colleges, four-year schools, public and private high schools, and community contexts. A few hope to teach abroad. They are working as teachers, teacher trainers, administrators, and academic advisors. Though we pride ourselves on a first-rate TA preparation program, and it has served our students well, this information helps us think beyond our own institutional environment to the broader range of contexts in which good educators are needed and to which we can therefore contribute. Survey respondents have recommended more frequent course offerings in areas such as writing program administration, literacy and community advocacy, and second language learning. Listening to this advice will enhance the currency and depth of our curriculum as we support a broader range of teaching ambitions.

But as we diversify our teacher preparation for a broader set of contexts, we must also acknowledge the nature of those contexts. Along with the rest of the discipline (Bousquet; Harris; Schell and Stock), we worry about directing students into a profession with dwindling numbers of full-time, secure positions (Penrose). The position titles reported by our alumni (e.g., adjunct English instructor, lecturer in English—3-yr. cap) reinforce that concern. We want our graduates to find fulfilling positions in which they are appropriately rewarded for their talents, and we know such positions are increasingly rare. At the same time, we want writing to be taught well wherever it is taught, and we know we can contribute well-prepared teachers to that cause. Our survey data

Student Ambitions and Alumni Career Paths

do not help us resolve this ethical dilemma, but a more deliberate focus on career mentoring in our program, as Moore recommends, can provide a forum for us to share these concerns with students and inform their professional explorations.

For example, we've begun gathering information about hiring practices in local community colleges and sharing it with students in our TA practicum and on our professional development webpage. We hope that students will have more realistic expectations about postsecondary teaching if they know that full-time teaching loads range from 12 to 22 credit hours per semester, that the North Carolina community college system does not award long-term contracts or tenure, and that more than 50 percent of recent hires at the responding schools have been on part-time appointments. We can point as well to local institutions where more professional working conditions are in place and encourage students to notice these variables as they explore the job market. It's also helpful for students hoping for careers in education to know that of the thirty-seven private and community college administrators in our regional sample, 97 percent noted that coursework in composition theory and pedagogy is essential for new hires, 84 percent look for experience teaching in computer-mediated environments, 73 percent value experience with adult learners, and 95 percent look for generalists who can teach in more than one area. Ideally, such information-based mentoring helps students make more purposeful decisions as they prepare themselves to enter this market.

We have even more work to do if we want our program to better support those students pursuing careers other than teaching. Though writing is basically what we do in English departments, most of us know surprisingly little about professional writing and editing occupations and the myriad contexts in which these skills are valued outside the academy. The survey data help us here too, identifying a wide range of fields that current students hope to enter: book publishing, magazine writing, film criticism, nonprofit communications, translating, corporate communications, Web work, and technical communications. Alumni list job titles such as writer, media producer, editor, associate editor, copy editor, and tech media publishing. We need to know more about these positions and the preparation they require. (What do book publishers look for in new employees? Corporate communications departments? Web design firms?)

More important, I would argue, we need to consider not just what kinds of writers these employers want, but what kinds we want them to have. For just as we aim to prepare knowledgeable, reflective teachers who will enhance the quality of education and the well-being of their students, so too we want to place thoughtful, creative thinkers into those public and private contexts where information is developed, corporate missions defined, stockholders informed, policies drafted, consumers educated, projects proposed, images created, and so forth. These contexts need not just good writers but also critical thinkers and thoughtful humanists who will enhance those organizational contexts as well. Fostering the development of these abilities and perspectives is well within the English department's mission.

This rich information from students and alumni inspires us to make the commitment to broaden the range of professional goals we aim to support through our master's program. Whether we do this by reeducating ourselves as mentors, revising individual courses, refocusing the curriculum, adding certificate programs, expanding internship opportunities, redesigning assistantships, consulting with career services, collaborating with local employers, or instituting other initiatives yet to be imagined, we have a clear mandate to help students explore their potential and the professions where that potential might best be realized. Supporting these explorations is a worthy goal for MA English programs to aspire to.

Notes

1. Current students were invited to participate in the eleven-item online survey via postings to the department's graduate program Google groups. The current discussion focuses on the thirty-seven respondents enrolled in the MA English program (41 percent of ninety active MA students in October 2012). Though the response rate was low, the proportional distribution of respondents across our MA concentrations was virtually identical to the distribution of the MA population at large at that time, offering a rough indicator of representativeness. Just under half of students in the MA program are enrolled in literature concentrations.

Because these subgroups are small, results are collapsed across concentrations except where indicated. The surveys and procedural details have been omitted for space but are available from the author on request.

2. The alumni survey included fifteen items and was also administered online. Alumni from all three of our master's programs were contacted via email in January 2013, using addresses obtained from the university's Alumni Office for graduates from 2008–2012. Of 233 addresses that appeared to be active, we received 66 completed surveys, for an overall response rate of 28 percent. The current discussion focuses on the 39 respondents who indicated they had graduated from the MA English program. Representativeness is harder to assess over the five-year period as enrollments have fluctuated, but the sample's distribution across concentrations is roughly comparable to enrollments in the MA program at large during this period. Nevertheless, the low response rate requires us to interpret trends with caution.

3. Responses paraphrased for length.

Works Cited

ADE Ad Hoc Committee on the Master's Degree. "Rethinking the Master's Degree in English for a New Century." *Modern Language Association*. MLA, June 2011. Web. 21 May 2013.

Anson, Chris M., and L. Lee Forsberg. "Moving Beyond the Academic Community: Transitional Stages in Professional Writing." *Written Communication* 7.2 (1990): 200–31. Print.

Beaufort, Anne. *College Writing and Beyond: A New Framework for University Writing Instruction*. Logan: Utah State UP, 2007. Print.

———. "Writing in the Professions." *Handbook of Research on Writing: History, Society, School, Individual, Text*. Ed. Charles Bazerman. New York: Erlbaum, 2008. 221–35. Print.

———. *Writing in the Real World: Making the Transition from School to Work*. Teachers College, 1999. Print.

Bérubé, Michael. "The Humanities, Unraveled." *Chronicle of Higher Education* 18 Feb. 2013. Web. 21 May 2013.

Bieber, Jeffery P., and Linda K. Worley. "Conceptualizing the Academic Life: Graduate Students' Perspectives." *Journal of Higher Education* 77.6 (2006): 1009–35. Print.

Bousquet, Marc. *How the University Works: Higher Education and the Low-Wage Nation*. New York: New York UP, 2008. Print.

Harris, Joseph. "Meet the New Boss, Same as the Old Boss: Class Consciousness in Composition." *College Composition and Communication* 52.1 (2000): 43–68. Print.

Moore, Cindy. "Mentoring for Change." *Rewriting Success in Rhetoric and Composition Careers*. Ed. Amy Goodburn, Donna LeCourt, and Carrie Leverenz. Anderson: Parlor, 2013: 158–74. Print.

Moore, Cindy, and Hildy Miller. *A Guide to Professional Development for Graduate Students in English*. Urbana: NCTE, 2006. Print.

Penrose, Ann M. "Professional Identity in a Contingent-Labor Profession: Expertise, Autonomy, Community in Composition Teaching." *WPA: Writing Program Administration* 35.2 (2012): 108–26. Print.

Schell, Eileen E., and Patricia Lambert Stock, eds. *Moving a Mountain: Transforming the Role of Contingent Faculty in Composition Studies and Higher Education*. Urbana: NCTE, 2001. Print.

CHAPTER ELEVEN

Disciplining the Community: The MA in English and Contextual Fluidity

JAMES P. BEASLEY
University of North Florida

Each year, admissions departments around the country, even in small liberal arts colleges, scramble for applicants and deposited undergraduate students, with recruitment spending often running into the millions of dollars. And in an age of narrowing market demands, many PhD programs can afford to be selective in their choice of applicants. However, recruitment strategies for MA programs have become increasingly more difficult to characterize. Some of this difficulty is linked to the identity of the degree itself. Some students seem to find their way to an MA program rather than programs finding them. I know that was my experience when I started my MA in English. Now, as a faculty member, I see the struggles of MA programs to justify their existence on a daily basis and the consequences of shifting priorities and institutional structures in which the tensions of balancing disciplinary learning and communal needs have been given programmatic focus. Whether through economic necessity or institutional restructuring, the justification for the MA in English has undergone readjustment in the last several years to focus on specific communal needs such as training local teachers or partnering with local businesses for internships and specific professional writing initiatives.

In an effort to explore these particular questions, Peter Vandenberg and Jennifer Clary-Lemon describe the relevancy of the MA in English in their 2010 *CCC*'s article, "Advancing by Degree." Their work has de-emphasized the disciplinary function of the MA in favor of its sustainability through localized community commitments, contending that MA's have "grown increasingly responsive to asserting their relevance on institutional, rather than disciplinary, terms" (268). For Vandenberg and Clary-Lemon, the MA functions in an "intra-disciplinary" context, able to bring structure to a loose conglomeration of courses in literature, literacy, rhetoric and composition, and creative writing. For them it also functions in an "interdisciplinary" context, able to create partnerships with new media, communications, business, journalism, and other professional fields both within the confines of the institution and in the community. I personally had the privilege of teaching at DePaul University in Chicago while Pete Vandenberg and the writing, rhetoric, and discourse (WRD) faculty developed and initiated the MA in writing studies he describes in this article. So when Vandenberg writes on the program in the following quotation, I understand the commitments that he and the WRD faculty have made to the Chicago community:

> The interdisciplinary relationships are unified by a commitment to rhetoric and writing studies among the WRD faculty. At the same time, however, the department is responsive to the immediate needs of a city with a range of teaching opportunities at all levels, as well as corporate and nonprofit demand for highly skilled technical communicators, project managers, and designers. It is also responsive, through a vertical internship program and a structured commitment to experiential learning, to an institutional mission to move the classroom into the city of Chicago and beyond. (276)

Not only have Vandenberg and DePaul's WRD faculty made significant commitments to the Chicago community, but through this responsive, reflexive program, they have also offered its students a model for community-based learning.

While Vandenberg and Clary-Lemon's contentions are productive for their purposes, their definitions of *intra-* and *interdisciplinary structures* could imply that the primary flow of the MA on an intradisciplinary level is its organizing effect on programs, while professionalization happens only on the interdisciplinary level as MA students come into contact with other departments and develop relationships with community business professionals.

— 198 —

Disciplining the Community: The MA in English and Contextual Fluidity

I contend that the opposite can also be true—that is, an MA's intradisciplinary function within the English department can be the most important professionalization a student receives while its "inter-disciplinary" function in the community can best give English programs identity, structure, and mission. To do so, I examine the contextual fluidity of four areas that Vandenburg and Clary-Lemon attribute to the MA in English: "practical and impractical" knowledge, English's response to market forces, English's understanding of intradisciplinarity, and, finally, inter-disciplinarity. What makes this multidirectional interpretation important is its further use of Vandenberg and Clary-Lemon's claims, which further their scope and application.

The Institutionalized MA

Vandenberg and Clary-Lemon argue that MAs in English seek to sustain themselves through localized community commitments, "asserting their relevance on institutional, rather than disciplinary, terms" (268). In this spirit, then, I wish to offer a description of my own institution's MA program and discuss the implications of that localized institutional context, rather than making an argument and offering my institution as an example of that argument.

At the University of North Florida (UNF), the concentration in rhetoric and composition (rhet/comp) comprises half of the MA students in English. The courses in this concentration are designed to work together in a sequence; a theory of composition course and a research methods course are the cornerstones of the concentration. The two required courses in the rhet/comp concentration require students to present their work at a conference in the form of a poster presentation or conference paper. While poster sessions are traditional outlets for research work, the rhetorical theory course also requires a poster presentation on any writing artifact, tracing its theoretical underpinnings throughout rhetorical history. The third component of the rhet/comp concentration requirement is a teaching practicum, wherein students design quizzes and writing workshops and lead discussions.

An introduction to rhetorical theory and history is especially revelatory for students, for the MA serves as a critique not only of

— 199 —

their own high school education, but also of their standard teaching practices. Rhetoric and composition's focus on institutional critique is an important element of students' professionalization into the field of English as they reflect on their current and future educational practices and, for teachers, their own pedagogical aims. This institutional awareness has led to a sense of professionalization among the rhet/comp students, tracking together not only in their coursework but also in professionalizing opportunities such as conference presentations.

Practical and Impractical Knowledge

Where "impractical" knowledge was once considered synonymous with a liberal arts education, the "practical" has now become synonymous with institutional relevancy connected to job placement, and it is within this institutional context that we as an MA program encounter the early assessments of the MA in English. Vandenberg and Clary-Lemon frame early MA programs through the work of Paula R. Feldman and Marcia A. Dalbey, noting that Feldman found the MA a place to "test the waters" (44), but for Dalbey the MA was a "consolation prize" (17) for those not able to be admitted into PhD programs (qtd. in Vandenberg and Clary-Lemon 257). In our experience, testing the waters is one of the very reasons many of our students enter the program. Much like myself at that stage in my academic career, the MA allows students to do the kind of work they might have hoped and expected to do in their BA but could not because of time constraints and graduation requirements. While a greater proportion of MA students still have a major time constraint in that they hold full-time jobs, many are going to school to continue to work. This is especially true for all English MA students, who are for the first time thinking about what they want to get out of a course of study rather than following what a department, college, or school thinks they should get out of a course or plan of study. This shift in motivation is precisely what Vandenberg and Clary-Lemon seem to be referring to when they write,

Disciplining the Community: The MA in English and Contextual Fluidity

> A comprehensive report sponsored by the Association of American Colleges in 1962 found that in liberal arts colleges at least, MA degrees "tend to be utilitarian and technical rather than to place emphasis on the acquisition or advancement of knowledge for its own sake," a reflection of the extent to which the research culture had come to dominate the province of post-baccalaureate education. (261)

There are those, however, who regard the MA in English as a practical degree. In other words, the defining qualities of an MA in English are exactly these pragmatic characteristics—i.e., the number of credits, the number of period requirements, skills transferable to careers outside the academy, etc. This could mean that the MA in English, at least when it focuses on rhetoric and composition, is understood as practical because of its close connection to pedagogy.

With market demands pressing for teachers of English composition at all educational levels, it seems that "utilitarian and technical" writing instructors are now what institutions actually want. But if the MA is precluded from the nonpractical "emphasis or advancement of knowledge for its own sake," then students risk never encountering the kind of thinking required in this liberal pursuit. What is worse, without an emphasis on or advancement of knowledge for its own sake, the only purpose of education is to fulfill prerequisites in order "to succeed in the workforce." While it is important that MA students secure jobs, some students are not pursuing the MA for that reason. In programs that recruit students, provide them funding, and give them choices among many MA options, "value for money" is an increasingly important consideration. Yet in our program, students are not recruited, receive little funding, and have chosen UNF mainly because we have the only graduate degree in English in the greater Jacksonville area. While Vandenberg and Clary-Lemon might see the passing on of disciplinary values as "impractical knowledge," many of our students find much value in being able to expand their circle of influence outside of the Jacksonville, Florida, area through those disciplinary connections.

Response to Market Forces

Since Vandenberg and Clary-Lemon locate the significance of the MA in its response to community needs as opposed to disciplinary conventions, it is necessary to evaluate what those community needs are and the role the MA has in responding to them. Vandenberg and Clary-Lemon are astute in implicating the market forces that drive the discipline and the historical willful ignorance of PhD programs in "minting" scholars without much flexibility outside of disciplinary knowledge, some of whom are unprepared to teach in MA programs that serve the market needs of their local communities. Their corrective, however, replaces one set of needs with another (i.e., the market needs of the community replace the market needs of the discipline). Most important to note, then, is that a redirection of the MA from the discipline to the community does not necessarily negate the influence of the market on the English MA; it merely shifts its focus in another direction by exposing the MA to market forces outside the discipline. Therefore, the position of the MA as communally driven rather than discipline driven is simultaneously productive and problematic, for what happens if the values of the community partners conflict with the values of the discipline or, more specifically for Vandenberg and Clary-Lemon's argument, the institution? What happens in a recession, when community partners are at a premium? Whose interests are given priority—corporate employers, students wanting a professional skill, or faculty wishing to teach to their interests? According to the 2011 report of the ADE Ad Hoc Committee on the Master's Degree, the majority of those entering the profession after graduation enter into teaching positions; fewer find positions in writing and publishing (30). While these findings are used to support more opportunities in writing and publishing, they could also suggest that students themselves highly value disciplinary attachment. In fact, what is often not mentioned in recent proposals to tie institutional funding to graduates' starting salaries is how often English majors care so much about their program of study that they often take lower-paying jobs in the discipline than they could get outside of

Disciplining the Community: The MA in English and Contextual Fluidity

English. That trend is not often accounted for because it escapes the "value-for-money" frenzy in US educational policy.

While much has been written about the corporate university, nothing has been more thoughtful than Bill Readings's 1996 *The University in Ruins*. Readings questions the effects of positioning the student as a consumer and the university as a product. If the student has already bought the product, then there is nothing left for the student to do but critique the "value-for-money" of his or her learning (27). Readings argues that because rhetoric itself has historically aligned with "Thought-as-a-question," rhetoric and the rhetor-teacher are *the* corrective for "Excellence" universities, which tend "to make Thought more and more difficult, less and less necessary" (175). Readings contends that it is the rhetor's concern with Thought that is the foil to the corporate culture of excellence:

> I want to insist that pedagogy is a relation, a network of obligation. In this sense, we might want to talk of the teacher as *rhetor* rather than *magister*, one who speaks in a rhetorical context rather than one whose discourse is self-authorizing. (158)

Readings is of course not suggesting that the field of rhetoric and composition will automatically respond in this way but is instead differentiating between faculty roles. By reimagining one's role from *magister* to *rhetor*, a faculty member will reorient academic and community needs toward student needs. Readings's description is particularly relevant to MA programs in writing studies or ones with rhet/comp specializations such as ours because of the efforts we make to professionalize our students. Faculty and students focused on literary studies often position themselves within the magisterial self-authorizing role of literary critic, whereas courses in rhetoric and composition can contextualize those roles both within the academy and without. With their focus on the seminar paper, literature courses speak with the unquestioned authority of the magister.

While Vandenberg and Clary-Lemon's MA students are not nearly as consumer driven as Readings's undergraduates, they are nonetheless enculturated in a symbiosis of consumption. Instead of merely positioning students as consumers, the entire MA in English could be the product that the community is purchasing, and the pressures of such signification could create an ethical dilemma for departments forced to serve the interests of a market overly reliant on "excellence" and productivity. While Readings concedes the inescapability of market pressures, he believes institutions can utilize their ineffectiveness to be "affective":

> We should be clear about one thing: nothing in the nature of the institution will enshrine Thought or protect it from economic imperatives. . . . But at the same time, if thinking is to remain open to the possibility of Thought, to take itself as a question, it must not seek to be economic. It belongs rather to an economy of waste than to a restricted economy of calculation. (175)

Readings does not necessarily imply that Thought is not a type of production, only that it is a "less restricted" type of production, which reveals why expenditures on admissions to MA programs are significant. Because MA programs can tolerate "wasteful" expenditures, the MA becomes the waste-ful space at the university. As rhetoric, defined by Readings, stimulates Thought, what had been considered wasteful becomes a productive position that complicates magisterial solutions. For example, while our rhet/comp concentration offers no courses in editing or publishing, many of the rhet/comp graduates have entered chief editorial positions with community publications. Part of their success in these positions is due to their understanding of rhetoric as a questioning, critiquing discipline. For the hierarchical and often patronistic political culture of a southern city, disciplinary transmission of these critical rhetorical values is essential to the journalistic community.

What I am contending here is not that serving the needs of the community is wrong, but that liberal arts institutions, like Vandenberg's and Clary-Lemon's, already possess a certain inertia toward Thought-production, whereas this imbalance in large public institutions becomes more pronounced through moves toward increasing productivity. "The question posed to the University," Readings writes, "is thus not how to turn the

Disciplining the Community: The MA in English and Contextual Fluidity

institution into a haven of Thought, but how to think in an institution whose development tends to make Thought more and more difficult, less and less necessary" (175). Any discipline can attune itself to community needs and even serve corporations through skill acquisition, practical training, and the ability to use their expertise. But because of rhetoric's unique position as the questioning discipline, it often runs contrary to the immediacy and efficiency of corporate culture. Literary study, with its focus on the production of critical interpretations, cannot escape an economy of production. Not only should an MA program whose purpose is to serve the needs of the discipline ask if it is making Thought more difficult, but MA programs that seek to serve community needs should also ask this question. In fact, because so many community needs center around productivity, success, and Excellence, a function of rhetoric for community partners could be demonstrated by how much waste it identifies, how much noise it can engender. If the MA is complicit in making Thought less necessary, then, according to Readings, it is not rhetorical, and this is where serving the needs of the community conflicts with emphasizing rhetorical disciplinarity. If the need of a community partner is to produce more efficient, more productive products, then that partner needs an MA program's *magisterial* function to provide authoritative instruction. However, in cooperating with community partners, an MA in rhet/comp can reveal that community partners need more complicated understandings of rhetoric itself. This is how rhetoric-as-thought functions to enculturate surrounding community partners into a broader rhetorical community, rather than enculturating the institution into a more magisterial community. An MA program may lose some of its effectiveness in serving the magisterial needs of the community rather than its rhetorical needs, but this is what makes rhetoric important in the first place. By responding to the demands by community employers for skill sets, for example, MA programs run the risk of acting as magisters rather than as rhetors in the lives of their students, especially for students whose prior educational history has been so wholly unconnected to the "waste" of Thought.

— 205 —

Intradisciplinarity and Centrifugal Force

While intradisciplinarity can certainly exert a centripetal force, imposing unity on divergent aspects of English studies, it also can exert a centrifugal force, moving the discipline outward into the community. It is not surprising, therefore, that issues of how English departments negotiate their relationship to market forces, whether that be toward an economy of calculation or an economy of waste, will consequently become an issue of disciplinarity. Readings writes, "My argument is that the market structure of the post-historical university makes the figure of the student as consumer more and more a reality and that the disciplinary structure is cracking under the pressure of market imperatives" (177). So far, then, Vandenberg and Clary-Lemon are with Readings, inasmuch as the disciplinary structure remains fixed. Their refiguring of the MA in English, however, merely reorients the economy of calculation, rather than reorienting fixed disciplinary structures. Vandenberg and Clary-Lemon observe:

> For those MA programs that do enjoy sustained success, it is often because they fill a distinct need in their region or community, respond to specific job prospects or undergraduate needs, or emerge out of a particular institutional exigence (rather than a discipline-specific one). In a current educational and economic climate that seeks to make degree programs relevant, this responsitivity to diverse constituencies is a clear strength of the writing studies MA. (269)

While Vandenberg and Clary-Lemon demonstrate the relevance of the MA to community needs, a shift in direction can also demonstrate how diverse constituencies can be aligned around the rhetorical values of Thought. An example of this multidirectional centrifugal force that writing studies can exert on a community can be found in our own local M.A in English. While some of the graduates of our rhet/comp concentration become local writing instructors, many have found work as advocates in the community. This seems to demonstrate the influence of the questioning function of rhetoric on a community.

Disciplining the Community: The MA in English and Contextual Fluidity

Rhetoric and composition occupies a central position as the professional and professionalizing aspect of English studies. This position has emerged, in part, from market forces and rhet/comp's response to those forces as partly defining the discipline, which differentiates it from literary studies. In the case of a small state MA program in the Southeast United States, I hope to demonstrate how a concentration in rhetoric and composition specifically functions on the intradisciplinary level as professional development for MA students. I hope to also demonstrate how a concentration in rhetoric and composition within the MA can actually instruct an entire community in the field of English itself. In other words, the MA functions in the community not only because it serves the interest of the community partners themselves, but also because it helps those outside the academy understand the complexity of English studies, its importance in and beyond the university, and the kinds of community projects it is prepared to undertake.

The fact that MA students receive important professionalization by making correlations to their other coursework in literature and literacy might seem counterintuitive at first. When viewed in light of the rhetorical notion "available means of persuasion," new implications for professionalization emerge. Vandenberg and Clary-Lemon write:

> A particularly striking feature of the MA in comparison with the PhD is the capacity of the degree to exert centripetal force, bonding potentially disparate elements of the English curriculum together or to stretch across disciplinary boundaries that the PhD cannot easily tolerate philosophically or structurally. (273)

The effect of this centripetal force is that English programs find cohesion in writing studies while students find their professionalization through centrifugal forces in working with other departments. In our MA program, the rhet/comp concentration exerts centrifugal force, calling attention to the disparate elements of the English curriculum and forcing those elements apart as much as possible.

By exerting centrifugal force within the department, the MA in writing studies draws attention to the disciplinary nature of literary studies. It is writing studies that mandates presenting at conferences, instruction in empirical research methods in English, and a teaching practicum. In many cases, these efforts combine to form the only opportunity for professionalization within the English MA. These efforts take place not in an interdisciplinary level outside the university but on an intradisciplinary level within the department. The MA in English functions not by drawing together other disciplines, but by helping MA students understand how to professionalize themselves. This professionalization takes place within the department, not by producing work for the community but through the production of disciplinary research and intellectual work that demonstrates to the other areas of English studies the significance of writing studies research. In other words, in institutions where writing studies is already seen by literature as moving outside the field of English in their service to the needs of professional colleagues in other departments, providing the same services to communities outside of the university only reinforces that stereotype.

Too often, however, rhetoric and composition programs have positioned themselves as uninterested in what happens outside its walls as a defense against becoming a service field. In liberal arts institutions, service to the community is the only arena in which writing studies functions on a service level. This does not mean, however, that rhet/comp programs in liberal arts institutions are without anxiety about working with other faculty in their departments or outside their departments. Vandenberg and Clary-Lemon observe:

> Of course, the potential for such fragmentation may be perceived as an opportunity—to re-envision dynamic programs, to revise and rethink our relationship to our colleagues, to enact "intradisciplinarity" by unifying subfields of English in the same course or program of study, to provide an integrated approach to [the] curriculum. (273)

While many departments think of literary studies as the "invention" and composition as its "delivery," an emphasis on rhetoric in the English department reconstitutes this ineffective binary. Writing studies programs provide an integrated approach to the curriculum because issues of practical and impractical knowledge,

– 208 –

Disciplining the Community: The MA in English and Contextual Fluidity

positions on market forces in the field of English, and issues of disciplinarity have become permanent questions to consider rather than "arguments" to be made. It is this very distinction, therefore, that demonstrates how rhet/comp serves a professionalizing function in the lives of its students.

Interdisciplinarity and Centripetal Force

As discussed, the MA in English exerts centrifugal force in interdisciplinary ways, and the result of their centrifugal force is professionalization into the discipline. Vandenberg and Clary-Lemon write:

> Firmly situated in the field of writing studies yet not singularly obligated to disciplinary reproduction, WRD's MA programming—and therefore its students—are enriched by a conception of MA-level education that turns on integrated praxis, distributing research in writing studies outward. (276)

If in a liberal arts tradition an MA in writing studies has a professionalizing centrifugal force carrying it outside the university, then it is also possible that it could exert a unifying centripetal effect on those outside the academy. In other words, raising awareness of disciplinary content benefits the community at large in a way that mere product delivery cannot.

James F. Slevin suggests that it is not just working together on a common project with different fields that constitutes interdisciplinarity, but a kind of consciousness about the process itself: "Such work becomes interdisciplinary not simply because diverse methodologies are used but because these methodologies are self-consciously directive of the project itself. Interdisciplinary work makes conscious and motivated what is otherwise only assumed and tacit" (206). His point is reflected in the description Vandenberg and Clary-Lemon provide of student work with community partners not in fields related to English that, when it occurs, achieves interdisciplinarity. If this work is to be interdisciplinary, it will be because rhetors question the methods themselves, inviting speculation on their effectiveness when

– 209 –

CHANGING STUDENT POPULATIONS

MA students serve the needs of their community partners (e.g., employers). Again, I note that in liberal arts institutions where English studies is traditionally associated with impracticality, creating and maintaining a program with this service-minded focus means it can more easily resist such market-driven needs. In institutions where service to a department or a university is the culture, however, service to corporate interests can be evidence of the unthoughtful continuation of the logic of efficiency and calculation. For those departments that have diverse critical approaches to literature, for example, the disciplinary function of rhetoric as a meta-awareness tool would not be as necessary. When students are introduced to and have practice in multiple theoretical approaches, their meta-awareness is already developed. In English departments where one critical approach is dominant, however, students have less practice in considering other ways of thinking about texts.

In the corporate partnership model of the English MA, how tolerant are corporate partners of a notion of "knowledge" as opposed to "production"? And not just knowledge as a product, but the notion of knowledge as "constantly becoming." This seems like a stretch for even the most progressive community partners, such as schools and community colleges. Slevin raises another, deeper issue in the corporate partnership model of the MA:

> Our failures are absolutely essential to our success in the ongoing study of the multiple and changing ways meaning is made by faculty and students through their writing. Working with colleagues in other fields, we are forced to examine our own assumptions about the way language works and to refine our ways of making sense of that process. Such knowledge as this is tentative and partial; it is also collaborative and dependent. It is a knowledge constantly becoming. (208)

Slevin defines interdisciplinarity within Readings's economy of waste, and Vandenberg and Clary-Lemon define interdisciplinarity within the economy of efficiency and calculation. The economy of waste is not tolerated well within the corporate culture, and it is imperative that programs entering into community partnerships consider what interdisciplinary characteristics of rhetoric

– 210 –

Disciplining the Community: The MA in English and Contextual Fluidity

are excluded because of those partnerships. The mapping of these pressures and their effects then become a large part of the MA's intradisciplinary function, demonstrating how service to the community can serve as disciplinary reproduction: when an MA program doesn't focus on what a corporate partner may immediately need and how the program can meet those needs, it opens that community partner to the possibility of Thought. This possibility of Thought, as a characteristic of both rhetoric and interdisciplinarity, questions modes of production. As more employers increasingly demand "critical thinking skills" from their entering workforce, they often do not understand how market forces preclude that kind of thinking. Inasmuch as it is focused on the production of waste, the rhetoric MA exposes employers to this paradox. As Readings observed about institutions "whose development tends to make Thought more and more difficult, less and less necessary" (175), resistance to the immediate demands of a community partner opens a space to make Thought within corporate cultures more possible. In other words, the community itself becomes "disciplined."

Contextual Fluidity

In this chapter, I argue that the key characteristics of the MA in English operate in a contextually fluid relationship with other constituencies. Readings himself underscores the importance of a dynamic interplay when he calls for a certain rhythm of disciplinary attachment and detachment designed so as not to let the question of disciplinarity disappear or sink into routine. Rather, disciplinary structures would be forced to imagine what kinds of thinking they make possible and what kinds of thinking they exclude (176). In other words, the very act of questioning Vandenberg and Clary-Lemon's definitions of intra- and inter-disciplinarity—or mine, or anyone else's—constitutes the nature of rhetorical study itself. If we settle on their definitions, or mine, or anyone else's, they become useful only in how they can be *magistered*; in our constant questioning of them, they have rhetorical significance.

– 211 –

One of the most important characteristics of Vandenberg and Clary-Lemon's claims is their attention to the needs of metropolitan centers such as Chicago:

> These responsive programs reinforce the connection between the master of arts degree and regional populations of students, whether they are rural students meeting in an urban center or suburbanites attracted to a small epicenter of a large metropolis. Programs like these have shown a keen responsiveness to situated student need while demonstrating the value of the MA in writing studies in its own right. Often such programs can attribute their success to their definition of writing, something that is intra-and interdisciplinary. (272–73)

When they use terms such as *rural, urban, suburban,* and *metropolis,* they are making visible specific students and specific spaces, or, as Sharon Zukin writes, "The look and feel of cities reflect decisions about what and who should be visible and what should not" (7). Interdisciplinarity cannot be understood in a vacuum of disciplinary (non)attention, which market forces usually dictate. In fact, market forces take up all the oxygen, so to speak, in the sense that their immediate desire for efficiency does not allow for any other consideration of disciplinarity than efficiency and calculation. What is needed for interdisciplinarity to be enacted is the absence, not of disciplinarity, as Vandenberg and Clary-Lemon suggest, but of calculation, for that is the only presence that would make "disciplinarity as a permanent question" impossible.

The resistance to disciplinary "reproduction" raises questions about the process of concealment itself. For example, Vandenberg and Clary-Lemon note the unique position the MA holds, generally free from the obligations of undergraduate general education studies requirements and the impetus to reproduce the professoriate. In their view, "[T]he MA can function on relatively autonomous ground, enabling community-based pedagogies that exploit intra- and interdisciplinary flexibility to link students to local exigencies and opportunities—ripe opportunities to realize the best of what writing studies has to offer" (278). Even this position, however, is not free of tension. Relations of power and

Disciplining the Community: The MA in English and Contextual Fluidity

discipline are hidden and simultaneously revealed in Vandenberg and Clary-Lemon's figuring of the MA in English. This chapter has attempted to examine the assumptions that Vandenberg and Clary-Lemon make about knowledge, about market forces, and about disciplinarity in their refiguring of the MA in writing studies. It also demonstrates the assumptions made about knowledge, market forces and disciplinarity in regional, public institutions. However, these multi-dimensional and multidirectional assumptions reveal differences between rhetorical disciplinarity based on measured, successful production and disciplinarity based on failed or wasted production.

In understanding this difference, the work of Henri Lefebvre can be helpful. One of the most applicable components of Lefebvre's theories of urban planning is that any plan tells us more about the planner than the population being planned. Lefebvre writes, "In particular, the displacements and distortions between practice and theory (ideology), between partial knowledge and results, come to the fore instead of being hidden. As does the questioning over use and users" (96). In other words, praxis exists not only when students are able to successfully take the education they have learned and reproduce it for practical advantage in the community; praxis also exists and functions multidimensionally and multidirectionally when those students consciously fail to do so, allowing them to reflect on the theory and alter it. Programs should be made aware of how ignoring market forces also ignores underlying politics and ideology, ignores how students are moving toward being consumers of education, how easily students can be made to serve other consumers, and how market forces are both hidden and revealed in their utilization through communal market needs. Programs should be aware of how obscuring structures of disciplinary reproduction also obscures an embedded politics and ideology, and how that ideology exerts centripetal forces in the rhetorical communities they seek to destabilize. Programs should be aware too of these elisions not only in Vandenberg and Clary-Lemon's claims, but also in the claims of all of us who strive to "realize the best of what writing studies has to offer."

– 213 –

Works Cited

ADE Ad Hoc Committee on the Master's Degree. "Rethinking the Master's Degree in English for a New Century." *Modern Language Association*. MLA, June 2011. Web. 22 June 2015.

Dalbey, Marcia A. "What Good Is the MA Degree?" *ADE Bulletin* 112 (1995): 17–20. Print.

Feldman, Paula R. "Response to John T. Day." *ADE Bulletin* 111 (1995): 43–45. Print.

Lefebvre, Henri. *Writings on Cities*. Ed. and trans. Eleonore Kofman and Elizabeth Lebas. Cambridge: Blackwell, 1996. Print.

Readings, Bill. *The University in Ruins*. Cambridge: Harvard UP, 1996. Print.

Slevin, James F. *Introducing English: Essays in the Intellectual Work of Composition*. Pittsburgh: U of Pittsburgh P, 2001. Print.

Vandenberg, Peter, and Jennifer Clary-Lemon. "Advancing by Degree: Placing the MA in Writing Studies." *College Composition and Communication* 62.2 (2010): 257–82. Print.

Zukin, Sharon. *The Culture of Cities*. Cambridge: Blackwell, 1995. Print.

CHAPTER TWELVE

An MA TESOL Program Housed in the English Department: Preparing Teacher-Scholars to Meet the Demands of a Globalizing World

GLORIA PARK AND JOCELYN R. AMEVUVOR
Indiana University of Pennsylvania

With globalization spreading English as the language of international communication in scholarly publications, scientific inquiry, and English language teacher preparation in the United States (Curry and Lillis; Park, "Situating the Discourses"; Uzuner), there is a continual increase in the number of multilinguals matriculating in MA programs specializing in Teaching English to Speakers of Other Languages (TESOL), applied linguistics, teacher education, or linguistics (Braine; Llurda; Park, *Unsilencing the Silenced*, "'I Listened to Korean Society'"). According to our preliminary institutional program website research on the number and types of TESOL programs available in the United States, we found 200 MA-level TESOL programs out of about 400 TESOL-related programs in the United States.[1] Furthermore, out of the 200 MA-level TESOL programs, only 39 are housed in the English department. Other TESOL-related programs are housed in a variety of departments, including English, but also in education, linguistics, foreign languages and literature, etc. However, curricular shifts in TESOL programs generally are often dictated by external factors, such as changes in student demographics and state mandates and policies aimed at teachers who work with English as an additional language learners (EALLs). Demographic changes are further affected by the influx of immigrant and international students in both K–12 and postsecondary educational contexts and by the trend toward globalization, which uses English as its language. The National Education Association confirmed this influx by showing that the number of EALLs has almost doubled in the last fifteen years, making it the fastest growing population in public schools. It is expected that by the year 2025, one in every four public school students will identify as an EALL. The increase in the number of EALLs in public schools is indicative of the need to prepare *all* teachers to work with EALLs. This increase also targets the roles and responsibilities of TESOL programs in the United States that prepare teachers to work in public schools as well as other post-secondary institutions. In addition to the demographic changes in the United States that have led to more EALLs in K–12 contexts, the number of international students gaining admission into US higher education institutions also continues to increase. The United States has become a popular destination for international students to earn degrees in higher education. This focus on US-based higher education institutions may be connected to how the world views the English language and its legitimate speakers and owners (Amevuvor, "Building"; Park, "'I Am Never'"; Phillipson and Skutnabb-Kangas; Widdowson).

Considering the growing number of students for whom English is not the first language, the main goal of the US TESOL professional organization and its academic degree programs, such as the master's level TESOL program (often identified as MA TESOL), is to prepare teachers to work effectively with multilinguals at all levels (K–16). However, depending on where an MA TESOL program is housed, there are institutional and departmental exigencies that affect the overall mission and curricula of MA TESOL programs. As a result, it is important to understand that not all MA TESOL programs are created equal—their heterogeneous disciplinary homes would likely dictate their curricular mission and philosophy. Our focus is on an MA TESOL program housed in an English department located in a four-year teaching university. The rationale for this specific institutional case is multifold: (1) our TESOL program's disciplinary focus in the English department, which provides students with a unique disciplinary experience; (2) the demographic changes occurring in our program in the past two years; and (3) the curricular changes as a result of the demographic shift in our program.

An MA TESOL Program Housed in the English Department

In this chapter, we focus on discussing the changes that have occurred in our program as they relate to our disciplinary foci, faculty expertise, curricular changes, and students' educational outcomes. We turn first to a brief review of the literature discussing MA-level TESOL programs and then to an institutional case study of Western Pennsylvania University's MA TESOL Program, which has gone through substantial curricular revisions to meet the needs of incoming students from around the world.

TESOL Programs in the United States

There is a growing trend to obtain an MA in TESOL from the United States. The programs in the inner circle countries (ICCs)—namely, the English-speaking countries such as the United States, the United Kingdom, Canada, Australia, and New Zealand—are some of the most sought-after by international teacher-candidates. Historically, even within the ICCs, the US and UK have been the powerhouses for preparing teachers of English due to the ways in which American English and British English have been perceived as "Standard English" (Kachru). Because of the sheer number of US postsecondary institutions and increased international focus on sounding like an "American," there has been heightened attention to US TESOL programs. As such, many teachers around the world seek admission into US TESOL programs, while students of all ages come to the United States for study abroad programs (Institute of International Education). As a result of this continual educational migration, there is an urgency to undertake national studies exploring various facets of it. This includes examining curricular areas, such as how the academic needs of K–16 EALLs are being met, but more important, how the teachers of EALLs around the world are being prepared. For this reason, we chose to focus solely on MA TESOL programs within the United States.

Much research has been conducted on the different entities of TESOL programs (e.g., courses, field experiences, teacher candidates' and supervisors' perspectives) and how together they can accommodate all teacher candidates. For instance, researchers have investigated how course sequences can improve the mission of programs (Ramanathan, Davies, and Schleppegrell). Other researchers have called for context-sensitive teacher education programs that connect their programmatic philosophy to teachers' future teaching contexts (Phillipson and Skutnabb-Kangas). Other scholars have examined the impact of a single course on the needs of TESOL students (Carrier; Kamhi-Stein).

Few studies, however, have explored the importance of the practicum in preparing teachers to teach English. Stoynoff called for an integrated practicum model, which incorporated not only the orientation of the practicum students, but also included both general and focused observations, mentored teaching, and portfolio development. Liu expanded Stoynoff's integrated model by offering different practicum sites to meet the need to address diverse teaching backgrounds. Moreover, Flowerdew raised a critical area of bridging theory from TESOL programs to practice implemented in authentic classrooms. Brady and Gulikers discussed the modifications of a practicum course designed and implemented in a university as a response to the experiences of teachers from diverse contexts. Finally, Park examined how student teaching under the mentorship of a non-native-English-speaking (NNES) teacher heightened the teacher's sense of her teaching and NNES teacher identity ("'I Am Never'").

While face-to-face residency programs constitute a majority of the MA TESOL programs in the United States, more and more institutions are working on either hybrid and/or online courses for diverse groups of teachers around the world. In her article "Looking to the Future of TESOL Teacher Education: Web-Based Bulletin Board Discussions in a Methods Course," Kamhi-Stein compared teacher candidates' participation in Web-based electronic discussions to in-class group discussions and discovered that teachers from diverse backgrounds need a variety of techniques to become more engaged in their TESOL programs. Both Nunan and Kouritzin examined the rewards and challenges of teaching MA TESOL courses online. With the continual development in making TESOL programs more appropriate and accessible for teachers all over the world in order to address the needs of their EALLs, there is an urgency to continue this line of inquiry. We respond to this urgency by exploring one institutional case in which the MA-level TESOL program is housed in the English department and how this program has continued to shape itself

An MA TESOL Program Housed in the English Department

in response to changes in the student population and their current and future educational needs. In particular, the program faculty at Western Pennsylvania University (WPU)[2] have completed a curricular revision to meet the needs of international students, specifically the influx of Fulbright Hayes Fellowship in graduate studies recipients needing to complete thesis research as part of their MA-level TESOL program.

WPU is one of the fourteen universities in the Pennsylvania State System of Higher Education (PASSHE). While there are other non-PASSHE institutions (e.g., Temple, Penn State) that award doctoral degrees, WPU offers the most PhD programs of all the schools in the PASSHE. Because of the geographical location of WPU and its identity as one of the PASSHE institutions, many applicants come from towns all over Pennsylvania. Table 12.1 provides a layout of undergraduate and graduate enrollment numbers for WPU as a whole, as well as for the College of Humanities and Social Sciences, from 2008 to 2013. These numbers illustrate WPU's steady growth in enrollment of both undergraduates and graduates in the College of Humanities and Social Sciences, where the English department is housed. Though tuition is competitive in the PASSHE, it is much lower than four of the other state-affiliated, non-PASSHE universities in Pennsylvania (i.e., Penn State University, University of Pittsburgh, Lincoln University, and Temple University).

In addition to the department's recruitment work in increasing

TABLE 12.1. WPU's Enrollment Numbers from 2008–2013

Academic Year	Undergraduate Enrollment	Graduate Enrollment	College of Humanities and Social Sciences Undergraduate Enrollment	College of Humanities and Social Sciences Graduate Enrollment
2008–09	11,928	2,382	1,704	526
2009–2010	12,291	2,347	1,793	552
2010–2011	12,827	2,299	1,865	580
2011–2012	12,943	2,189	1,820	582
2012–2013	13,058	2,321	1626	574

the number of undergraduate English majors and minors as well as English education majors (a joint program with the College of Education), the English department houses the following graduate programs: the MA in TESOL Program, the MA in literature, the MA in composition and literature, the TESOL Graduate Certificate Program, the PhD in composition and TESOL, and the PhD in literature and criticism. Out of the five MA programs housed in the English department, the MA in TESOL Program has had the largest number of international students; more than 80 percent of the program's students are considered international students, with F1 student visa status. Countries represented in our TESOL program during the last five years are Afghanistan, Saudi Arabia, China, Iraq, Japan, Korea, Russia, South Africa, Niger, Ivory Coast, Indonesia, Thailand, Togo, United Arab Emirates, Algeria, Taiwan, and the United States. Our noninternational, US students, due to their experiences teaching and living abroad, are mostly bilingual or multilingual. For instance, Amevuvor, a US student and 2014 graduate of the MA TESOL Program, was active in the Ghanaian community on campus, so she focused her thesis on experiences of Ghanaian international students (*Exploring*). Table 12.2 shows the enrollment numbers of WPU's MA TESOL Program from 2008 to 2014. The data were gathered by Park during her time as program director for the MA in TESOL.

TABLE 12.2. Enrollment Numbers and Thesis-Track Numbers for WPU's MA TESOL Program

Entrance Semester	Approximate Enrollment	Countries	Thesis
Spring 2008	3	USA (1)	0
Fall 2008	12	Korea (1)	1
Fall 2010	13	Algeria (1); Ivory Coast (1); Indonesia (1); Taiwan (1); China (2); Korea (1)	6
Fall 2011[3]	11	Taiwan (2); Niger (1); Iraq (1); Togo (1); Indonesia (1); Japan (1); China (2); USA (1); South Africa (1)	9
Fall 2012	12	S Arabia (4); China (3); Indonesia (1); US (4)	9
Fall 2013	12	Russia (1); Turkey (1); S Arabia (5); Japan (1); US (4)	8
Fall 2014	12	Afghanistan (1); Indonesia (2); China (1); S Arabia (1); US-multilingual (6)	8 as of the end of May 2015

Faculty Expertise

Our English department is the largest department in the entire university. Our department has more than seventy tenured, tenure-track, and temporary faculty as well as teaching associates (TAs). However, temporary faculty and TAs are hired to teach only liberal studies English courses, which are the undergraduate writing courses required by the university. As a result, master's-level and doctoral-level program courses are taught by tenured and tenure-track faculty members who have a certain disciplinary expertise and specialization. In the PhD in composition and TESOL program that houses the MA TESOL, there are thirteen full-time faculty, out of which only six have expertise working with MA-level TESOL program students; four have been here anywhere from five to fifteen years and two are new faculty as of fall 2013. Five faculty have earned terminal degrees from the United States and possess different degrees of linguistic proficiency (Hebrew, Korean, Hindi, Spanish) in addition to English.

In 2008, when Park began her tenure-track position at WPU, MA-level students were admitted throughout the academic year. Thus, most of the students began in the fall semester and some began in the spring semester. As a result of admitting students in both fall and spring, we noticed the need to offer certain required courses more frequently, which raised issues of staffing and having either too many or not enough students in each of the required courses, depending on the semester. In fall 2008, the following courses were required as the core TESOL courses: (1) Introduction to TESOL; (2) TEFL/TESL Methodology; (3) ESL Materials and Media; (4) Second Language Acquisition; (5) American English Grammar.

In addition to the five required core courses, there were two required teacher education courses: (1) Observation of Teaching, and (2) Practicum. Each student also developed a graduating portfolio, which did not earn credit hours and was not assessed. Finally, students completed 15 credits of TESOL and/or education electives. Many elected to take some of the following courses: Second Language Teaching; Second Language Literacy; Special Topics: ESL Assessment; Cross Cultural Communication; Language and Social Contexts; Writing Assessment; and courses in other programs with the approval of the program directors. The PhD program created dual-level courses to serve both PhD and MA TESOL students as a way to add more collaboration and interdisciplinarity to both programs. However, this led to other problems, which we discuss later.

In May 2011, Park began her new role as a program director of TESOL while teaching as its core faculty member. At that time, we were down to four permanent TESOL faculty due to three retirements. In one of the programmatic meetings, the TESOL faculty discussed the need to reexamine our existing curriculum to look for ways to meet the demands of students being admitted and to make our program more competitive in the state. The first issue the faculty discussed was creating a cohort of about fifteen students who would be admitted only in the fall semester. Given the limited number of faculty teaching the MA-level TESOL courses, the cohort model would allow us to streamline courses offered during fall and spring. Depending on the caliber of applications, we have had anywhere from thirteen to fifteen students since the fall 2011 cohort, with only one domestic student in the 2011 cohort, four domestic students in the 2012 cohort, and four domestic students in the 2013 cohort. The ratio of international to domestic students fluctuates from time to time; however, more than 50 to 70 percent of students come from outside of the United States and consider themselves multilinguals.

Another major factor influencing the reconceptualization of our curriculum was our students and their backgrounds. In the past three years, our program has had an increase in the number of students sponsored by the Fulbright Foreign Student Program. Because these Fulbright students are funded by the Fulbright Office in conjunction with their governments, the students are often required to complete a thesis as a culminating research project. These graduate students who opt to conduct thesis research are often funded by their government, their home university, or the Fulbright Foreign Student Program. Therefore, their research often focuses on exploring the educational dilemma emerging from their native contexts. Through their thesis research, graduate students can begin to shed some light on what is occurring in their home countries and share their findings with their colleagues, administrators, and others in their home educational institution as they attempt to internationalize English language education. For example, Amevuvor shared her thesis results about Ghanaian international student experiences with administrators in the Office of International Education (OIE), and a subsequent study on all African students' experiences was initiated by the OIE (*Exploring*).

Finally, with more students opting to conduct thesis research, program faculty discussed the changes that took place from 2011 to 2014 to meet the demands of admitted students who wished to conduct thesis research as their culminating project in earning their MA in English studies with a TESOL specialization degree. We proposed an initial research course for all MA TESOL program students, Introduction to Research in TESOL and Applied Linguistics. The following have been approved as the five core required courses for the MA TESOL program students:

- ◆ Introduction to TESOL (Fall, 1st Year)
- ◆ TESOL Methodology, Materials, and Instructional Technology (Fall, 1st Year)
- ◆ Introduction to Research in TESOL and Applied Linguistics (Fall, 1st Year)
- ◆ Second Language Acquisition
- ◆ Second Language Literacy

We also saw the need to offer courses on teacher education. Although our program is housed in an English department, the program's devotion to theory-to-practice preparation made a practicum course essential in our program. Such a mission came in part from our students, who, in classes and exit interviews, problematized the application of some theories, particularly in their home contexts. Even though many graduate students came into our MA TESOL program with teaching as well as tutoring experience from their own countries, all of them desired to improve their teaching in multicultural contexts like the United States. Thus, it was clear there was a need for students to practice teaching in order for them to experience the challenges of moving from theory to practice. Despite this need, for the past several years there has been a lack of practicum sites for our MA TESOL program students. This was especially problematic since the English department does not offer TA positions to master's students. In assisting our MA TESOL students to observe, team-teach, and reflect on teaching practices, Park designed a year-long practicum context in which the second-year MA TESOL students who are registered for Observation of Teaching (fall) and Practicum (spring) would be assigned to a mentor in one of the university's disciplinary departments. Thus far, our MA TESOL program has worked closely with faculty in the English department as well as the American Language Institute housed in our university. All of the faculty and instructors who participate volunteer to be mentors for MA TESOL students who observe and team-teach in their classes.

Although the required teacher education core components consist of only two courses, a lot of teamwork as well as field-work is involved. As part of culminating projects in both courses, program students and mentor teachers coauthor a reflective paper describing the focus of the observed incidents and including reflections on lessons learned by both mentor and mentee. This paper allows them to think about what teaching is and how mentees should be mentored by veteran mentor teachers. This opportunity also allows for further reflection on professional development for both mentors and mentees.

Another critical component (newly proposed as of fall 2011) focuses on research for thesis-track students. In addition to the introductory research course that all MA TESOL program students need to take during their first semester in the first year, we have decided to have two additional courses (as electives for all and required for thesis students). Advanced Research Seminar allows students to work on a three-chapter research proposal (introduction, literature review, and methodology), which follows the successful completion of the Introduction to Research in Applied Linguistics and TESOL course. During this course, students learn about the importance of the Institutional Review Board (IRB) application, research ethics, writing and reviewing the literature, and methodological design of their proposed research, and they gain access to participants and sites relevant to their research. The final research course is Quantitative and Qualita-

An MA TESOL Program Housed in the English Department

tive Data Analysis, which allows students to complete their data analysis and write Chapters 4 and 5 of their theses.

Graduates of our MA TESOL Program

Since May 2009, upon securing IRB approval of studying the experiences of our MA TESOL Program graduates, we have been conducting exit interviews with interested graduates who want to discuss their educational and professional experiences journeying through our program. Table 12.3 is a snapshot of the participants of our exit interviews. Following is a brief discussion of the selected participants' demographics and their academic experiences in our MA TESOL program.

Six Multilingual Women

To reveal how our program's curriculum has impacted the professional work of our graduate students, we provide six short cases of students' professional development as it pertains to their

TABLE **12.3.** Study Participant Numbers, Thesis-Track Numbers, and Home Countries

Entrance Semester	Participants	Countries	Thesis
Fall 2006–2007	3	Japan (1); Brazil (1); Jordan (1)	0
Spring 2008	1	US (1)	0
Fall 2008	1	Korea (1)	1
Fall 2010	7	Algeria (1); Ivory Coast (1); Indonesia (1); Taiwan (1); China (2); Korea (1);	6
Fall 2011	11	Taiwan (2); Niger (1); Iraq (1); Togo (1); Indonesia (1); Japan (1); China (2); US (1); South Africa (1)	9
Fall 2012	12	Saudi Arabia (4); China (3); Indonesia (1); US (4)	9
Fall 2013	12	Russia (1); Turkey (1); Saudi Arabia (5); Japan (1); US (4)	8
Fall 2014	11	Afghanistan (1); Indonesia (2); China (1); Saudi Arabia (1); US-multilingual (6)	8

researcher and teacher identities. We selected the following six women to illustrate Fulbright student teacher-scholars who completed thesis research and student teacher-scholars who did not opt to do thesis research. In their interviews, Fulbright students focused on discussing their thesis research studies connected to the perceived educational issues in their native countries, whereas the three practicing teachers honed in on theory to practice (dis)-connections as they related to their past and future teaching contexts in their home countries.

Three Multilingual Women Fulbright Student Teacher-Scholars

All three Fulbright graduate students were enrolled in the fall 2010 cohort and were selected by their governments to represent their countries as Fulbright graduate students. All three came with some teaching experience in their home country, but in order to be promoted in their countries, they needed a TESOL degree from the United States. Allison, Malua, and Nia are all multilingual women who excelled in schools growing up in Algeria, Ivory Coast, and Indonesia, respectively. Although they were supported by their family members, as educated women who wanted to continue to pursue higher education outside of their home contexts, they were often relegated to the margins by individuals in academic and social contexts in their native countries. All three believed that pursuing thesis research related to their home contexts and experiences would provide them with a solid foundation in knowledge and legitimize them as experts in specialized areas. Allison is from Algeria, and she chose to research the Algerian administration's control over students' rights. Malua focused on pedagogical strategies for teaching in large classes. Her topic was inspired by her own teaching experiences in the Ivory Coast, where she often had to teach large classes. Nia, from Indonesia, chose to examine hegemonic practices of the Test of English as a Foreign Language (TOEFL). Her research was influenced by the field of democratic assessment as well as her own experiences as a non-native English speaker who had to take the TOEFL in order to study in the United States. Although these women chose their research topics based on their lived experiences and home

An MA TESOL Program Housed in the English Department

contexts, their reasons for deciding to pursue thesis research differed. In Allison's case, she conducted a thesis because it was a requirement for validating her US degree in Algeria. Malua and Nia, on the other hand, both pursued thesis research as a personal and professional endeavor.

Three Multilingual Graduate Students

Mika, from Japan, Priscilla, from Brazil, and Samantha, from Jordan, were from the fall 2006 and 2007 cohorts, so Park was able to conduct interviews with them before they left the program. In their interviews, all three women discussed the challenges of applying theory to practice in their local contexts. Because of their educational cultures' mandates on how to teach English, they came into our MA TESOL program seeking teaching approaches that would liberate the students from rote learning and memorization. For instance, both Mika and Priscilla specifically discussed the need to raise awareness of the theory to practice connection and its challenges in their native countries. Mika stated that while the Japanese Ministry of Education wants all teachers to use the communicative language teaching (CLT) approach in teaching English, the ministry does not understand the disconnect that exists between the underlying philosophy of CLT and the linguistic realities of ELLs in Japan. Furthermore, both Mika and Priscilla discussed the need to focus on learners and context when they are teaching English in their home countries. Specifically, Priscilla discussed a variety of language teaching ideas, especially learning via authentic engagement in communities in which the students and teachers live. She mentioned, for example, how students created their own community newspaper to promote multimodal language use. Because of her gendered experiences in Brazil, Priscilla wanted to raise awareness of gender discourses dominant in the Brazilian context. Similarly, Samantha came to understand the need to "be critical about the world around us." She focused on educating the mind as opposed to memorizing and learning linguistic skills. In particular, she focused on educating women through teaching and mentoring as one way to help them change perspectives about the world around them. In addition to finding relevant pedagogical approaches for teaching English in their native contexts through their MA TESOL program, these teacher-scholars sought specific ways to continue their professionalization in academic literacies.

These narratives do not do justice to the rich layers of experience and knowledge constructed by these six women who graduated from our program. However, all six, given the appropriate tools and environment to develop, were committed to promoting critical consciousness-raising activities that place language and literacy education of all students at the fore by raising awareness of the hegemonic practices that challenge both teachers and learners as they attempt to make education and its implications more authentic, learner centered, and humanistic.

Lessons Learned from Our Students

Preparing teachers from all walks of life to embrace and teach English as an international language (EIL) is a complex endeavor. Our program faculty's mission and philosophy centers on preparing teachers to understand their learners in a global context that continues to privilege the use of EIL. Thus, reexamining our curriculum, sharing our perspectives with our students and colleagues, and disseminating theory and practice emerging from our program are critical components of our work as MA TESOL program teacher-scholar faculty. Although it prepares graduate students to teach EIL and disseminate their thesis research as a form of knowledge within their home contexts, our MA TESOL program with a thesis research option becomes an added responsibility to the existing mission of teacher preparation. This option raises awareness of what an ideal MA TESOL program curriculum should focus on in relation to knowledge domains and core competencies, the heart of preparing teacher-scholars to work in EIL contexts.

Through this short chapter, we share our voices, perspectives, and programmatic changes in an effort to challenge our teacher-scholar endeavors as we continue to admit TESOL students from all over the world and work to meet the demands of our globalized communities. We conclude this chapter with a brief discussion of what we have learned and what we continue to learn from the

An MA TESOL Program Housed in the English Department

students who enter our classrooms, challenging practices that have often emphasized skill-based rote learning as opposed to opening the mind to a variety of perspectives that allow for questions that emerge from lived experience.

One of the ways our students challenge the sociocultural and sociopolitical aspects of EIL is by continuing to call attention to the coexistence of privilege (multilingual graduate students' forms of capital) and marginalization (the positioning of TESOL in a variety of [inter]disciplinary departments). For instance, though our students come with their own sets of privilege, including Fulbright scholarships and the means and experiences required to study abroad, their stories also reveal not only the marginalization associated with the TESOL field, in that it is often housed in a variety of departments, but also the marginalization associated with being a non-native English teacher in a field with a great demand for native teachers.

Given the juxtaposition of privilege and marginalization in our students' experiences, we call for the inclusion of life history narrative writings through the MA TESOL curriculum as a way to raise (self)awareness of multilingual graduate students' multiple identities and realities. Through such writing, students are able to engage their multiple identities, whether they be marginalized or privileged, and come to an understanding of how they impact their teacher identities. Thus, life history writing assignments not only help teachers understand the positionality of their students, but, more important, they also help students unpack these identities in their own professional and personal lives.

Along with including life history narratives in the TESOL program curricula, we need to reexamine existing program curricula in order to address the research demands and abilities of multilingual graduate students planning to do thesis or other empirical research work. In the context of this study, it was the increase of students interested in conducting thesis research, whether for their own purposes or as a scholarship requirement, that spurred the development of the two research-oriented courses in our program. Therefore, MA TESOL programs need to understand students' previous research experiences in order to discover what research skills and US research socialization they may need to develop before conducting research in the United States.

Professional Work of Our Graduate Students

Whether our graduate students choose to take the thesis route or not, our graduate program supports their professional endeavors. Those who choose not to conduct thesis research, like Mika, Priscilla, and Samantha, are supported as they connect theory to the actual practice of teaching. Likewise, those who choose to write a thesis, such as Allison, Malua, and Nia, are encouraged to consider the practical implications of their research. No matter what our students' professional endeavors, our main goal in supporting their professional work is to guide them to expand that work within the program to contexts outside of the program where they can have an impact. Throughout our program's curriculum changes, we attempted to reflect those needs by including research and practical teaching options for students wishing to develop their researcher and teacher identities.

While this is just one institutional case study of an MA TESOL program housed in an English department at a doctoral-granting institution, our experiences with students who come from all over the world may serve as a window into understanding how to work with other institutions with vibrant TESOL programs across disciplinary departments. We believe that the key to maintaining a robust MA TESOL program is to provide opportunities for students to have a voice in their educational journeys. Giving students that voice is a way to improve student learning outcomes and to continue to (re)shape curricular practices that meet the needs of all students who are being trained to work with EALLs around the world. It is worth noting, however, that our program needed to find creative ways to transform while still operating within the constraints of its resources. By understanding the limitations of our program and faculty, we have been able to work within those constraints to meet the needs of students. This is a lesson that any department can take away. Although a program may have the number of applications needed to expand a cohort, it is better to be mindful of the program's capabilities and to allow it to grow with available resources. Despite some lack in resources, our program has found creative ways to accommodate students' needs. For instance, by partnering with the American Language

An MA TESOL Program Housed in the English Department

Institute and the English department as a whole, we have been able to develop practicum options that were previously unavailable. Therefore, we measure the success of our program by its ability to work within its resource constraints and still find creative ways to meet students' needs and (re)shape the curriculum.

Acknowledgment

We thank editors Margaret Strain and Rebecca Potter for their willingness to work with us to share our program experiences. We also thank the reviewers of this manuscript and David Hanauer for his support in our MATESOL program endeavors. Most important, we are thankful to all our students, who have impacted our lives as teacher-scholars.

Notes

1. This approximation comes from a preliminary search of the existing institutional and program websites available as of May 2013.

2. All names and institutions are pseudonyms.

3. Beginning with fall 2011, the program admitted students only into the fall cohort program due to offering more thesis-related research courses and responding to the demands of an increase in the number of thesis-track students.

Works Cited

Amevuvor, Jocelyn. "Building a Cultural Bridge between Ghana and the United States in the Writing Center." *Tutoring Second Language Writers.* Ed. Shanti Bruce and Ben Rafoth. Boulder: UP of Colorado, 2015. 174–79. Print.

————. *Exploring the Continuity of Experiences within Ghanaian International Students' Voiced Narratives.* MA Thesis. Indiana U of Pennsylvania, 2014. Print.

Brady, Brock, and Goedele Gulikers. "Enhancing the MA in TESOL Practicum Course for Nonnative English-Speaking Student Teachers." *Learning and Teaching from Experience: Perspectives on*

Nonnative English-Speaking Professionals. Ed. Lía D. Kamhi-Stein. Ann Arbor: U of Michigan P, 2004. 206–29. Print.

Braine, George, ed. *Non-Native Educators in English Language Teaching*. Mahwah: Erlbaum, 1999. Print.

Carrier, Karen A. "NNS Teacher Trainees in Western-Based TESOL Programs." *ELT Journal* 57.3 (2003): 242–50. Print.

Curry, Mary Jane, and Theresa Lillis. "Multilingual Scholars and the Imperative to Publish in English: Negotiating Interests, Demands, and Rewards." *TESOL Quarterly* 38.4 (2004): 663–88. Print.

Flowerdew, John. "The Practicum in L2 Teacher Education: A Hong Kong Case Study." *TESOL Quarterly* 33.1 (1999): 141–45. Print.

"Fulbright Foreign Student Program." Institute of International Education, n.d. Web. 27 Jan. 2014.

Institute of International Education. "Data Sources 2009." Institute of International Education, 10 Aug. 2010. Web. 28 Jan. 2014.

Kachru, Braj B. "English as an Asian Language." *Links & Letters* 5 (1998): 89–108. Print.

Kamhi-Stein, Lía D. "Looking to the Future of TESOL Teacher Education: Web-Based Bulletin Board Discussions in a Methods Course." *TESOL Quarterly* 34.3 (2000): 423–55. Print.

Kouritzin, Sandra G. "The Personal, Practical, and Professional Rewards of Teaching MA-TESOL Courses Online." *TESOL Quarterly* 36.4 (2002): 621–24. Print.

Liu, Dilin. "Multiple-Site Practicum: Opportunities for Diverse Learning and Teaching." *TESOL Journal* 9.1 (2000): 18–22. Web.

Llurda, Enric, ed. *Non-Native Language Teachers: Perceptions, Challenges, and Contributions to the Profession*. New York: Springer, 2005. Print.

National Education Association. *An NEA Policy Brief: English Language Learners Face Unique Challenges*. Washington: NEA, 2008. Web. 28 Jan. 2014.

Nunan, David. "Teaching MA-TESOL Courses Online: Challenges and Rewards." *TESOL Quarterly* 36.4 (2002): 617–21. Print.

Park, Gloria. "'I Am Never Afraid of Being Recognized as an NNES': One Teacher's Journey in Claiming and Embracing Her Nonnative-Speaker Identity." *TESOL Quarterly* 46.1 (2012): 127–51. Print.

———. "'I Listened to Korean Society. I Always Heard That Women Should Be This Way. . .': The Negotiation and Construction of Gendered Identities in Claiming a Dominant Language and Race in the US." *Journal of Language, Identity, and Education* 8.2 (2009): 174–90. Print.

———. "Situating the Discourses of Privilege and Marginalization in the Lives of Two East Asian Women Teachers of English." *Race Ethnicity and Education* 18.1 (2015): 108–33. Web. 28 June 2016.

———. *Unsilencing the Silenced: The Journeys of Five East Asian Women with Implications for TESOL Teacher Education.* Diss. U of Maryland, 2006. Print.

Phillipson, Robert, and Tove Skutnabb-Kangas. "English Only Worldwide or Language Ecology?" *TESOL Quarterly* 30.3 (1996): 429–52. Print.

Ramanathan, Vai, Catherine Evans Davies, and Mary J. Schleppegrell. "A Naturalistic Inquiry into the Cultures of Two Divergent MA-TESOL Programs: Implications for TESOL." *TESOL Quarterly* 35.2 (2001): 279–305. Print.

Stoynoff, Stephen. "The TESOL Practicum: An Integrated Model in the U.S." *TESOL Quarterly* 33.1 (1999): 145–51. Print.

Uzuner, Sedef. "Multilingual Scholars' Participation in Core/Global Academic Communities: A Literature Review." *Journal of English for Academic Purposes* 7.4 (2008): 250–63. Print.

Widdowson, H. G. "The Ownership of English." *TESOL Quarterly* 28.2 (1994): 377–89. Print.

CHAPTER THIRTEEN

When the MA Is Enough: Considering the Value of Graduate Education

SHARON JAMES MCGEE, REBECCA BURNS, KISHA WELLS,
NANCY THURMAN CLEMENS, AND JEFF HUDSON
Southern Illinois University Edwardsville

Increasingly, for many graduate students, the master's degree is becoming a "terminal" career degree. The Council of Graduate Schools notes that "[m]aster's education is the fastest growing and largest component of the graduate enterprise in the United States."' With the *right* graduate master's degree, graduates can secure or maintain viable employment in a field and have successful careers. One such valued degree is the master's in rhetoric and composition (aka writing studies, composition studies, teaching of writing, and other nomenclature). The MA degree provides access to teaching positions at community colleges, credentials for corporate positions in editing and writing, and advancement for middle and high school teachers. While determining exactly how many of these programs exist is difficult, anecdotal evidence suggests that the number of these programs has increased significantly since the 1980s. In their survey of MA-level rhetoric and composition programs, Brown, Torres, Enos, and Juergensmeyer estimate that 216 stand-alone MA programs existed in 2004, although not all of those programs had a specialization in rhetoric and composition (6).

As more and more students are taking out larger loans to finance their graduate education, considerable attention has focused on the "value" of a graduate degree generally. *The Chronicle of Higher Education, Time* magazine, various newspapers, and the blogosphere share stories of students graduating from prestigious

– 234 –

When the MA Is Enough: Considering the Value of Graduate Education

universities hundreds of thousands of dollars in debt and making student loan payments tantamount to mortgage payments each month. While the value of a graduate education, particularly in the humanities, has always been in question to many in the general public, an intense focus is now being placed on the cost of a graduate education, and so the question takes on new and pressing meaning. Nonetheless, as those of us in the academy know, intrinsic value exists in a graduate education, value that cannot (and perhaps should not) be determined based on fair market price or other quantitative indices. And yet those of us in the academy do have an ethical obligation to consider the cost of debt ratio for graduate students. This chapter explores the value of a master's degree in rhetoric and composition by examining the local program at Southern Illinois University Edwardsville (SIUE), a master's comprehensive university in the metropolitan St. Louis area, where Sharon is a faculty member and where Rebecca, Kisha, Nancy, and Jeff completed their MA degrees. After a program overview, Rebecca, Kisha, Nancy, and Jeff give accounts of how the degree has provided added value to their current lives. We do not intend to suggest that SIUE is the only MA program in rhetoric and composition that has successful graduates, nor do we claim to have a unique approach to our program or course of study. Yet we do believe that SIUE's MA Teaching of Writing Program positions students well for success as MA graduates.

The Teaching of Writing MA Specialization at SIUE

The teaching of writing MA specialization in SIUE's Department of English Language and Literature began in 1986 (Office of Institutional Research 12), making it a long-standing MA program not connected to a PhD program in rhetoric and composition. This distinction is useful, for a stand-alone MA program can have different challenges from those of an MA program that feeds into a doctoral program at the same institution. Typically, the latter programs provide professional development opportunities to future graduates, opportunities that MA students can also participate in. These programs also often have funding to bring

– 235 –

high-profile scholars in the field to campus for research presentations. Students in a stand-alone MA program, on the other hand, may have fewer of these kinds of opportunities, may have fewer peer role models, and, quite frankly, often differ in their professional aspirations from those who attend an MA-to-PhD program.

The original degree at SIUE, although named "Teaching of Writing," had, like probably many other programs at the time, as many requirements in literature as in composition pedagogy. Emeritus Professor Isaiah Smithson, who was instrumental in designing the original program and shepherding it through the approval process, recalls that most of the faculty in the department at the time had their degrees in literature and wanted to teach only literature. A specialization in teaching of writing would, they feared, draw students away from the literature specialization, threatening enrollments in upper-division and graduate-level literature courses. So the new program had a fair number of required literature courses for political, not pedagogical, reasons. We suspect that departmental politics played a role in the creation of many early rhetoric and composition programs, which involved negotiations and peace offerings designed to allay the fears of literature faculty.

From 1986 to the late 1990s, the teaching of writing specialization proved that it could recruit and retain strong students without eating into the graduate specialization in literature. Simultaneously, faculty in the department came to realize that other MA and PhD programs were incorporating rhetorical studies into their curricula as well. And, of course, the general attitude toward rhetoric and writing studies by younger faculty, many of whom had received training in composition teaching in their graduate programs, viewed composition and rhetoric as both a legitimate intellectual enterprise and a valuable contributor to the life of the department. By 2000 the program had been revised significantly, a revision that led to Sharon's hire as a specialist in empirical research methods and writing in the disciplines. Since 2001 the specialization has been tweaked several times although none of those revisions has altered the basic structure of the program.

While certainly not unique, the MA specialization requires students to take courses in composition pedagogy, empirical research methods, rhetorical theory, and history of rhetoric and

When the MA Is Enough: Considering the Value of Graduate Education

to complete a practicum in the teaching of writing as well as exit work (typically three long papers). Students also select three secondary courses. As our program's title suggests, we emphasize composition pedagogy, but the program grounds students in what the faculty feel are the essential components of a well-rounded graduate training in rhetoric and composition: pedagogy, theory, research methods, and history. Further, faculty members in the program stress professional development to students. Because of the students' makeup (about half are working middle or high school teachers) and because of our faculty's general interest in literacy studies, literacy—for secondary, basic writing, and university students—permeates many courses, either explicitly or implicitly. We mentor students in preparing conference proposals and developing the kinds of professional documents they will need to obtain and maintain a position (e.g., CVs, statements of teaching, and teaching portfolios).

Students in our MA specialization can be classified into three general categories: (1) working middle or high school teachers who seek master's-level credentialing to retain state licensure and who are drawn to know more about writing pedagogy and theory, (2) students who want to seek employment at one of the many local community colleges in the area (and beyond) and realize that an MA in literature will not open as many doors for them, and (3) students who wish eventually to pursue a PhD in rhetoric or writing studies. Many, if not all, of our students reside within a 100-mile radius of campus; they choose our program because of its reputation, its proximity, and the relatively low cost of graduate tuition. Some of our students attend the program full-time and graduate in two years, but many others attend part-time, taking one or two classes a semester while working full-time. Most students who enroll in our program have not had an undergraduate rhetoric and composition emphasis, and some, it is safe to say, are not exactly sure what the discipline of rhetoric and composition is when they begin. We have an excellent placement rate for graduates who seek either part-time or full-time community college employment. However, we make no claim to placing all of our graduates in the position of their dreams (which is most often a tenure-track job at a regional community college) or in a position at all. Other graduates teach in local high school English departments. The few who wish to pursue a PhD get accepted into one of their choice schools.

The program has a strong reputation in southern Illinois and the metropolitan St. Louis area; in fact, some community colleges recommend our program to their current faculty who do not have a degree in rhetoric and composition or others interested in a position there. Since most of our graduate students originate from the area, many wish to remain local upon graduation. With at least four community colleges (some with multiple sites) within a fifty-mile radius of SIUE, employment opportunities have been available nearby. Admittedly, while the faculty are poor record keepers of official numbers, we do a good job of staying in contact with our graduates. Both graduates who remain local and those who move away have fared well in the job market, demonstrating that external audiences recognize the quality of our program and our graduates.

In brief, our MA program offers graduates the opportunity to enter into or remain in the life of the academy, whether that be as middle or high school educators, community college professionals, or PhD graduate students. A few graduates take another route, choosing corporate or industry options. Aside from those few who enter doctoral programs, the MA alone opens an important door for career advancement. As our graduates attest in the following sections, the MA degree can be enough for a satisfying professional life.

The Graduates Speak

But do graduates feel that their degrees have added value to their professional lives and opened doors for them? When Sharon originally proposed this chapter, she had envisioned interviewing graduates to discover their thoughts on the program, but it became clear that the graduates should themselves become coauthors on this project. Although four graduates were asked to collaborate on this project, many others could have been invited. Those chosen represent an array of experiences. Rebecca returned for an undergraduate degree in English after having worked in social services for several years. She then chose the MA specialization in

When the MA Is Enough: Considering the Value of Graduate Education

composition and rhetoric at SIUE because it was geographically convenient and because she knew that it would position her well in the local job market. Rebecca held a teaching assistant position within the department, completed the MA degree in two years, and began a position as an assistant professor at a local community college in the first fall following graduation. Kisha, on the other hand, took a slower path to degree completion, as she describes in her narrative. Kisha worked full-time as a preschool teacher and pursued her coursework as a part-time student. Her interest in African American rhetoric and developmental writers influenced her selection of elective courses as well her choice of exit paper topics. While Kisha's search for a community college position took longer than Rebecca's, it ended successfully. As an officer in the United States Air Force, Nancy was offered the opportunity to attend a master's program in English so that she could teach at the Air Force Academy. Given a definitive timeline for completion, Nancy graduated in two years, and one of her exit papers won the department's Edwin Graham Memorial Award for best paper. Although she did not begin her teaching assignment immediately, she found that the value of her degree was being utilized even when she was not in the classroom. Jeff took courses part-time because he taught high school. Having attended a National Writing Project Summer Institute before beginning his MA work, Jeff came to the program knowing that he wanted to learn more about writing pedagogy and how to improve writing instruction for his students. In the next sections, Rebecca, Kisha, Nancy, and Jeff tell stories of their professional growth.

Rebecca's Story: *When the MA Is Enough*

I more fully recognized the value of my MA degree in nearly the same way that I gained new respect for my parents after leaving home. While my parents taught me countless life lessons, everything from the importance of helping others and standing up for my beliefs to tying my shoes and managing money, all of which prepared me to live on my own, the SIUE Teaching of Writing MA program equipped me with the experience and the theoretical and pedagogical tools necessary to succeed in the academy on my own.

– 239 –

Entering the academy in a full-time capacity is not easy, but SIUE's Teaching of Writing program facilitates that process for students like me. I received instruction not only in my coursework but also, through hands-on application, during my teaching practicum, an opportunity that allowed me to co-teach with and learn from an experienced professor. I received more targeted instruction, as well, such as how to incorporate visual and digital rhetoric into the classroom; how to teach technical writing; and how to compile a teaching portfolio and write a curriculum vita, a statement of teaching philosophy, and an application letter. But I still had to demonstrate myself a qualified and worthy colleague, and the Teaching of Writing curriculum and professors prepared me for that. In addition to sharing valuable interview advice, professors also encouraged me to join committees, attend conferences, and present papers. This complete academic immersion provided me with the substance, experience, and confidence I needed to demonstrate my strength as a teacher and establish a dialogue with potential colleagues during interviews.

After seven interviews and two full-time offers, I settled into a full-time faculty position at a local community college, and then, more than ever, the value of my MA degree became obvious. Suddenly, nearly everything we read and discussed in my composition theory and pedagogy classes felt relevant and crucial. What I learned began guiding and shaping my pedagogical decisions and practices. I started emphasizing writing as a process and finding ways to give writing value *beyond* the grade. Since my graduate coursework exposed me to theorists such as Andrea Lunsford, Lisa Ede, and Linda Bergmann, I knew helping students recognize the value in writing would make their writing better. To convince them that they would, in fact, write for real people beyond college (not for their professors), I found writing opportunities for my students within the community. One semester, for instance, my second semester composition students and I worked with the City of Kirkwood, Missouri, Landmarks Commission to design brochures to help Kirkwood homeowners identify Sears houses. Upon completion of the project, the mayor and commissioners presented my students and me with a certificate of appreciation at the city's annual awards ceremony, and we were featured in local

When the MA Is Enough: Considering the Value of Graduate Education

newspapers. Engaging my students in a real-life writing experience helped them take personal and active responsibility for learning because they recognized that they were not just completing an assignment: they were completing work that their community may read and use every day. Fortunately for my students, I could contextualize terms from my coursework such as the *rhetorical triangle,* enabling them to grasp abstract concepts applicable to the work they were doing, as in the brochure project. The experience of writing for a real audience to fulfill a real purpose can forever change the way students think about writing.

SIUE's MA program and professors prepared me for working outside of the classroom. Those outside of the academy and new to the program may not realize how much labor is expected of teachers *beyond* the classroom. I didn't. Fortunately, throughout my teaching practicum—and honestly, in all of my courses—professors stressed the importance of working with colleagues to build and maintain effective writing programs. I realized how crucial continued scholarship and hard-working committee members are to a writing program. SIUE's MA program helped me understand that becoming an effective teacher involves far more than learning how to teach. Effective teaching is often the product of what happens outside the classroom and inside meeting rooms. It is in such places where committees discuss ways to help students succeed and where faculty pursue opportunities to stay current in our field.

We often hear people say, "I wouldn't trade my experiences for the world," and we think, "How cliché." But I understand what they mean. My MA degree, while relatively inexpensive, proves itself more valuable each academic year. My coursework and experience prepared me for employment at the community college level by immersing me in the academic community and providing me with knowledge, practical experience, and the resources to succeed in the classroom and beyond. But as I learned from a committee interviewer several months after my hire, simply possessing the Teaching of Writing MA specialization gave me a notable edge over others competing for the position. How does one quantify the value in that?

CHANGING STUDENT POPULATIONS

Kisha's Story: My Degree Isn't for Me

My seventh year as an instructor at Prairie State College also became my first year as an assistant professor of English. During those seven years, I missed at least two opportunities to become a full-time professor because I hadn't yet earned my MA. With all of my graduate courses completed, I was only sixty short pages away from receiving the piece of paper that would change the course of my career, but before I was able to complete my thesis, life happened: I found myself having to relocate—twice. I had two surgeries and, later, two children. My MA had been delayed, first for a year, but that year quickly proliferated into seven. But one year after earning my degree, I was offered a position as an assistant professor of English at Prairie State College. Being qualified to receive a full-time teaching position at a community college is definitely a result of earning my MA, but with that degree comes so much more.

Rebecca mentions receiving more "targeted instruction" when working toward the MA, and I couldn't agree more. In hindsight, however, one of my first experiences with targeted instruction came as an undergraduate at the hands of an English professor who would change the course of my life. This professor was greatly impressed by my work. She called me into her office and explained to me the difficulties many African American students have with English. This was something I had never thought about before, and I wanted to be part of the solution. She encouraged me to consider a major in English. I did and quickly received my BA.

Later, when I entered my MA studies, I wasn't aware in the way I am today of how, as an African American woman, I could be part of change within the academy. One of the benefits of an MA, however, is that it helps one to home in on specific social, economic, and cultural inequities that influence how our society works. The theoretical and pedagogical studies offer students a greater insight into the world. One of the "hows" of our society is the treatment of those who are disempowered. In my required theory course, I read Freire and learned about the disempowered. I remember learning that most developmental writers are minorities who struggle to learn a language quite different from their home language, thus stripping them of power. I remember learning

— 242 —

When the MA Is Enough: Considering the Value of Graduate Education

about the inequities women face and how those inequities will sometimes cause us to silence ourselves in the classroom, stripping us of our voices, thus stripping us of power. In learning those things, I was reminded of why I needed this degree—to help all of those who have been marginalized gain access to and become successful in the academic community, but also to empower them so they can become successful in our society.

That desire to help and the knowledge I acquired as a graduate student is what still drives me today as a teacher. I now spend my days not simply teaching students, but empowering them. I teach developmental courses and help students gain access to a culture they may never before have been able to enter. Every semester, when I see the success of a former student, I am reminded that my MA has done much more for others than it will ever do for me. Like me, Rebecca sees the value in learning how to reach the disempowered, and Nancy used this same knowledge to reach women in Afghanistan. This in-depth study of racism, classism, feminism, and other -isms isn't taught at the baccalaureate level.

Understanding the hows and whys of the world makes me not just a better teacher but also a better person. I enter the world with my eyes open. I am aware, and my presence in the academic community positions me to act and to promote change. I am not just a teacher who is well trained in the different learning styles and different ways to teach grammar. I am a teacher who understands how the social ladder works, and I am now able to empower those who don't understand how to climb it. That doesn't happen in my classroom only; it happens with anyone I meet. That is the value of an MA.

Nancy's Story: Wide Awake

I had served in the military for nearly eight years when I received an email asking if I would teach English to cadets at the Air Force Academy. The director of English at the Air Force Preparatory School also asked whether I would be interested in pursuing a degree in rhetoric and composition at a university of my choice. I had an undergraduate degree in English, a subject I've always loved, but I frankly didn't expect the military to be impressed with my area of study. After all, what good is an English degree

– 243 –

in a world where expert marksmanship, strategic military planning, and gravitational force are kings? The answer is simple: an MA makes me a more valuable asset to our nation's fighting force because I am a better thinker, and better thinking translates across all areas of leadership.

The military encourages and expects its officers to pursue higher education. To become a commissioned officer in the military, one must have a baccalaureate degree. This level of education is enough to open doors to a higher military tier, but more locked doors await once one reaches the place between company grade officer and the next level, field grade officer. In fact, to attain promotion past the junior officer ranks, a master's is expected. Largely, officers can acquire a degree in any field they choose. The academic exposure becomes less about acquiring tactical knowledge and more about the act and art of learning honed in pursuit of a master's.

During a time when the nation's military had its hands full in two countries in the Middle East, the Air Force released me for eighteen months to pursue an MA in English, rhetoric and composition. In all operations, the military weighs the rewards against the risks of loss, and in this case, the Air Force calculated that the reward gained from allowing me such an experience outweighed the temporary loss of an officer, an asset. The military, specifically the United States Air Force, comprehends the intrinsic value of a master's degree. After all, it daily reaps the benefits of the innovative problem-solvers, creative leaders, and well-informed service members who are returned to the mission after such a degree is completed. I was no exception.

After graduating from the program, I went back to my military duties and waited for my assignment to teach cadets at the Air Force Academy. Much like Rebecca, Kisha, and Jeff, I was eager to show myself as a "qualified and worthy colleague" when I arrived at the Academy, and I didn't want to lose what I had learned in pursuit of the MA in the interim, so I obtained a second civilian job teaching English through an online university. In the role of online instructor, I was able to apply the knowledge I gained in the MA program by helping students recognize their individual writing processes and how best to work within them. I had many consultations with students who were frustrated with

When the MA Is Enough: Considering the Value of Graduate Education

writing, often sheepishly confessing to being "bad writers." But for most, their writing processes improved significantly simply because they were able to recognize that it was a continual process. This additional teaching experience, made possible because of my degree, further reinforced the Air Force's belief that a master's degree would make me a better contributor to our mission.

Inevitably, I was deployed to Afghanistan, from January 2011 until January 2012. I certainly didn't anticipate that my English teaching skills would be put to use there, with the exception of a well-written email or proposal, but they turned out to be highly sought-after tools. About three months into my yearlong deployment, I was asked to build relationships with the local Afghan community by establishing a program in which female volunteers from the US forces worked with teachers at a local girls' school in Kabul. I was asked to lead the group of volunteers because I had an MA in English and experience teaching online. Despite my protests that teaching English online to English-speaking students was not the same as teaching English to non-native speakers in a foreign country, like most things in the military, when asked to do something, one does it. We traveled to the girls' school once or twice a week as the war would allow and practiced reading and speaking English with the Afghan teachers. While we were supposed to be teaching them English, I often found I was learning far more than I was teaching.

My degree, and the skills I gained in its pursuit, put me in the perfect position to contribute to the effort in Afghanistan on an interpersonal level. I certainly grew in my practical knowledge of writing through SIUE, but I also gained new ways to approach information on a deeper level. As Kisha indicates, in SIUE's MA program we studied the ways in which learning happens in oppressed societies and that literacy does not refer only to one's reading ability. The awareness of complex literacy was a priceless tool in a society where women had not been allowed to attend school for nearly thirty years and only about 12 percent of the female population could read something written on a page (Central Intelligence Agency). I recognized that the citizens of Afghanistan, especially the women, knew more ways to move through the oppressive state that Al-Qaeda enforced, and their

– 245 –

literacy was displayed in the things they created with their hands, not the letters they could write with them.

Although beneficial to my personal growth, being attuned to multiple literacies was also valuable to the military because I was able to transfer a certain awareness to the environment around me. During a time when a misstep of cultural sensitivity severed relationships that took months to build, each positive tie we had to the local community aided our ability to help the Afghan nation. In training sessions with other female service member volunteers who would work at the school, we discussed the importance of not dismissing the women because they "didn't know how to read" or because they had a more reserved demeanor than we were used to encountering from American women. I tried to make the American women aware of how much space we would take up with our uniforms, our uncovered heads, our insouciant confidence, our American-ness. In preparation for visiting the Afghan teachers, we frequently discussed the ways in which the women adapted to their oppressive reality and how our job was more important than simply teaching them to read and speak English. We were creating a safe space for them to thrive out of the shadows of decades of maltreatment and despotism. I would have been ill-equipped to fulfill these duties without the hours I spent with the professors, students, and materials in my quest for the MA. Because of the art and act of thinking and communicating that I learned in the master's program, I could lead a team that built a joint partnership with the Afghan teachers, empowering them and creating a lasting impact that is rippling through a new Afghanistan.

I have since returned from my tour in Afghanistan, and I am settled into my current duty as an English teacher at the US Air Force Preparatory School. The English department is filled with a mixture of skilled instructors, both military and civilian, and all have higher-level degrees in the tradition of the military's expectations for leadership and education. Together, we are propelling a different group of people to a new, hopeful future as Air Force officers. My students, both females and males, are younger than the women in Afghanistan, but no matter. I consistently draw on the same tools in my classroom.

– 246 –

When the MA Is Enough: Considering the Value of Graduate Education

The demographics of the Prep School consist of students from diverse backgrounds, of all nationalities, educational opportunities, and financial hardships. The school is a place for students who do not fit the standard "mold" of an academic. They attend the Prep School to learn military discipline and new math, science, and English skills. Coming from underrepresented minorities, they have stories of oppression and marginalization of their own. Once again I find myself relying on the knowledge gained during my MA to teach them more than how to write a collegiate-level essay. Much like the cross-cultural and gender awareness I applied in Afghanistan, I find myself keenly alert to my varied students' needs in a way I would not be without my educational experience. I am able to validate their thoughts, past experiences, current insecurities, and struggles, which in turn gives them the ability to move forward in a new, positive direction.

Before beginning my rhetoric and composition studies at SIUE, I didn't know how to leverage my education fully to benefit myself or my mission as an airman. With each academic experience, however, I improved. I began to want more for myself and from myself in service to my nation. Seeds were planted, making me aware of the "more" that was available to me if only I could practically apply my knowledge. The value of my MA is incalculable. At its core, it helped me develop insightful awareness of and sensitivity to the world I encounter, which makes me more fully present in all experiences of my life.

Jeff's Story: What Happens at SIUE Doesn't Stay at SIUE

Barb Gillian, my former principal, retired last spring. As the school year wrapped up, we had the chance to talk briefly one morning. She dropped her principal persona in a way she'd rarely been able to do and shared with me what she considered the one regret of her administration. "You know," she said, "I never was the *instructional* leader I wanted to be. I was always dealing with schedules or facilities or budgets. I've always seen myself as a teacher." Like Barb, I am a teacher first. I am thankful for school leadership embodied in people like Barb who understand teaching and learning. The MA I earned at SIUE positioned me to take on leadership roles within our Writing Project site and

— 247 —

within my own school. With my school's support, I have been able to pursue teacher leadership and literacy instruction.

This work began during my graduate study at SIUE when Dr. McGee introduced me to Dr. Ralph Córdova in the School of Education. Not long after I completed my MA, Dr. Córdova began work to bring a National Writing Project (NWP) site to SIUE, and together we began building what has become a vital and relevant new site. Among other things beyond the scope of this chapter, my work with Dr. Córdova has had us presenting papers and doing site work on such national stages as the American Educational Research Association and NWP annual conferences. These experiences shaped my professional identity and helped me contribute to the professional development of my colleagues.

Schools tangled in the knots of accountability and assessment mandates sometimes have difficulty seeing the value of innovative work like that of the National Writing Project. In the summer of 2012, for example, we brought together an elite group of educators and teacher leaders representing eight Writing Project sites, two museums, classrooms, and libraries, for a first-of-its kind weeklong institute, 3RDSpace, to explore innovation and creativity and to envision ways for these processes to be applied to instructional needs and challenges within the home contexts of the participants (Córdova, Kumpulainen, and Hudson).

Building on the curricular foundation of my MA and guided by the responsive design theory of action I am creating with my colleagues in the Writing Project, I have been leading a series of professional development workshops at Alton High School for the purposes of exploring literacy practice across the curriculum in order to appropriate the Common Core State Standards (CCSS) in humane and generative ways. We hope to shift the educational discussion from one of assessment to one of instruction. The Literacy Laboratory brings teachers together twice a month, voluntarily, to inquire into practice and build a repertoire of literate practice across the curriculum so that we might live up to the promise of the CCSS (Córdova, Hudson, Swank, and Sabo-Lay).

Holding an MA degree has conferred upon me an ethos that creates opportunities I would not otherwise have, such as teaching our dual credit composition course. I know, however, that I cannot lead from the authority of a title, department head, or

When the MA Is Enough: Considering the Value of Graduate Education

degree alone. When Teresa (pseudonym) was accidentally placed in my dual credit composition course, the fact that a scheduling mistake had been made was immediately apparent. Without a foundation in basic and developmental writing (one area of emphasis in my graduate work), I might likely have referred her to the guidance department and had her schedule corrected. Had I done so, Teresa would have endured a semester of worksheets and disruptive classrooms. Instead, I had both the empathy and theoretical foundation to support Teresa in the dual credit course. Although she might not have passed the placement exam to earn college credit, for possibly the first time in her academic career, she had the chance to learn with and from a population of students with whom she had never worked before.

When our area's dual credit teachers meet, the agenda is nearly always dominated by talk of assessment. We norm papers and study the rubric. With both the ethos and the theoretical and practical foundations of my graduate degree, I have been able to work with these colleagues to shift our conversation to one of instruction rather than assessment. Such a shift in the agenda has the potential to transform practice, to affect what gets enacted in the classroom.

Last, and most significant, an MA in teaching writing has allowed me to forge and name what I believe about writing and learning. I continue to shape and reinvent a pedagogy informed by the critical, process, and feminist pedagogies I explored at SIUE. My students use language to both discover what they know and express that knowledge. They come to understand the power of language, the importance of voice, *their* voices. It doesn't get better than that.

Reflecting on the Narratives

Rebecca's, Kisha's, Nancy's, and Jeff's stories are personal, certainly, but represent the range of experiences that one who obtains an MA degree might experience. Some paths to employment have been easier than others. Of course, jobs—with salaries to pay the bills—are important, and graduate educators need to be mindful that most, if not all, students attend graduate programs with some kind of end employment in mind—whether that be continuing to a PhD and ultimately landing a (probably academic) job or moving on with just the MA degree. Ethically, we cannot promise students job placement, and for the sake of full disclosure, some of SIUE's graduates are still looking for full-time employment. While the stories told here may seem nearly evangelistic, for some students the reality is that employment eludes them for many reasons, not the least of which is that the recent economic downturn has affected community college, public school, and university budgets and frozen hiring efforts.

However, an MA in a specialization like rhetoric and composition that has a focused curriculum balanced between theory and application offers many graduates a more immediate path to the kind of fulfilling professional (and balanced personal) life they desire. As these graduates have illustrated, our curriculum provides students with the essentials needed to become effective teachers and colleagues, yet it is diverse enough to offer a range of courses that target individual interests (e.g., teaching with computers, teaching African American literature, teaching creative writing, teaching ESL students, and so on). And as the graduates indicate in their narratives, their MA degrees were enough to situate them squarely within their desired fields with the tools needed to help empower their students and shape the future of our country.

Employment notwithstanding, what strikes us about these narratives when considered collectively is that the MA opened the door to jobs, yes, but also added intrinsic value. Those who complete a doctoral program often talk about "the experiences" of the program—those intangible aspects of professional development, camaraderie, late-night discussions about new and visionary questions, the faculty mentoring—as being as important a part of their education as the courses they took. It seems a legitimate question to ask whether MA students, who may take different timelines through coursework, who have diverse career and life experiences, and who often have less time on campus together, have the same kind of "experiences," the kind with intrinsic value that is immeasurable to personal, academic, and professional growth. In a graduate program, students build personal networks that tend to last them throughout their professional lives. Rebecca,

When the MA Is Enough: Considering the Value of Graduate Education

Kisha, Nancy, and Jeff have had, to varying degrees, the same kind of professional foundation and network building that a PhD program might offer. Through the program—which integrates five of the six strategies outlined for doctoral programs by the Council of Graduate Schools Preparing Future Faculty initiative (Gaff et al. 6–7)—they were encouraged to attend and present at regional and national conferences and to become active, vibrant members of their institutions.

More important, perhaps, they share the knowledge they gained. Rebecca has used composition theory to design assignments meant to actively engage students in the writing process as they shape real texts for real audiences. Kisha works with developmental writers and African American students, the ones who inspired her to pursue her MA. Nancy put the education she gained to use in providing literacy and educational opportunities for women in war-torn Afghanistan. Jeff has used his growth to become a leader at his own school and for other teachers in a National Writing Project site. As Kisha notes in her narrative, her degree has had even more of an impact on the students she has taught than it has had on her, which holds true for all of these (and other) graduates. These examples, as well as others, demonstrate the added value of an MA degree and the way in which the degree has an impact on myriad lives.

Works Cited

Brown, Stuart C., Monica F. Torres, Theresa Enos, and Erik Juergens-meyer, eds. Spec. issue of *Rhetoric Review* 24.1 (2005): 5–127. Print.

Central Intelligence Agency. "Facts on Women from the World Fact Book." *CIA.gov*. Central Intelligence Agency, 7 Mar. 2013. Web. 14 June 2014.

Córdova, Ralph A., Jr., Jeff Hudson, Patricia Swank, and April Sabo-Lay. "Inquiring into My Practice (iimp) Protocol Scaffolds Teachers' Innovative Lessons." 9th Qualitative Research Conference. U of Missouri-St. Louis. 7–9 Mar. 2013.

Córdova, Ralph A., Jr., Kristiina Kumpulainen, and Jeff Hudson. "Nurturing Creativity and Professional Learning for 21st Century

Education: *ResponsiveDesign* and the Cultural Landscapes Collaboratory." *LEARNing Landscapes* 6.1 (2012): 155–78. Web. 14 June 2013.

Council of Graduate Schools. "Master's Completion Project." *Council of Graduate Schools.* CGS, 2012. Web. 13 June 2013.

Gaff, Jerry G., Anne S. Pruitt-Logan, Leslie B. Sims, Daniel D. Denecke, and Program Participants. *Preparing Future Faculty in the Humanities and Social Sciences: A Guide for Change.* Washington: Council of Graduate Schools land the Association of American Colleges and Universities, 2003. PDF file.

Office of Institutional Research and Studies. *Southern Illinois University Edwardsville Fact Book, 2012 Edition.* Edwardsville: Southern Illinois U, 2012. Print.

Smithson, Isaiah. "Hello and Question." Message to Sharon J. McGee. 26 Aug. 2014. E-mail.

Afterword

ADAM KOMISARUK
West Virginia University

During the decade or so that I spent as an undergraduate advisor, I developed a standard speech for students thinking about pursuing a PhD in English. Its outlines will be familiar: If you hear the call, hearken to it, but do so with your eyes wide open. Know that you will be delaying your entrance into the workforce for no fewer than five, typically seven, possibly ten years. Your existence will be a lonely one. Positive reinforcement will be scant. Expect to gain twenty pounds. You will likely go into debt, with or without a fellowship. All this will be for employment prospects that could be charitably described as uncertain. Nor, at present, does an English PhD have applications outside academia that are worth the sacrifice. If you know all these things and still want to take the plunge, then God speed. If, however, you feel neither sure this life is for you nor quite done with your education, then by all means consider the MA. It will give you a taste of what goes on in the world of advanced literary scholarship. It can easily be parlayed into future applications to PhD programs, where it is often a prerequisite. And if, having "scratched an intellectual itch or achieved a personal milestone" (FitzGerald and Singley 146), you prefer to try your fortunes as a doctor, a lawyer, a business owner, a world traveler, or what have you, you will be free to do so without having frittered away your youth.

This vision of the MA—as a degree of more intrinsic than extrinsic value, more postbaccalaureate than preprofessional—is one that I sustained through my transition to director of graduate studies and in which I suspect I am not alone. It turns out, however, to bear little resemblance to the realities that the fascinating essays collected here adduce. "Many MA students are looking

– 253 –

for an intellectual challenge," says Ann M. Penrose of her own program at North Carolina State, "but none . . . have the luxury of pursuing graduate education solely for their own knowledge or enrichment" (184). The overwhelming majority of respondents to Penrose's survey (70 percent) see the MA as a way to enter or advance in the teaching profession, and an overlapping majority (54 percent) see it as preparation for the PhD (182). Her separate survey of NCSU alumni reveals 38 percent actively employed as teachers and 36 percent continuing their studies, a result not far from the ADE Ad Hoc Committee on the Master's Degree figures of roughly 40 percent and 43 percent, respectively (Penrose 185; ADE Ad Hoc Committee 32). Further evidence supports the picture of MA student intentions (not to say outcomes) as relatively homogeneous. Again and again, the authors in this collection report student frustration with the disparity between the work they are trained to do and the work they end up doing, as well as a shared desire by students and faculty to orient the MA curriculum toward more practical ends. Is it not high time, per the title of the ADE report, to be "Rethinking the Master's Degree in English for a New Century"—a century in which the MA already constitutes the highest degree held by half of all postsecondary English faculty members (ADE Ad Hoc Committee 20)?

I confess to being one who places the humanities, as Mark Mossman puts it, "in an oppositional posture that pushes against the structure of academic capitalism"; who indeed finds "repellent" the suggestion that the English MA be "more professionalized and recognized as the commodity that in so many ways it already is" (50, 54, 54). I wince at the instrumentalist language, asserting itself on nearly every page of this collection, that construes the English MA in terms of *training, preparation, application, certification, translation,* and so forth. My knee-jerk response to the consumerist reinvention of the university is defiantly to embrace what James Beasley, quoting Bill Readings, calls an "economy of waste" (204). The lament of the newly minted English MA about a theory–praxis disconnect is not unique to the teaching profession, as attested by the long-standing "law school vs. lawyer school" debate, and by the legend of a "July effect" that correlates the start of the medical residency cycle with a spike in hospital errors (Bronner; Chen). The perceived insularity of

Afterword

these professions certainly bears evaluation, but it seems to me precipitous to interpret insularity per se as a crisis.

I do not mean to suggest that because I am skeptical of a "practical" MA I am indifferent to practical considerations. On the contrary, what gives me pause is the question of how such an MA would work in actual fact. Programmatic changes are rarely resource-neutral; zero-sum games are more common than we might like to admit. An adjustment made to accommodate something someone wants can have budgetary, curricular, and personnel implications for an entire department, often at the expense of something someone else wants. Rebecca Potter raises the "question of faculty readiness to provide expert guidance in the kind of work that most of their master's students will undertake"; "very few tenured faculty have attended and/or taught in a community college, and some of the literature professors may consider teaching composition to be a necessary evil. Many may not be required to teach composition at all. Very few have taught high school English" (68, 68). If this situation is to be redressed in the name of enhanced MA professionalization, either new faculty will need to be hired or existing faculty retrained accordingly (with concomitant clarification of workload, merit, and promotion and tenure expectations). Moreover, if professionalization is to become a structural rather than a voluntary feature of the MA program, presumably in the form of required courses, it is likely to mean either an extended time to degree or a curtailment of course offerings in literature (lest chronic underenrollment draw unwanted scrutiny from the administration).

A broader definition of MA professionalization, one that looks beyond composition-heavy positions at two-year colleges, has the potential to amplify these problems. "What do book publishers look for in new employees?" asks Penrose. "Corporate communications departments? Web design firms?" (193–94). These are good questions, but I fear that in attempting to answer them we will face an endlessly proliferating range of possibilities for which MAs, duly supported by curricular offerings and qualified faculty, are expected to be prepared. The aspirational English department thus starts to resemble the poet described by Imlac, the learned man in Samuel Johnson's *Rasselas*, who

– 255 –

AFTERWORD

> must be acquainted . . . with all the modes of life. His character requires that he estimate the happiness and misery of every condition; observe the power of all the passions in all their combinations, and trace the changes of the human mind as they are modified by various institutions and accidental influences of climate or custom, from the spriteliness of infancy to the despondence of decrepitude. (1.69–70)

This is also to assume that the corporate world is monolithic; that any given employer necessarily knows *what* it is looking for at any given moment; that the rules are rational and not subject to change without notice, just as we were promised that our 401(k)s were always safe, our pensions were always inviolate, and our homes would always appreciate. Mossman's solution is essentially to use the master's tools to dismantle the master's house: "Ours will be a professionalism that privileges issues of social justice," with "unfettered intellectualism" somehow "transform[ing]" the "utilitarian paradigm" (54, 56). My instincts tell me that this is playing in a rigged game, and that if we try to make the argument for what we do according to corporate definitions of utility, we have already lost. If I am to wax idealistic, I would rather do so through a kind of Kantian professionalism-without-a-profession: instead of trying to anticipate every contingency, awaken students' imagination; cultivate an environment in which, instead of fretting about how their studies might be applied, they might conduct them with excellence, integrity, and passion.

And yet. Am I not speaking from a position of extreme privilege? The ethos in which I was reared—do your work, and your future will take care of itself—is a luxury most students can ill afford. I salute the contributors of the present volume and their home departments for successful innovation at the master's level—at Missouri Western, a master of applied arts in written communication (Adkins); at Bowling Green and Clemson, new or enhanced online presences (Blair; Scheg); certificates or specializations in the teaching of writing at Indiana University–Purdue University Indianapolis (Fox and Lovejoy) and at Southern Illinois University Edwardsville (McGee, Burns, Wells, Clemens, and Hudson); certificates and a portfolio-based capstone project in composition at San Francisco State (Ching, Lockhart, and Roberge). Of the more theoretical approaches, I respect Mossman's

– 256 –

Afterword

and Beasley's provocative and conscientious arguments that we ignore the socioeconomic determination of the English MA at our peril: "[O]bscuring structures of disciplinary reproduction also obscures an embedded politics and ideology" (Beasley 213). *Contingency* may seem a dirty word in some respects, denoting an "inevitably abusive" condition of academic labor with which "our common quarrel as one faculty" must be, or any other unforeseeable condition of the postgraduation world (ADE Ad Hoc Committee 16). But in another respect, it is vital that we recognize ourselves as "contingent" beings, as interdependent parts of what Adkins calls an "ecological network" comprising students, faculty, administration, and, of course, the academics and nonacademics outside one's own institution (80). The call by Ching, Lockhart, and Roberge for MA programs to be "locally responsive and socially productive" resonates throughout this collection, with several contributors describing the reciprocal needs of their programs and the communities in which they are situated (5). Those of us who teach at land grant institutions, as I do, have a special fiduciary responsibility to the publics that, at whatever dwindling level, keep them fed.

Assuredly, as Miller and Carter say, "one size doesn't fit all" (172). I presume to offer no unified theory of how the MA in English might become more engaged with its material conditions. But I would like to pose a series of what I consider diagnostic questions for those interested in reforming their programs along such lines.

1. *Che vuoi?*

What, exactly, is your objective? Is it to climb the ever-elusive *U.S. News & World Report* rankings? to boost overall graduate enrollment in your department? to boost the number of applications and, thus, your rejection rate ("selectivity")? to populate your graduate courses with a "better" caliber of student? to increase graduate funding levels in the form of assistantships, fellowships, etc.? to improve departmental morale and/or student satisfaction? to hire additional faculty? to protect and/or increase the variety of graduate-teaching opportunities available to faculty? to improve MA placement in PhD programs? to improve the rate and/or gainfulness of

AFTERWORD

MA employment (the computation of which, like the statistics for PhD employment, lacks good national protocols)? to keep specific employers or consortia of employers in the region, with whom you may have come to develop a tacit or overt understanding, well stocked with prospects? It is no secret, and no shame to say, that programmatic decisions are often made inductively rather than deductively. For example, it is fair to say that the undergraduate linguistics requirement in my department is justified by the presence of a linguist on our faculty rather than the other way around, whatever the motives behind his original hiring; nor, given his stature as an internationally renowned scholar, a heavily decorated teacher, and an indispensable university citizen, would we have it any other way. It is important that, in assessing "need," we can answer "Whose?" and "According to whom?" and do so honestly.

2. What are you willing to do?
Institutional reform requires sacrifice, and sacrifice must be shared. In what my associate chair calls the "sliding-puzzle game" of departmental administration, an adjustment to even the smallest feature of a program usually requires adjustments everywhere. The closer this process comes to home, the more resistance it can encounter. Of the professionalization efforts in her own MA program, Blair reports that many faculty members "did not want to focus on courses such as The Teaching of Literature, preferring instead to teach special topics courses in their literary specialties" (29). Staffing our graduate research methods course is an annual struggle—so much so that faculty volunteers may claim it as a "bonus" outside their regular graduate teaching rotation—and I shudder to think what would befall us if we were to develop courses perceived as even more peripheral to "real" scholarly work. Would you personally teach such courses, or are you assuming it will be someone else's responsibility? Would you teach them if it meant fewer turns at bat in your area of expertise? if it meant conducting additional research—with or without a modification of your current research expecta-

– 258 –

Afterword

tions—and even undergoing additional training to acquire the appropriate skill sets?

Pedagogical pressures should also be anticipated at the level of the individual literature classroom. The ADE survey reports that the two most common courses required of all or most MA students are Research Methods (63.6 percent) and Literary Theory (51.4 percent) (23) and asks, nonrhetorically, whether these are "the most urgent need in the MA curriculum, especially for those students who do not pursue the PhD" (10). If these requirements were to become electives, students might enter your advanced literature courses lacking a foundation that could heretofore be assumed; would you be prepared to accommodate them?

Finally, there is the matter of MA students as members of the departmental teaching force themselves. Ninety-five percent of the respondents to Penrose's survey of Raleigh, North Carolina–area "private and community college administrators . . . look for generalists who can teach in more than one area" (193). This is a tall order when student and faculty teaching assignments are interdependent. In my department, all graduate students are fully funded through assistantships, though with a heavier teaching load (2-2) than is typical at peer institutions. MA students teach only composition; PhD students begin with composition and then, usually in their third year, become eligible for first-year and sophomore-level literature courses—specifically, the courses that remain unclaimed after we make faculty assignments, which we do a year in advance. Historically this system has served well; but as undergraduate humanities majors decline, existing courses are being consolidated or offered with less frequency, faculty are occupying a greater share of those courses, and so fewer are left over for PhD students. I cannot see us broadening these already straitened opportunities, let alone to MA students in the name of producing better "generalists," except by putting the entire faculty into the composition sequence, which we have not done for the past decade or so. I happen not to think this is a bad idea—places like the University of Michigan do it, and it would keep our department invested in our educational mission at all levels—but I do not expect

AFTERWORD

it would be an easy pill to swallow. Indeed, I have a strong suspicion that the prospect of tenured and tenure-track faculty teaching composition is the elephant in the room of the academic jobs-crisis debate.

3. Are you listening to one another?

Dispositionally and institutionally, we tend to work alone. Collaboration is far more uncommon and inconsistently rewarded in the humanities than in the sciences. It is not surprising that the contributors to this volume advert frequently to interdisciplinarity, which represents the exciting possibility of coming out of one's shell. Michael Bérubé, as director of the Institute for the Arts and Humanities at Penn State, believes in a visionary reinvention of interdisciplinary itself: conventional pairing, such as that of literature with film or art history, "doesn't come close to what I mean. . . . I want French and metallurgy. And we almost got there." In the shorter run, as Adkins points out, "interdisciplinarity may exist within one department" as well as across departments or schools (93).

Still, I would urge that in our zeal to forge new alliances we not become unmindful of the *otherness* of the disciplines. Every institution will have its idiosyncratic configuration even of ostensibly proximate fields: at mine, literary and writing studies are housed within the English department as separate majors; linguistics and TESOL in the Department of World Languages; and English education in an altogether separate college where, en route to the master's degree, students take many English courses and earn a BA in English without ever having been English majors. Inhabitants of these different demesnes will each have their own research questions, methodologies, conventions, vocabularies, agendas, aspirations, challenges, territorialities, quirks, insecurities. By acknowledging the fault lines that can exist or emerge, we prevent interdisciplinarity from becoming simple colonization—what Princeton historian Sean Wilentz waggishly calls "the recent trend for literary critics to write about any subject they please, and in a tone of serene authority." As we contemplate a more "interdisciplinary" MA, we might take a moment to imagine

— 260 —

Afterword

the shoe being on the other foot: would we respond cheerily or defensively to a secondary English education specialist, or a historian, or a neuroscientist who ventures into literary criticism? to the implication that one might become a competent teacher of our discipline by osmosis rather than by undergoing a meticulous training regiman oneself?

The sense of humility that I am counseling vis-à-vis interdisciplinarity applies to the culture of the MA program more broadly. The essays in this volume have been a revelation to me, because many MA students' assumptions—let alone their prospective employers'—turn out to have been wildly at variance with my own. It had seldom occurred to me that the English MA might be conceptualized as a professional credential, or that it was functioning as such in so many cases already. I do not know how widespread my illusions may be, but it strikes me as of the utmost importance that all stakeholders in a program be on the same page. Special heed must be paid to student voices, which the ADE report notably omits and which the essays by Fox and Lovejoy, Penrose, Park and Amevuvor, and McGee et al. do us a great service to include. Do we know what our MA students are doing there? Do we ask them? If they are expecting preparation to teach at the community college level, are they aware of the probability of their receiving a position in that sector, of that position being tenurable versus not, of a nontenurable position being rehirable/renewable versus not, of the assignments being to literature versus composition courses? As with alt-ac guidance for PhD students, I believe this information should be provided upon matriculation or, better yet, upon recruitment, so that departmental identity becomes defined by transparency rather than a perceived bait-and-switch.

Indeed, I concur with the advice of Anne Krook and others that our reconception of alt-ac (alternatives to academic employment), for both PhD and MA students considering such a pathway, begin with the term itself and its undue stigma of a "Plan B" or consolation prize. I like "public humanities" as a point of departure because it evokes the outward-directedness—the "centrifugal force," in Beasley's phrase (206)—from which our discipline would benefit at

– 261 –

AFTERWORD

every level. This is true alike of traditional and nontraditional programs of study, oriented toward careers inside academia, careers outside academia, or no careers in particular. Whether the genre in which we are working is the first-semester seminar paper, the conference abstract, the service learning report, the dissertation prospectus, the academic job letter, the corporate interview, the press release, the journal article, the book proposal, the grant application . . . no audience ever craved *less* clarity, *less* concision. Nor, having accommodated them, were we ever the worse for it. Learning to emerge, cicadalike, from our shells in all our vulnerability not only makes professional sense: it is our duty. We should be good at it.

Works Cited

ADE Ad Hoc Committee on the Master's Degree. "Rethinking the Master's Degree in English for a New Century." *Modern Language Association*. MLA, June 2011. Web. 14 Aug. 2013.

Adkins, Kaye. "From Political Constraints to Program Innovation: Professionalizing the Master's Degree in English." Strain and Potter 79–98.

Beasley, James. "Disciplining the Community: The MA in English and Contextual Fluidity." Strain and Potter 197–214.

Bérubé, Michael. West Virginia University. Morgantown, WV. 26 Oct. 2015. Address.

Blair, Kristine L. "English Online/On-the-Line: The Challenges of Sustaining Disciplinary Relevance in the 21st Century." Strain and Potter 22–40.

Bronner, Ethan. "A Call for Drastic Changes in Educating New Lawyers." *New York Times*. New York Times, 10 Feb. 2013. Web. 28 June 2016.

Chen, Pauline W. "Are Med School Grads Prepared to Practice Medicine?" *New York Times*. New York Times, 24 Apr. 2014. Web. 28 June 2016.

Ching, Kory Lawson, Tara Lockhart, and Mark Roberge. "The Locally Responsive, Socially Productive MA in Composition." Strain and Potter 3–21.

Afterword

FitzGerald, William T., and Carol J. Singley. "Crafting a Program That Works (for Us): The Evolving Mission of the Master's in English at Rutgers University–Camden." Strain and Potter 138–56.

Fox, Steve, and Kim Brian Lovejoy. "Boundary Crossings and Collaboration in a Graduate Certificate in Teaching Writing." Strain and Potter 99–119.

Johnson, Samuel. *The Prince of Abissinia: A Tale*. 2 vols. London, 1759. *Eighteenth-Century Collections Online*. Web. 4 Sept. 2016.

Krook, Anne. "Alt-Ac Q&A." West Virginia University, Morgantown. 11 Nov. 2015. Address.

McGee, Sharon James, Rebecca Burns, Kisha Wells, Nancy Thurman Clemens, and Jeff Hudson. "When the MA is Enough: Considering the Value of Graduate Education." Strain and Potter 234–52.

Miller, Hildy, and Duncan Carter. "'There and Back Again': Programmatic Deliberations and the Creation of an MA Track in Rhetoric and Composition." Strain and Potter 157–75.

Mossman, Mark. "Academic Capitalism, Student Needs, and the English MA." Strain and Potter 41–58.

Park, Gloria, and Jocelyn Amevuvor. "An MA TESOL Program Housed in the English Department: Preparing Teacher Scholars to Meet the Demands of a Globalizing World." Strain and Potter 215–33.

Penrose, Ann. "Student Ambitions and Alumni Career Paths: Expectations of the MA English Degree." Strain and Potter 179–96.

Potter, Rebecca C. "But Can You Teach Composition? The Relevance of Literary Studies for the MA Degree." Strain and Potter 59–75.

Scheg, Abigail G. "TextSupport: Incorporating Online Pedagogy into MA English Programs." Strain and Potter 120–37.

Strain, Margaret M., and Rebecca C. Potter, eds. *Degree of Change: The MA in English Studies*. Urbana IL: NCTE, 2016. Print.

Wilentz, Sean. "Who Lincoln Was." *New Republic*. New Republic, 15 July 2009. Web. 28 June 2016.

INDEX

Academic capitalism. *See also* New Economy
effects of, 41
English program as external to, 50
and English programs, 48, 50
vs. public good of knowledge/ learning, 44–45
and terminal MA degree, 41–42, 46–48, 56
Academic literacy, 8
ADE Ad Hoc Committee on the Master's Degree, xiv, xv, xxi, xxvn2, xxvn5, xxvin6, 22–23, 59–60, 62, 73nn1–2, 80–81, 87, 95, 138–39, 182, 184, 186, 191, 202, 254
Adjunct faculty
employment prospects for, 114–15
MA degree holders as, 22
as online instructors, 123
and Portland State University MA track, 170
Adkins, Kaye, xix, 60, 61, 86, 256, 257, 260
Allen, I. Elaine, 129
Allen, Nancy, 90
Alvarez, Deborah M., 25, 37
Amevuvor, Jocelyn R., xxiii, 60, 216, 220, 223, 261
Anson, Chris M., 190
Aronowitz, Stanley, 50
Asch, Evelyn D., 43
Atwell, Nancie, 118n4

Baker, Jason, 84
Ballif, Michelle, 80
Ballou, Jeffrey P., 43
Barrett, Bob, 132
Bartlett, Anne Clark, xii, xiv
Bawarshi, Anis, 80
Beard, David, 125
Beasley, James, xxii, 254, 257, 261
Beaufort, Anne, 190
Begum, Khani, 31
Benninghoff, Steven T., 90
Berelson, Bernard, xii, xviii
Berlin, James A., xi, 161, 166
Berlinerblau, Jacques, 29, 30
Berthoff, Ann E., 161
Bérubé, Michael, 191, 260
Bieber, Jeffery P., 191
Bishop, Wendy, 161, 162
Blair, Kristine L., xvii, 25, 37, 256, 258
Boettcher, Judith V., 132
Boroch, Deborah, 19
Bousquet, Marc, 164, 192
Bowling Green State University (BGSU) online MA program
economic impact of, 35–36
faculty resistance to, 28–30, 36–37
nontraditional students of, 26–27
overview of, 24–27
and professional development, 33–34
quality control measures for, 32–33

INDEX

as student-centered, 27–28,
    37, 38
student demand for, 27–28
technological challenges of, 30,
    32, 33–35
Bradburn, Ellen M., 73
Brady, Brock, 218
Braine, George, 215
Bronner, Ethan, 254
Brown, Heath, 123
Brown, Stuart C., xxvn3, 234
Burns, Rebecca, xxiii, 72, 239–
    41, 256, 261

California State Assembly Bill
    (AB) 1725, 13
Career paths. *See also* Teaching
    of MA degree holders, 73n3,
        89, 91, 184–85
    nonacademic, 24, 89, 91,
        170–71, 182–83, 185,
        193–94
    student expectations vs. out-
        comes for, 186–90
Carlo, Rosanne, 159
Carrier, Karen A., 218
Carter, Duncan, xxi, 59, 60, 257
Certificate program in writing
    pedagogy. *See also*
        Indiana University–Purdue
        University Indianapolis's
        (IUPUI) graduate
        certificate program
    benefits of, 102–3, 106–7
    need for, 101–2
    overview of, 117–18n3
    purpose of, 104–5
    value of, 101, 116–17
CGS. *See* Council of Graduate
    Schools (CGS)
Chen, Pauline W., 254
Ching, Kory Lawson, xvii, 60,
    71, 256, 257
Civic engagement. *See also* Local
    responsiveness
    and Portland State University

MA track, 168–69
and Rutgers University–Cam-
    den MA program, 148–49
Clark-Ibáñez, Marisol, 132
Clary-Lemon, Jennifer, 4, 19, 71,
    125, 203
    on autonomy of MA degrees,
        xvii
    on diversity of MA students,
        123
    on interdisciplinarity, 210
    on intradisciplinarity, 208, 209
    on MA degrees as impractical,
        201
    on MA in composition, xxii, 3
    on MA's value as fulfilling
        community needs, 199–
        200, 202, 206, 212
    on MA vs. PhD, 207
    on relevance of MA in English,
        197–98
Clemens, Nancy Thurman, xxiii,
    72, 243–47, 256, 261
Community colleges
    diversity of students as chal-
        lenge, 7–9
    enrollment growth of, 62
    grammar and language devel-
        opment issues in, 9–13
Composition programs. *See also*
    English programs; specific
    programs
    faculty biases against, 68
    focus of, vs. TESOL, 12
    historical trajectory of, 10
    vs. literary studies programs,
        63–64
    relevancy of, to employment
        opportunities, 61–62,
        64–68
Connors, Robert J., 11, 161
Conrad, Clifton F., xix
Conrad, Rita-Marie, 132
Córdova, Ralph A., Jr., 248
Council for Programs in
    Technical and Scientific

Index

Communication (CPTSC), 96n3
Council of Graduate Schools (CGS), 81, 88–89, 92
Cronk, Brian, 83
Crowley, Sharon, 161, 170
Cuban, Larry, 99–100
Curry, Mary Jane, 215

Dalbey, Marcia A., xii, 91, 120, 200
Damrosch, David, 151
David, Jane L., 99–100
Davies, Catherine Evans, 217
Dayton, David, 91
Delbanco, Andrew, 62, 63
Delfino, Manuela, 132
Denecke, Daniel D., 251
Desrochers, Donna M., 62
Digital humanities, 125–26
Digital Wharton project, 154–55
Distance learning. *See* Online MA programs; Technology
Diversity, 7–9
Donahue, Patricia, 163
Donhardt, Tracy, 103
Donoghue, Frank, 51, 52
Dunn, John S., Jr., xiv, xv, 123

EALLs. *See* English as an additional language learners (EALLs)
Ecological networks, 92–96
Economic impact, 35–36
Economic opportunities, 42–44. *See also* New Economy
Edminster, Jude, 33
Elbow, Peter, 165
Employment. *See also* Career paths
  literary studies' relevancy to, 71
  and MWSU MAA program goals, 92–95
  nonacademic, 24, 89, 91, 170–71, 182–83

prospects for, 114–15, 192–93
relevancy of composition vs. literary studies for, 61–62, 64–68
of SIUE graduates, 239–49
English, James F., 151
English as an additional language learners (EALLs), 215–16
English programs, 48, 50. *See also* Composition programs; MA programs
Enos, Theresa, xxvn3, 159, 234
Enrollment rates, 23–24, 49–50
Environmental factors, 80–81

Faculty. *See* Adjunct faculty; Teachers
Fahimi, Mansour, 73n3
Fairfield, Hannah, xvi
Falconer, Isobel, 132
Feldman, Paula R., 200
FitzGerald, William T., xx, 59, 61, 116, 253
Flowerdew, John, 218
Forrest Cataldi, Emily, 73n3
Forsberg, L. Lee, 190
Fox, Steve, xix, xx, 60, 108, 256, 261
Freckleking (online user name), 37
Frick, Jane, 86
Friedman, Audrey A., 106
Friend, Christy, 166
Fulkerson, Richard, 10

Gaff, Jerry G., 251
Gallagher, Kelly, 118n4
Gaylord, Mary M., xiv, 57n3
Gellin, Laura, 104
German university model, xi
Giddens, Elizabeth J., 23
Giles, Clark, 105
Gillian, Barb, 247
Gillotte-Tropp, Helen, 14
Giordano, Michael J., xiv, 79
Glazer, Judith S., xii

– 267 –

INDEX

Glazer-Raymo, Judith, 46, 47
Goen-Salter, Sugie, 14
Gorbunov, Alexander V., 35
Graff, Gerald, 55, 166
Grammar and language
    development, 9–13
Grant, Abigail A., 127, 131, 132, 133
Greene, Stuart, 161
Guillory, John, 55
Gulikers, Goedele, 218

Hammond, Betsy, 172
Hampel, Regine, 132
Hampton, Johnna, 104
Hardy, Donna, 129
Harner, Sandi, 90
Harris, Joseph, 192
Hawisher, Gail E., 128
Haworth, Jennifer Grant, xix
Hearn, James C., 35
Hieronymi, Pamela, 36
Higher education
    and economic opportunity, 42–44
    for-profit institutions, 57n1
    as global industry, 45
    history of, in US, xi
    tiered degree system in, xi–xii
Higher Learning Commission, 100
Hudson, Jeff, xxiii, 72, 247–49, 256, 261
Hunter, Susan M., 23
Hurlburt, Steven, 62

Indiana University–Purdue
    University Indianapolis's
    (IUPUI) graduate
    certificate program. *See
    also* Certificate program in
    writing pedagogy
    assessments of, 111–12
    challenges of, 112–16
    cross-level collaboration of, 103–6, 112–13

vs. MA degree, 107
overview of, 108–11
texts for, 118n4
value of, 116–17
Integrated reading and writing
    (IRW) programs, 14
Interdisciplinarity
    as centripetal force, 209–11
    of MA degree, 198–99
    and MA programs, 260–62
    of MWSU MAA program, 92–93
Internships, 93–94
Intradisciplinarity
    as centrifugal force, 206–9
    of MA degree, 198–99
    Vandenberg and Clary-Lemon on, 208
IRW. *See* Integrated reading and
    writing (IRW) programs

Jackson, Brian, 73–74n4, 93
Jacobs, Jane, 44
Johns Hopkins University, xi
Johnson, Samuel, 255
Johnson-Eilola, Johndan, 90, 92
Juergensmeyer, Erik, xxvn3, 234

Kachru, Braj B., 217
Kamhi-Stein, Lía D., 218
Kennedy, David M., 132
Knowledge, practical vs.
    impractical, 200–201
Ko, Susan, 130, 131
Kohl, Kay J., 80, 87, 89, 92, 95
Kolowich, Steve, 123
Komisaruk, Adam, xvi
Kouritzin, Sandra G., 218
Krook, Anne, 261
Kumpulainen, Kristiina, 248

LaPidus, Jules B., 89, 92
LeBlanc, Paul, 128
Lefebvre, Henri, 213
Lentricchia, Frank, 170
Leslie, Larry L., xviii, 41, 47

– 268 –

Index

Lillis, Theresa, 215
Lindemann, Erika, 118n4
Literary studies programs
vs. composition programs, 63–64
relevancy of, to employment opportunities, 61–62, 64–68, 71–72
Littlejohn, Allison, 132
Liu, Dilin, 218
Llurda, Enric, 215
Local responsiveness. *See also* Civic engagement
of literary studies, 71–72
of SFSU composition program, 4–6, 12, 13–14, 15, 18–19
terminal MA degree's focus on, 19
Vandenberg and Clary-Lemon on, 3
Lockhart, Tara, xvii, 60, 71, 256, 257
Lorenz, Chris, 45
Lovejoy, Kim Brian, xix, xx, 60, 108, 256, 261
Loyola University Chicago, 126

MA degree holders
as adjunct faculty, 22
career expectations vs. outcomes for, 186–90
career paths of, 73n3, 91, 184–85
employment prospects for, 114–15, 192–93
nonacademic career paths of, 24, 89, 170–71, 182–83, 185, 193–94
teaching as primary career for, 62, 90, 123
writing skills improvement as goal for, 63
MA degree in English
benefits of, 187–89
contextual fluidity of, 211–13
and history of higher educa-

tion, xi–xii
interdisciplinarity of, 198–99
intradisciplinarity of, 198–99
marginal place of, in graduate education, 51
and market forces, 202–5
number awarded, vs. PhD, xiii
as professional degree, 153–54
rates of, vs. PhDs, among faculty, xii, xxvn2, 52, 62
relevance of, 197–98
revision of, for New Economy, 52–57
studies on changes in, xiv–xv
value of, xii, 145, 234–35
MA degree in English (stand-alone). *See* MA degree in English (terminal)
MA degree in English (terminal)
and academic capitalism, 41–42, 46–48, 56
career path for, 70
as credential for economic participation, 44–45, 46–48, 49–50, 53, 188–89
focus of, on local responsiveness, 19
nonacademic trajectory for, 24, 89–92, 170–71
relevancy of literary studies to, 61
use of term, xxvn4
Mangieri, Jackie, 129
MA programs. *See also* specific programs
ecological networks of, 92–96
economic impact of, 35–36
enrollment rates, 23–24, 49–50
environmental influences on, 80–81
as inadequate preparation for teaching, 68–69
objectives for, 257–58
in online pedagogy, 127–28
online pedagogy as absent from, 122–25, 130–31

– 269 –

INDEX

specialization within, 59–60
student recommendations for changes to, 189–90
theory–praxis disconnect in, 191–94, 254
work of faculty vs. students in, 70
MA TESOL programs. *See also* Western Pennsylvania University MA TESOL program
online, 219
overview of, in US, 217–220
Matsuda, Paul Kei, 12
McComiskey, Bruce, 128, 166
McGee, Sharon James, xxiii, 72, 256, 261
Mcgill, Lou, 132
Meloncon, Lisa, 90
Michigan State University, 126
Millar, Susan Bolyard, xix
Miller, Hildy, xxi, xxii, 59, 60, 173n1, 192, 257
Miller, Susan K., 118n4
Miller, Thomas P., 73–74n4, 93
Missouri Western State University, 61, 81–84
Missouri Western State University MAA program
as applied professional degree, 86–92
development of, 84–86
employment goals of, 92–95
as interdisciplinary, 92–93
and internships, 93–94
overview of, 80
technical communication track, 90–91, 94
Monske, Elizabeth, 25, 37
Moore, Cindy, xxii, 173n1, 188, 191, 192, 193
Moran, Charles, 128
Mossman, Mark, xviii, 60, 254, 256
Moxley, Joseph M., 161

Mrvica, Ann, 96n2
Mueller, Derek N., xiv, xv, 123
Munger, Roger, 91
Myers, David Gershom, 161
Myers, Jimmy, 82
Myers-Wylie, Danan, 129

Nachmias, Rafi, 127
Nagin, Carl, 101–2, 105
National Center for Education Statistics (NCES), 49–50, 73n3
National Council of Teacher Quality, 114
National Writing Project (NWP), 101–2, 105
NCES. *See* National Center for Education Statistics (NCES)
New Economy. *See also* Academic capitalism
critical writing/reading as key to, 48
higher education as competitive entity in, 45
MA degree as credential for, 44–45, 46–48, 49–50, 53
MA degree as revised for, 52–57
Niemczyk, Mary, 132
North Carolina State University, 73n3
North Carolina State University MA program
aspirations for, 190–94
surveys administered by, 180–81, 194–95nn1–2
Nunan, David, 218
NWP. *See* National Writing Project (NWP)
Nystrand, Martin, 161

Olina, Zane, 132
O'Meara, Kerry Ann, 149
Online Learning Consortium,

– 270 –

Index

128–29

Online MA programs
at Bowling Green State University (BGSU), 24–38
and MA TESOL programs, 218
and Rutgers University–Camden MA program, 151–52
Scheg on, 70

Online pedagogy. *See also* Technology
absence of, from MA programs, 122–25, 130–31
In's and Out's of Online Instruction, The (Myers-Wylie, Mangieri, and Hardy), 129
MA-level programs in, 127–28
proposed MA curriculum for, 131–34
Teaching Online: A Practical Guide (Ko and Rossen), 130

Orleans, Antriman V., 132
Owens, W. R., 31, 33

Pantoja, Veronica, 118n4
Park, Gloria, xxiii, 60, 215, 216, 218, 220, 221, 222, 224, 227, 261
Parker, William Riley, xi
Pedagogy, applied, vs. theory, 113
Penrose, Ann M., xxii, 62–63, 73n3, 192, 254, 255, 259, 261
Persico, Donatella, 132
PhD degree
and history of higher education, xi–xii
number awarded, vs. MA, xiii
as professional goal of MA students, 182
rates of, among faculty, xii, 52, 62
value of, vs. MA, xii, 145

Phillipson, Robert, 216, 218
Portland State University MA track
and civic engagement, 168–69
department mission and identity of, 164–66
effect on undergraduate curriculum, 167–68
faculty strengths as basis for shaping, 158–60
literary vs. composition focus of, 160–64
student requirements for, 169–72
Potter, Rebecca C., xviii, 255
Professional development, and teachers' salaries, 99–100, 113–14
Pruitt-Logan, Anne S., 251

Ragan, Lawrence C., 31
Rainey, Kenneth T., 91
Ramanathan, Vai, 217
Readings, Bill, 203, 204–5, 206, 211
Reiff, Mary Jo, 80
"Report on the 2012 Survey of Programs," xiv–xv
Reynolds, Luke, 106
Rhee, Michelle, 113
Rhetoric programs. *See* Composition programs
Rhoades, Gary, xviii, 41, 44, 47
Rich, Anne, 90
Richards, Erin, 114
Roberge, Mark, xvii, 60, 71, 256, 257
Robertson, Linda R., 170
Robidoux, Charlotte, 91
Roen, Duane, 118n4
Rose, Mike, 168
Ross, Andrew, 42, 43, 45
Rossen, Steve, 130, 131
Rutgers University–Camden MA program
and campus shift toward PhD

– 271 –

INDEX

programs, 144–45
and civic engagement, 148–49
curriculum of, 142–48
Digital Studies Center, 150
Digital Wharton project,
154–55
future paths for, 148–56
and MFA program creation,
139–40, 146–47
regional campus location of,
140–41
as stand-alone MA program,
141
student demographics of, 141

Sabo-Lay, April, 248
Salvatori, Mariolina Rizzi, 163
San Francisco State University
(SFSU) composition
program
challenges of student diversity
for graduates, 7–9
graduate certificates offered
by, 4
grammar and language development issues for gradu-
ates, 9–13
local responsiveness of, 4–6,
12, 13–14, 15, 18–19
Post-Secondary Reading (PSR)
certificate, 13–18
as site of tension, 3–4, 6–7, 10,
12, 15–18
study of graduates, 6
Savenye, Wilhelmina C., 132
Scheer, Sam, 106
Scheg, Abigail G., xx, 60, 70,
122, 133, 256
Schell, Eileen E., 170, 192
Schleppegrell, Mary J., 217
Scholes, Robert, 29, 51
Schön, Donald A., 5
Scott, Linda, 132
Seaman, Jeff, 129
Selber, Stuart A., 34, 90
Selfe, Cynthia L., 24, 128

Shaughnessy, Mina P., 10
Sides, Charles H., 96n2
Sims, Leslie B., 251
Singley, Carol J., xx, 59, 61, 116,
154–55, 253
Skutnabb-Kangas, Tove, 216,
218
Slaughter, Sheila, xviii, 41, 44, 47
Slevin, James F., 209, 210
Smith, Sidonie, 24, 35
Smithson, Isaiah, 236
Southern Illinois University
Edwardsville (SIUE) MA
program
overview of, 235–38
student demographics of,
237–38
students on, 239–47
Steinberg, Erwin R., 16
Steward, Doug, xii, 23, 25, 49,
51
Stimpson, Catharine R, xii, 43
Stock, Patricia Lambert, 192
Storr, Richard J., xi
Stoynoff, Stephen, 218
Strain, Margaret M., 61, 160
Students
career expectations vs. outcomes for, 186–90
as commodities, 45
as consumers, 203–4
diversity of, as challenge for
faculty, 7–9
English as an additional language learners (EALLs),
215–16
faculty biases against nontraditional, 29–30
faculty biases against online,
32
grammar and language development issues for, 9–13
motivations of, 9, 91–92
multilingual English learners,
12
nontraditional, for online MA

– 272 –

Index

programs, 26–27
professional goals of, 181–84
of WPU MA TESOL program, 225–31
Swank, Patricia, 248

Teachers. *See also* Adjunct faculty
biases of, against composition studies, 68
biases of, against nontraditional students, 29–30
biases of, against online programs, 32
rates of PhD vs. MA degrees among, xii, xxvn2, 52, 62
resistance of, to online education, 28–30, 36–37, 128–29
resistance of, to online MA program at BGSU, 28–30, 36–37
salaries of, and graduate degrees, 99–100, 113–14
Teaching
as career path for MA degree holders, 62, 90, 123, 184–85, 192
literary studies' relevancy to, 71–73
MA programs as inadequate preparation for, 68–69
and Portland State University MA track, 171–72
as professional goal of MA students, 182
Teaching English to Speakers of Other Languages (TESOL). *See* TESOL programs
Technical communication, 86, 90–91, 94, 96n3, 171, 189
Technology. *See also* Online pedagogy
challenges of, for online pro-

grams, 30, 32, 33–35
and digital humanities programs, 125–26
faculty resistance to, 28–30, 36–37, 128–29
Teres, Harvey, 63
TESOL programs, 12. *See also* MA TESOL programs
Therber, Angie, 104
Thomas, Arthur, 114
Torres, Monica F., xxvn3, 234
Tremmel, Robert, 105
Tulley, Christine, 37
Turner, Roy K., 91

University of Maryland University College (UMUC), 127
University of Michigan-Flint, 127
University of North Florida, 199
University of Virginia, 126, 134n1
U.S. News & World Report, 22
Uzuner, Sedef, 215

Vandenberg, Peter, 4, 19, 71, 125, 203
on autonomy of MA degrees, xvii
on diversity of MA students, 123
on interdisciplinarity, 210
on intradisciplinarity, 208, 209
on MA degrees as impractical, 201
on MA in composition, xxii, 3
on MA's value as fulfilling community needs, 199–200, 202, 206, 212
on MA vs. PhD, 207
on relevance of MA in English, 197–98
Villanueva, Victor, 117n2, 118n4

Waggoner, Eric, 118n4

– 273 –

INDEX

Walters, Margaret B., 23
Warnock, Scott, 30, 33
Weisbrod, Burton A., 43
Weisser, Christian, 80
Wells, Kisha, xxiii, 72, 242–43, 256, 261
Western Pennsylvania University MA TESOL program. *See also* MA TESOL programs
  faculty expertise, 221–25
  graduate interviews, 225–28
  overview of, 219–20
  professional work by students, 230–31
  required courses of, 223
  student recommendations for changes to, 228–29
Widdowson, H. G., 216
Wiemelt, Jeffrey, 161
Wilentz, Sean, 260

Wolf, Amie, 25, 37
Worley, Linda K., 191
Wright, Erika, xiv, 120
Writing pedagogy
  IUPUI graduate certificate program, 99–118
  SIUE MA program, 235–38
Writing skills
  improvement in, as goal of MA degree holders, 63
  and New Economy participation, 48
Writing studies. *See* Composition programs

Yena, Lauren, 118n4
Young, Richard E., 16

Zukin, Sharon, 212

Editors

Rebecca C. Potter is an associate professor of English and American literature at the University of Dayton, where she is also associated with the Sustainability, Energy and the Environment (SEE) program. In the 2015–16 academic year, she was a visiting scholar at the Rachel Carson Center for the Environmental Humanities in Munich, Germany. She has published work on subjects ranging from early modern poetry to contemporary environmental writers, where her main interest lies. Her work has appeared in *Pedagogy; American Studies: Culture, Society and Art;* and *Studies in Literature*. She is currently completing a book, *The Cassandra Effect*, which intersects narrative and social responses to global climate change. Together with Margaret M. Strain, she has taught and mentored graduate students in an English master's program, work that inspired this publication.

Margaret M. Strain is a professor of English at the University of Dayton, where she teaches undergraduate and graduate courses in writing, composition theory, histories of rhetoric, and Irish drama. She has edited *Principles and Practices: Discourses for the Vertical Curriculum* (2013). With Alexis Hart, she coedits the Interviews section of *Kairos: A Journal of Rhetoric, Technology, and Pedagogy*. Her work on the disciplinary rise of composition studies, research methods, oral narratives, and graduate writing instruction

EDITORS

has appeared in *Rhetoric Society Quarterly*; *JAC: A Journal of Rhetoric, Culture, and Politics; Writing on the Edge*; *Composition Forum; Pedagogy*; and several edited collections.

CONTRIBUTORS

Kaye Adkins is a professor of English focusing on technical communication at Missouri Western State University, where she served as the first director of the master of applied arts in written communication. Adkins is the coauthor of two technical communication textbooks, *Technical Communication: A Practical Approach* and *Technical Communication Fundamentals*. She has presented and published on curriculum design, ecocomposition and environmental rhetoric, metaphor theory, and policy and procedure writing, and she consults and conducts training workshops on policy and procedure writing and compliance documentation. Adkins serves on the Executive Committee of the Council for Programs in Technical and Scientific Communication.

Jocelyn R. Amevuvor is a graduate of Indiana University of Pennsylvania's master's in TESOL program. She is currently an instructor at IUP's American Language Institution. She has also developed and supervises a tutoring program for all of the university's international students. Her research interests include international student experiences, African studies, and tutoring centers. Amevuvor's experience in the MATESOL program, "The Difference a Year Makes: The Transformative Journey of an MA TESOL Student," was published in *TESOL Journal*.

James P. Beasley is an associate professor of English at the University of North Florida, where he teaches graduate courses in rhetorical history, theory, and research. His work has been published in *College Composition and Communication*, *JGE: The Journal of General Education*, and *Rhetoric Review*. His 2010 essay, "Demetrius, Deinotes, and Burkean Identification at the University of Chicago" won the Theresa J. Enos award for the best essay of 2010 from *Rhetoric Review*. His upcoming publications include articles on materiality and assessment and assessment as social justice.

Kristine L. Blair is a professor of English and dean of the College of Liberal Arts and Social Sciences at Youngstown State University and former chair of the English Department at Bowling Green State University. The author or coauthor of numerous publications on

— 277 —

CONTRIBUTORS

gender and technology, the politics of distance learning, electronic portfolios, and feminist pedagogies, Blair serves as editor of both the international print journal *Computers and Composition* and its separate companion journal, *Computers and Composition Online*. She is also a recipient of the Conference on College Composition and Communication's Technology Innovator Award and the Computers and Composition Charles Moran Award for Distinguished Contributions to the Field.

Rebecca Burns is an associate professor of English at St. Louis Community College–Meramec, where she teaches composition and literature. She received her master's degree in English with a specialization in the teaching of writing at Southern Illinois University Edwardsville. Her most recent publications include "Surefire Class: Projecting Gender," *Teaching Seeing & Writing 4* (2010) and *Forbidden* (pseudonym Bailey Grey, 2013). In 2014 she presented at the University of Missouri's annual Focus on Teaching and Technology conference and edited *Black Girls Can: An Empowering Story of Yesterdays and Todays* (as Rachel Garlinghouse). She is currently editing a collection of artwork and writing for the well-known midwestern composer, conductor, artist, and professor Gary Gackstatter, author of *Pen and Ink*.

Duncan Carter is an emeritus professor of English who taught at Portland State University from 1987 to 2013. He served as director of writing for six years. Later he became English department chair and, for ten years, associate dean of the College of Liberal Arts and Sciences. Interested in writing across the curriculum, program administration, and the relationship between thought and language, he has published a number of articles on these topics, along with two composition texts.

Kory Lawson Ching taught for eight years as a faculty member at San Francisco State University, where he offered undergraduate and graduate courses in ethnographic writing, blogging, composition theory, teaching with technology, and qualitative research methods. His research interests include teacher preparation and digital literacies, and his work has appeared in the journals *Composition Studies*; *Computers and Composition*; *Computers and Composition Online*; *JAC: A Journal of Rhetoric, Culture, and Politics*; and *Rhetoric Review*, as well as the website *Inside Higher Ed*. He is currently on the faculty of the University Writing Program at the University of California, Davis.

Nancy Thurman Clemens is a third-year doctoral candidate at the University of Denver. She plans to analyze in her dissertation the rhetorical theory within the Department of Defense's sexual assault

Contributors

program. Nancy has currently served seventeen years in the United States Air Force, deploying to Kuwait, Saudi Arabia, Bosnia/Herzegovina, and Afghanistan.

William T. FitzGerald is an associate professor of English, director of first-year writing, and director of the Teaching Matters and Assessment Center at Rutgers University–Camden, where he teaches courses in rhetoric and writing studies. He is the author of *Spiritual Modalities: Prayer as Rhetoric and Performance* (2012) and coeditor of *The Craft of Research*, 4e. His current book project is a reception study of the familiar "Serenity Prayer."

Steve Fox is an associate professor of English at Indiana University–Purdue University Indianapolis (IUPUI), where he directs the writing program. He also directs the Hoosier Writing Project, a site of the National Writing Project. He is a member of the Labor Caucus of the Conference on College Composition and Communication. Fox has written and co-written articles and book chapters on teaching writing, language diversity, and teaching portfolios, and he coedited *Teaching Academic Literacy: The Uses of Teacher-Research in Developing a Writing Program.*

Jeff Hudson has been teaching high school English in Alton, Illinois, since 1996. In 1997 he became a fellow of the National Writing Project and soon after became co-director of the Piasa Bluffs Writing Project at Southern Illinois University Edwardsville. In recent years, his work and research interests have focused on the development of collaborative, reflective professional development cultures supporting teachers to grow into their practice. He is a member of the Cultural Landscapes Collaboratory (CoLab) leadership team. The CoLab (www.ourcolab.org) is a consortium of teacher-researchers exploring practice and redefining professional development and teacher preparation.

Adam Komisaruk is an associate professor and MA/PhD program supervisor in the Department of English at West Virginia University. His research has appeared in *Eighteenth-Century Life, Law and Literature, Studies in Romanticism,* and *Nineteenth-Century Contexts,* among other venues. He is working on a critical edition of Erasmus Darwin's *The Botanic Garden* (forthcoming) and on a study of sexuality and the public sphere in British Romanticism.

Tara Lockhart is an associate professor at San Francisco State University and director of composition; she coordinates and teaches first-year writing, as well as teaching graduate courses in composition, literacy studies, and pedagogy. Her scholarship focuses on writing–learning transfer, hybrid forms of the essay that promote writers' rhetorical

CONTRIBUTORS

and stylistic awareness, and pedagogies for graduate-level writing instruction. She is the senior editor of the journal *Literacy in Composition Studies* (licsjournal.org). Lockhart's work has appeared in *College English, Enculturation,* and several edited collections; along with her co-researcher, Mary Soliday, she is the recipient of a 2013 CCCC Research Initiative Grant. *Informed Choices: A Guide for Teachers of College Writing* (Lockhart and Roberge) was published in 2015 as part of the Bedford/St.Martin's professional resource series.

Kim Brian Lovejoy is an associate professor of English in the School of Liberal Arts at Indiana University–Purdue University Indianapolis, where he teaches undergraduate and graduate courses in the writing program. He directs the Graduate Program in Writing and Literacy and the Graduate Certificate in Teaching Writing, and is the editor of the *Journal of Teaching Writing.* He serves on the Executive Committee of the Research Network Forum of the Conference on College Composition and Communication (CCCC) and co-chairs the CCCC Language Policy Committee. He coauthored *Other People's English: Code-Meshing, Code-Switching, and African American Literacy* (2014) and *Writing: Process, Product and Power* (1993). His chapter "Practical Pedagogy for Composition" appeared in *Language Diversity in the Classroom: From Intention to Practice* (2003), his article "Self-Directed Writing: Giving Voice to Student Writers" in *English Journal* (2009), and his coauthored "From Language Experience to Classroom Practice: Affirming Linguistic Diversity in Writing Pedagogy" in *Pedagogy: Critical Approaches to Teaching Literature, Language, Composition and Culture* (2009), reprinted in *Students' Right to Their Own Language: A Critical Sourcebook* (2015).

Sharon James McGee is a professor and current chair of the Department of English Language and Literature at Southern Illinois University Edwardsville, where she has taught since 2001. Her scholarship has appeared in *CCC* and *Rhetoric Review* among other venues. She counts writing this chapter with Becky, Kisha, Nancy, and Jeff as one of the highlights of her career so far!

Hildy Miller is a professor of English, former writing program administrator, and department chair at Portland State University. Her research interests include history of women in rhetoric, particularly in nineteenth-century America; Gothic studies; and composition/English administration. She teaches graduate and undergraduate courses in rhetoric, composition, literature, and film.

– 280 –

Contributors

Mark Mossman received his PhD from Saint Louis University in 1998 and joined the faculty at Western Illinois University in 2001 after two years at Bethany College in West Virginia. He became chair of English at WIU in 2010. He is the author of *Disability, Representation and the Body in Irish Writing, 1800–1922* (2009), and he has had research published in such journals as *College English*, *Nineteenth-Century Feminisms*, *Postmodern Culture*, *European Romantic Review*, and *Victorian Literature and Culture*.

Gloria Park is an associate professor of TESOL and applied linguistics at Indiana University of Pennsylvania. Since 2008 she has taught undergraduate English, MATESOL, and composition and TESOL doctoral courses. She served as an MATESOL program director (2011–2015) and created and directs the TESOL Graduate Certificate Program. Park's research areas include world Englishes, critical and feminist pedagogy, teacher narratives, and qualitative research. Specifically, her goal is to help multilingual learners and teachers understand themselves as knowledgeable, reflective individuals who are critical of how the English language is situated in worldwide contexts. Her work appears in *TESOL Quarterly*; *TESOL Journal*; *Journal of Language, Identity, and Education*; *Race Ethnicity and Education*; and *Journal of Pedagogic Development*.

Ann M. Penrose is professor and director of graduate programs in English at North Carolina State University. She teaches graduate and undergraduate courses in composition theory, writing pedagogy, writing research methods, academic discourse, and communication in the sciences. Her research interests include teacher preparation and program administration, writing and reading processes, and socialization in disciplinary communities. These interests converge in her programmatic research on English graduate students' professional ambitions. Her work has appeared in *College Composition and Communication*, *Research in the Teaching of English*, *WPA Journal*, and *Written Communication*.

Mark Roberge is a professor of English at San Francisco State University, where he currently serves as the coordinator of the MA composition program. He is coauthor of *Informed Choices: A Guide for Teachers of College Writing* (2015), coeditor of *Generation 1.5 in College Composition: Teaching Academic Writing to U.S.-Educated Learners of ESL* (2009), and coeditor of *Teaching U.S.-Educated Multilingual Writers: Pedagogical Practices from and for the Classroom* (2015). He has also served as coeditor of the California/Nevada TESOL Association's *CATESOL Journal* for the past twelve years.

CONTRIBUTORS

Carol J. Singley is a professor of English at Rutgers University–Camden, where she served as director of the MA program. She also was associate director of the writing program at Swarthmore College and helped design the nation's first PhD program in childhood studies at Rutgers–Camden. An internationally known scholar of Edith Wharton, Singley is the author of *Edith Wharton: Matters of Mind and Spirit* (1995); coauthor of *House of Mourning, House of Mirth* (2013), and editor of four books on Wharton. She also coedited *Anxious Power: Reading, Writing, and Ambivalence in Narrative by Women* (1993) and *The Calvinist Roots of the Modern Era* (1997). Her work in childhood studies includes the authored book *Adopting America: Childhood, Kinship, and National Identity in Literature* (2011) and the coedited collection *The American Child: A Cultural Studies Reader* (2003). She is also the author of articles on peer tutoring, and composition.

Abigail G. Scheg is a course mentor for general education composition at Western Governors University. She has also served as a dissertation chair for doctoral students at Grand Canyon University and Northcentral University. Scheg has authored and edited a number of texts on online pedagogy, educational technology, and popular culture, including *Reforming Teacher Education for Online Pedagogy Development, Implementation and Critical Assessment of the Flipped Classroom Experience, Critical Examinations of Distance Education Transformation across Disciplines,* and *Bullying in Popular Culture: Essays on Film, Television and Novels.*

Kisha Wells is a recently tenured associate professor of English at Prairie State College, where she serves on several committees and served as portfolio coordinator for two years. She is a proud graduate of Southern Illinois University Edwardsville, where she received both her BA and MA degrees.

This book was typeset in Sabon by Barbara Frazier.
Typefaces used on the cover include Trajan Pro and Times.
The book was printed on 50-lb. White Offset paper
by Versa Press, Inc.